Lincoln Christian College

CHAPTERS IN THE HISTORY OF
NEW TESTAMENT TEXTUAL CRITICISM

NEW TESTAMENT TOOLS
AND STUDIES

EDITED BY

BRUCE M. METZGER, Ph.D., D.D., L.H.D.

Professor of New Testament Language and Literature
Princeton Theological Seminary

VOLUME IV

GRAND RAPIDS 3, MICHIGAN
Wm. B. EERDMANS
1963

CHAPTERS IN THE HISTORY OF NEW TESTAMENT TEXTUAL CRITICISM

BY

BRUCE M. METZGER

GRAND RAPIDS 3, MICHIGAN
Wm. B. EERDMANS
1963

Copyright 1963 by E. J. Brill, Leiden, Netherlands.

All rights reserved. No part of this book may be reproduced or trans-lated in any form, by print, photoprint, microfilm or any other means without written permission from the publisher.

PRINTED IN THE NETHERLANDS

225.4
m59

Rebatore

3 91

87 may 61

TO

MY WIFE

20975

CONTENTS

PREFACE

The purpose of these essays is to survey certain significant areas within the broad field of the history of New Testament textual criticism. By tracing the history of research on a given subject— such as the Caesarean text or Tatian's Diatessaron—one will often gain new insight as to what is or is not a profitable topic for further investigation. Obviously the more comprehensive the survey is, the more likely it will provide fresh points of view and suggest new combinations of evidence. For this reason the bibliographical net has been cast wide in the effort to bring together as complete a conspectus of relevant literature as was practicable.

It is well known that a beneficial cross-fertilization of ideas not infrequently takes place when the problems and methodology in different fields of research are compared. It is hoped, therefore, that what is set forth regarding the textual criticism of the Septuagint (in chapter I) or of the Homeric and Indian epics (in chapter VI) will stimulate further discussion among New Testament scholars. Moreover, an attempt has been made (particularly in chapters III and V) to break through the provincialism—if this is the correct word—of restricting one's attention only or chiefly to what has been published in German, French, and English and of neglecting to take into account significant research undertaken by Slavic and Hispanic scholars. The Appendix deals in a biographical manner with the unsung contributions to textual criticism made by the famous English printer, William Bowyer, Jr., whose name is worthy to be mentioned alongside those of the Stephanus and Aldine dynasties of printers.

What may be called the first draft of the chapters of this book appeared as articles during the past fifteen years in several American and British journals. For permission to utilize this material the author is grateful to the editors of the *Journal of Biblical Literature* (Philadelphia), *Journal of Religion* (Chicago), and *New Testament Studies* (Cambridge). The discussion of the subject matter of each chapter has been expanded to a greater or less extent, and the bibliographical research has been brought up-to-date. In 1962 the manuscript of this book was awarded a prize by the Christian Research Foundation.

During the present generation the discipline of New Testament textual criticism has attracted relatively few students. Here it is lamentably true that, though "the harvest is plentiful, the laborers are few." One of the aims of the author will be attained if the diversity and range of subjects treated in these essays should stimulate students of various backgrounds and talents to pursue further the fascinating and rewarding tasks associated with investigating the transmission of the text of the Greek New Testament. To this end, throughout the chapters and particularly at the close of the first two chapters, doctoral candidates will find more than a score of problems, all of which clamor for attention and some of which might well provide appropriate subjects for research projects and dissertations.

BRUCE M. METZGER

Princeton Theological Seminary
Princeton, New Jersey

ABBREVIATIONS

ATR	*Anglican Theological Review*
B	*Biblica*
BBC	*Bulletin of the Bezan Club*
Byz	*Byzantinoslavica*
BZ	*Biblische Zeitschrift*
CD	*Ciudad de Dios*
CQR	*Church Quarterly Review*
CSCO	*Corpus scriptorum christianorum orientalium*
CSEL	*Corpus scriptorum ecclesiasticorum latinorum*
EB	*Estudios Bíblicos*
EE	*Estudios Eclesiásticos*
HTR	*Harvard Theological Review*
JBL	*Journal of Biblical Literature*
JR	*Journal of Religion*
JTS	*Journal of Theological Studies*
NTS	*New Testament Studies*
OC	*Oriens Christianus*
PG	Migne, *Patrologia Graeca*
PO	*Patrologia Orientalis*
RB	*Revue Biblique*
RF	*Razón y Fe*
S	*Sefarad*
SD	*Studies and Documents*
TS	*Texts and Studies*
TU	*Texte und Untersuchungen*
U	*Universidad* (Zaragoza)
ZNW	*Zeitschrift für die neutestamentliche Wissenschaft*

CHAPTER ONE

THE LUCIANIC RECENSION OF THE GREEK BIBLE[1]

Among the several scholars of the ancient Church who occupied themselves with the textual criticism of the Bible, one of the most influential was Lucian of Antioch. Though not as learned or as productive in a literary way as either Origen or Jerome, Lucian's work on the text of the Greek Bible proved to be of significance both in his own day and, to an even greater extent, during the centuries following. In fact, his recension of the text of the New Testament, with only minor modifications, continued to be used widely down to the nineteenth century, and still lives on in the so-called Ecclesiastical text of the Eastern Orthodox Church.

Little is known of the life of Lucian of Antioch. Born probably at Samosata in Syria about the middle of the third century, he was educated at Edessa under a certain Macarius, who, according to Suidas, was a learned expounder of holy Scripture. After a period when he may have studied at Caesarea, Lucian transferred to the famous theological school of Antioch, of which he and Chrysostom, Diodorus, Theodoret, and Theodore of Mopsuestia were to be some of the more distinguished alumni.

Apparently Lucian was in sympathy with the theological views of his fellow townsman, Paul of Samosata, and when Paul was deposed for Christological heresy in A.D. 268 (or 270), he too withdrew from the Church. During his later years Lucian seems to have become more orthodox, and under the episcopate of Cyril of Antioch (A.D. 283-304) he was restored to ecclesiastical fellowship. He died in the peace of the Church, suffering martyrdom for the faith at Nicomedia, Bithynia, probably on January 7, 312.

Many are the historical and theological problems connected with the person and influence of Lucian of Antioch. The question has even been raised as to whether Lucian the excommunicated heretic was the same person as Lucian the martyr and Biblical scholar.[2]

---

[1] The substance of this chapter was presented as a lecture at the Symposium on Antioch of Syria held during May, 1959, at the Dumbarton Oaks Research Library and Collection, Washington, D.C.

[2] This view, suggested earlier by Ceillier, Fleury, De Broglie, and Oikonomos, has been revived by D. S. Balanos in Πρακτικὰ τῆς ᾿Ακαδημίας ᾿Αθηνῶν,

There is no need, however, to suppose the existence of two Lucians, one orthodox and one heretical; the somewhat conflicting reports can be easily reconciled by the assumption that Lucian was a critical scholar whose views on the Trinity and on Christology differed from what was later defined at Nicea as the orthodox position, but that he wiped out all stains of doctrinal aberrations by his heroic confession and martyrdom.[1] It is quite understandable that during his connection with the school at Antioch he exerted a pervasive influence upon the theological views of those who came to adopt Arian theology. Indeed, Arius himself, a former pupil of Lucian's, declared (in a letter to Eusebius of Nicomedia) that he was merely following Lucian's views regarding Christology. Along with Arius, other sympathizers of Lucian's point of view—such as Eusebius of Nicomedia, Maris of Chalcedon, Leontius of Antioch, Eudoxius, Theognis of Nicaea, Asterius—became a closely-knit group that were dubbed "Collucianists."

It is, however, not the vicissitude of doctrinal disputes[2] that is our concern here, but the part that Lucian played in editing the text of the Greek Bible. Though not a little has been written on the subject, it is unfortunate that, with only a few exceptions,[3] scholars have confined their attention either to problems relating to his recension of the Greek Old Testament or to those relating to the New Testament. Such restrictions of interest have worked to the disadvantage of both groups of scholars. Just as the grammarian and the lexicographer of the New Testament can learn much from an examination of the language of the Septuagint, so too the tex-

VII (1932), 306-311, and by Gustave Bardy, *Recherches sur saint Lucien d'Antioche et son école* (Paris, 1936).

[1] So, for example, Albert Ehrhard, *Die Kirche der Märtyrer* (Munich, 1932), pp. 304f., and Adhémar d'Alès, "Autour de Lucien d'Antioche," *Mélanges de l'université Saint Joseph* (Beyrouth), XXI (1937), 185-199, who point out that it is extremely unlikely that two persons of the same name should have played important roles in Antioch at the same time without leaving in the sources a trace of their differentiation from each other.

[2] For discussions of Lucian from a doctrinal point of view, reference may be made to E. Buonaiuti, "Luciano martire, la sua dottrina e la sua scuola," *Rivista storico-critica delle scienze teologiche*, 1908, pp. 830-836, 909-923; 1909, pp. 104-118; Friedrich Loofs, *Das Bekenntnis Lucians, des Märtyrers* (= *Sitzungsberichte der königlich preussischen Akademie der Wissenschaften*, Berlin, 1915), pp. 576-603; Adolf von Harnack, *Dogmengeschichte*, 5te Aufl., II (Tübingen, 1931), 187-190; and, especially, Bardy, *op. cit.*

[3] E.g. M. Spanneut's recent study, "La Bible d'Eustathe d'Antioche — Contribution à l'histoire de la 'version lucianique,'" *Studia Patristica*, ed. F. L. Cross, IV (*TU*, LXXIX [Berlin, 1961]), 171-190.

tual critic of the New Testament will profit from considering the problems and tasks of Septuaginta-Forschung. As an exploration in methodology, therefore, the aim of the present chapter is to shed light upon the text of the New Testament by giving attention to one specific type of text common to both Old and New Testaments, the Lucianic text.

The following pages will present, first, a résumé of ancient testimonies relating to Lucian and his work as textual critic; second, a survey of research on the Lucianic or Antiochian text of the Greek Bible; third, the influence of this text outside the Greek Church; and fourth, a critical evaluation of the Lucianic recension. The chapter will conclude with a list of some of the problems that remain to be solved.

I. Ancient Testimonies to Lucian and his Textual Work

The earliest references to Lucian are two brief and highly favorable estimates which Eusebius includes in his *Church History*. Here Lucian is described as a presbyter of Antioch, "whose entire life was most excellent (ἄριστος)" (VIII.xiii.2), and as "a most excellent (ἄριστος) man in every respect, temperate in life and well-versed in sacred learning" (IX.vi.3).

Later in the fourth century Jerome makes three references to Lucian which differ considerably in temper and appreciation of his work. The differences are no doubt to be accounted for by considering the several contexts and Jerome's immediate purpose in referring to Lucian. On the one hand, when Jerome is comparing his own work as reviser of the Old Latin text with similar work by others in Greek, he is rather severe in his judgment of Lucian. Thus in his Preface to the Four Gospels, which takes the form of an open letter addressed to Pope Damasus and which was composed perhaps about the year 383, he refers somewhat contemptuously to the "manuscripts which are associated with the names of Lucian and Hesychius, the authority of which is perversely maintained by a few disputatious persons." Continuing in the same vein Jerome condemns the work of Lucian and Hesychius as infelicitous: "It is obvious that these writers could not emend anything in the Old Testament after the labors of the Seventy; and it was useless to correct the New, for versions of Scripture already exist in the languages of many nations which show that their additions are false."[1]

---

[1] Praetermitto eos codices quos a Luciano et Hesychio nuncupatos paucorum hominum adserit peruersa contentio: quibus utique nec in ueteri in-

Subsequently, in the Preface to his translation of the books of Chronicles, Jerome makes a more temperate allusion to the work of Lucian and other Biblical scholars. In referring to the diversity of the editions of the Greek Old Testament, he declares that three are current in various parts of the Empire: "Alexandria and Egypt in their [copies of the] Septuagint praise Hesychius as author; Constantinople to Antioch approves the copies [containing the text] of Lucian the martyr; the middle provinces between these read the Palestinian codices edited by Origen, which Eusebius and Pamphilus published."[1]

In his valuable *Lives of Illustrious Men*, written soon after A.D. 392, Jerome is still more generous in his description of Lucian. Here, in a biographical sketch devoted to the martyr from Antioch, he characterizes him as "a man of great talent" and "so diligent in the study of the Scriptures that even now certain copies of the Scriptures bear the name of Lucian."[2] What is of special importance is the declaration that copies of the Scriptures (and not just of the Septuagint, as Jerome is sometimes quoted) passed under the name of *Lucianea*.

strumento post septuaginta interpretes emendare quid licuit nec in nouo profuit emendasse, cum multarum gentium linguis scriptura ante translata doceat falsa esse quae addita sunt (edita sunt, ms. E; John Wordsworth and H. J. White, *Novum Testamentum Domini Nostri Iesu Christi Latine*, I [Oxford, 1889], 2). There has been a curious reluctance among many scholars to admit that Jerome here refers to any more than the Lucianic text of the Old Testament. But, as B. H. Streeter pointed out, "seeing that Jerome is writing a careful and considered Preface to a revised version of the Four Gospels, and that he only mentions the Lucianic and Hesychian versions in order to contrast their inferior text with that of the 'ancient codices' he himself has used, I simply cannot understand why some scholars have raised doubts as to whether the Lucianic and Hesychian recensions included the New Testament as well as the Old" (*The Four Gospels* [London, 1936], p. 591). As regards the much more nebulous figure of Hesychius, whom no Greek author mentions, the situation is different. Despite the popularity of Wilhelm Bousset's suggestion that the so-called "Neutral" text is to be attributed to Hesychius, most scholars today are inclined to agree with Sir Frederic G. Kenyon, who concluded his study of "Hesychius and the Text of the New Testament" (*Mémorial Lagrange* [Paris, 1940], pp. 245-250) with the words: "The title of 'Hesychius' rests in fact upon what is little more than a shadow of a shade."

[1] Alexandria et Aegyptus in LXX suis Hesychium laudat auctorem; Constantinopolis usque Antiochiam Luciani martyris exemplaria probat; mediae inter has provinciae Palaestinos codices legunt, quos ab Origene elaboratos Eusebius et Pamphilus vulgaverunt (Migne, *PL*, XXVIII, 1392 A, and Friedrich Stummer, *Einführung in die lateinische Bibel* [Paderborn, 1928], p. 239).

[2] Lucianus, vir disertissimus, Antiochenae ecclesiae presbyter, tantum in Scriptuarum studio laborat, ut usque nunc quaedam exemplaria Scripturarum Lucianea nuncupentur (*de Viris inlustribus*, 77 [*TU*, XIV, pp. 41f., ed. E. C. Richardson]).

Information of the widespread use of Lucian's recension of the Psalter is contained in Jerome's letter to Sunnias and Fretela (about A.D. 403). These two Gothic churchmen had inquired of Jerome why his own Latin Psalter (the so-called Roman Psalter) differed so frequently from the Septuagint. In his reply Jerome points out that they have been misled by their edition of the Septuagint, which varied widely from the critical text of Origen given in the Hexapla and used by himself. Jerome writes: "You must know that there is one edition which Origen and Eusebius of Caesarea and all the Greek commentators call κοινή, that is common and widespread, and is by most people now called Lucianic; and there is another, that of the Septuagint, which is found in the manuscripts of the Hexapla, and has been faithfully translated by us into Latin."[1] Here Jerome distinguishes the Lucianic text from that of the Hexapla, and indicates that the former met with such universal acceptance that it received the name of the Vulgate or common text.

Later testimonies refer to Lucian's competence in Hebrew. For example, Suidas and Simeon Metaphrastes (in the *Passio S. Luciani martyris*) assert that "he translated [literally, renewed] them all [i.e. the books of the Old Testament] again from the Hebrew language, of which he had a very accurate knowledge, spending much labor on the work."[2] Though Lucian may have consulted the Hebrew in connection with his revision of the Septuagint, this statement is obviously exaggerated in the manner of hagiographers. More sober, and doubtless nearer to the truth of what Lucian attempted to do, is the description of pseudo-Athanasius in his *Synopsis sacrae scripturae*: "Using the earlier editions [i.e. of Aquila, Theodotion, and Symmachus] and the Hebrew, and having accurately surveyed the expressions which fell short of or went

---

[1] Illud breuiter admoneo, ut sciatis aliam esse editionem, quam Origenes et Caesariensis Eusebius omnesque Graeciae tractatores κοινήν—id est communem—appellant atque uulgatam et a plerisque nunc Λουκιάνειος dicitur, aliam septuaginta interpretum, quae et in ἑξαπλοῖς codicibus repperitur et a nobis in Latinum sermonen fideliter uersa est (*Epist.* 106, § 2, 2 [*CSEL*, vol. LV, p. 248, ed. Hilberg]).

[2] Both Suidas and Simeon, who here agree (except in inconsequential details) in their accounts of Lucian, depend upon earlier hagiographical sources. The variant ἐπανεσώσατο, which Adler adopts into her text of Suidas, is clearly the inferior reading; either Simeon's ἀνενεώσατο or ἐπανενεώσατο is to be preferred. For the text of both see Joseph Bidez's ed. of Philostorgius, Anhang VI (= *Griechische christliche Schriftsteller*, 1913, p. 187).

beyond the truth, and having corrected them in their proper places, he published them for the Christian brethren."[1]

Among testimonia of uncertain origin there is an unequivocal statement that Lucian concerned himself with the New Testament as well as the Old. Under the date of October 15, the Menaeon of the Greek Church (this is a liturgical volume which includes short accounts of saints and martyrs to be read on their festivals) states that Lucian made a copy with his own hand of both the Old and New Testaments, written in three columns, which afterwards belonged to the Church in Nicomedia.[2] Substantially the same information in a more extended hagiographical context is contained in the Synaxarium ecclesiae Constantinopolitanae for October 15.[3]

This list of testimonies may be brought to a close[4] with a reference to the condemnation of Lucian in the so-called *Decretum Gelasianum*, where mention is made of *Evangelia quae falsavit Lucianus, apocrypha, Evangelia quae falsavit Hesychius, apocrypha* (v, iii, 8-9). It is generally agreed that this statement rests upon a misunderstanding of the critical remarks of Jerome.[5]

By way of summarizing ancient testimonies concerning Lucian's textual work, we find that his contemporaries generally regarded him as an able scholar, entirely competent to undertake such a recension. As a native Syrian he could, of course, have consulted the Syriac version; he also appears to have had some acquaintance with Hebrew. As would have been expected, he made use of previous Greek translations of the Old Testament, and sought to adjust the Greek to the underlying Hebrew text. But we are told nothing as to the amount of revision which he undertook in either Old or

---

[1] Theodor Zahn dated this document not later than the fifth or sixth century; see his *Geschichte der neutestamentlichen Kanons*, II (Erlangen, 1890), 311. The text is printed in Migne, *PG*, vol. XXVIII, col. 433; see also H. Dörrie's discussion of the textual transmission of this passage in his article, "Zur Geschichte der Septuaginta im Jahrhundert Konstantins," *ZNW*, XXXIX (1940), 79-87.

[2] The relevant passage is a follows: εἰς κάλλος δὲ γράφειν ἐπιστάμενος βιβλίον κατέλιπε τῇ Νικομηδέων ἐκκλησίᾳ, γεγραμμένον σελίσι τρισσαῖς (εἰς τρεῖς στήλας διῃρημένης τῆς σελίδος), περιέχον πᾶσαν τὴν παλαιάν τε καὶ τὴν νέαν διαθήκην.

[3] Edited by Hippolyte Delehaye, *Propylaeum ad Acta Sanctorum, Novembris* [vol. LXI], 1902, pp. 138ff.

[4] For several other ancient testimonies to Lucian, see M. J. Routh, *Reliquiae sacrae*, 2nd ed., IV (Oxford, 1846), 5-10.

[5] See Ernst von Dobschütz, *Das Decretum Gelasianum* (= *TU*, XXXVIII, 4), pp. 51 and 292.

New Testament text, the nature of the manuscripts which he consulted, the relation of his work to the Hexapla, and other similar matters. For information bearing on such problems, we must turn to the manuscripts which have been thought to contain the Lucian recension.

II. SURVEY OF RESEARCH ON THE LUCIANIC OR ANTIOCHIAN TEXT

A. *The Old Testament*

Our account begins with the first printed edition of the entire Greek Old Testament; namely, that contained in the famous Complutensian Polyglot Bible sponsored by the Spanish Cardinal Francisco Ximenes de Cisneros (1437-1517), Archbishop of Toledo, and published at Complutum (now Alcalá de Henares). The four folio volumes containing the Old Testament in Hebrew, Latin, and Greek were printed between 1514 and 1517. As it happened, one[1] of the two manuscripts of the Greek Old Testament which Pope Leo X sent from the Vatican Library for the use of the editors of the Polyglot, and which forms the basis of a large part of their text, contains the type of text now thought to be Lucianic, at least in Samuel and Kings. In other parts of the Old Testament, however, this manuscript departs from the Antiochian type of text. Furthermore, the Spanish editors frequently adopted readings from several other Greek witnesses, and occasionally even conformed the Greek to the Hebrew without any manuscript authority. This Complutensian text was followed on the whole in subsequent Polyglot Bibles (those published at Antwerp, 1569-72; Heidelberg, 1586-1616; Hamburg, 1596; and Paris, 1645).

During the seventeenth and eighteenth centuries scholars laid the basis for subsequent investigations by collecting variant readings from manuscripts of the Greek Old Testament, from the early versions, and from the quotations of the Fathers. Brian Walton's Polyglot Bible (London, 1654-57), Humphrey Hody's valuable researches into the text of the Septuagint (Oxford, 1703), and the collection by Bernard de Montfaucon of the remains of Origen's Hexapla (Paris, 1713) were climaxed by the publication of the monumental *Vetus Testamentum Graecum cum variis lectionibus* edited by Robert Holmes and James Parsons (5 vols., Oxford, 1798-1827). The variant readings of about three hundred separate

[1] Namely, Cod. Vat. gr. 330 (= Holmes 108).

codices, of which twenty are uncial, are given. In addition to patristic citations, evidence is also supplied from the Old Latin, the Coptic, Arabic, Slavonic, Armenian, and Georgian versions, obtained partly from manuscripts, partly from printed texts. This immense apparatus now made it possible to group manuscripts by families; indeed, it became necessary to do so if only to bring some kind of order out of the chaotic mass of evidence.

During the latter part of the nineteenth century, through the researches of Ceriani, Field, and that polymathic scholar, Lagarde,[1] a beginning was made in the assigning of extant manuscript witnesses to each of the major recensions of antiquity. In the case of the Lucianic text, two touchstones were available for identifying the paternity of variant readings. One was the frequent agreement between this text and the quotations of the Fathers of the fourth and fifth centuries who almost certainly used the Antiochian Bible, in particular Chrysostom and Theodoret. A second means of identifying certain individual readings was supplied by the presence of the siglum $\kappa\alpha\grave{\iota}\ \lambda$ which is found prefixed to marginal readings in several Greek manuscripts, as well as the letter lomadh (λ) marking variants in certain Syriac manuscripts. Although in some instances the Greek siglum is to be interpreted as meaning $\kappa\alpha\grave{\iota}\ \lambda o\iota\pi o\acute{\iota}$, most scholars are agreed that in other instances it is to be resolved as $\kappa\alpha\grave{\iota}\ \Lambda o\upsilon\kappa\iota\alpha\nu\acute{o}\varsigma$. The key to this resolution of the siglum was discovered in the nineteenth century in a note[2] prefixed to the Arabic translation of the Syro-Hexaplar, which states, "Lucian compared with the greatest care these Hebrew copies, and if he found anything different or superfluous he restored it to its place, prefixing to the part which he emended the initial letter L." In the same passage reference is made to the marks by which the readings of Aquila,

---

[1] The literary activities of this scholar were immense. He published books in no less than ten languages. As the Prorector of the University said at his funeral, probably no one of his colleagues could spell out the alphabets of all the languages in which Lagarde had edited texts; see p. 170 of the address delivered by George Foot Moore, entitled "Paul Anton de Lagarde," on the occasion of the opening of the Lagarde Library in the University of the City of New York, April 29, 1893 (*The University Quarterly*, July, 1893, pp. 166-179). An (incomplete) bibliography of his publications, compiled by R. J. H. Gottheil (*Proceedings of the American Oriental Society*, 1892, pp. ccxi-ccxxix), includes 297 major publications.

[2] A Latin translation of this Arabic note is found in Field, *Origenis Hexaplarum quae supersunt ... fragmenta* (Oxonii, 1875), pp. lxxxiv sq.; cf. Giovanni Card. Mercati, "Di alcune testimonianze antiche sulle cure bibliche di San Luciano," *B*, XXIV (1943), 1-17, especially pp. 7ff.

Symmachus, Theodotion, and the other Greek versions are denoted; and then the writer proceeds: "but if [the letters] elif, vaw, ra are used, these are Origen's readings; if the letter lomadh, that is Lucian's."

Making use of this aid in identifying Lucianic readings, scholars were able to isolate and classify witnesses to the Antiochian recension. Thus, for the historical books of the Old Testament Ceriani[1] and Field[2] discovered that the text of the cursive Greek manuscripts 19, 82, 93, 108 agrees frequently with the form of text quoted by the Antiochian Fathers, and that these same manuscripts contain readings marked as Lucianic in the Syro-Hexaplar. Working independently Lagarde had come to almost the same results, and on the basis of evidence from these four manuscripts plus another, codex 118, he reconstructed the Lucianic recension of about one half of the Old Testament (Genesis to II Esdras, and a double text of Esther).[3] Unfortunately, except for the Book of Esther and, in another publication, the first fourteen chapters of Genesis, Lagarde provided no *apparatus criticus*. Thus, the scholar who wishes to check the variants in order to evaluate Lagarde's judgment must still go to Holmes and Parsons' thesaurus of variant readings.

In the Prophets another group of manuscripts has been found to contain the text of Lucian. Field satisfied himself that codices 22, 36, 48, 51, 62, 90, 93, 144, 147, 233, 308 offer in more or less pure form the Antiochian text. Later scholars, however, have criticized Field's grouping, and some of the manuscripts have been removed from his list of Lucianic witnesses. Thus, Cornill[4] struck out four (62, 90, 147, 233), and in this he was supported by Lagarde. In the Minor Prophets, the doctoral research of a young Dutch scholar, Schuurmans Stekhoven, indicated a slightly different grouping of manuscripts (22, 36, 42, 51, 62, 86, 95, 147, 153, 185, 238, 240, and in Zech. ch. 13 also 231).[5] He also pointed out that they do not all supply the Lucianic text in an equally pure form.

During the first decade of the twentieth century a group of scholars in Germany, many of them under the leadership of Alfred

---

[1] *Monumenta sacra et profana*, II, 2 (1864), pp. 76, 98, 102; *Rendiconti del R. Istituto Lombardo*, Ser. 2, vol. XIX (1886), 206 ff.

[2] *Op. cit.*, p. lxxxvii.

[3] *Librorum Veteris Testamenti canonicorum pars prior graece* (Göttingen, 1883).

[4] C. H. Cornill, *Das Buch des Propheten Ezechiel* (Leipzig, 1886), pp. 65-66.

[5] J. Z. Schuurmans Stekhoven, *De alexandrijsche vertaling van het Dodekapropheton* (Leiden, 1887), p. 44.

Rahlfs, Lagarde's successor at Göttingen, began a systematic investigation of the Lucianic text within certain books of the Bible. For example, Johannes Dahse attempted a classification of the manuscripts in Genesis, and assigned codices 53, 56, 129 to Lucian.[1] His reasons for this assignment, however, rested on a narrow selection of evidence, and subsequent scholars have indicated their dissatisfaction with his judgment. On the basis of a large induction of evidence, Ernst Hautsch found that, for the Book of Joshua, the quotations of the Antiochian Fathers agree with codices 44, 54, 75, 76, 84, 106, 134, while in the Book of Judges, the Bible of Theodoret (and Chrysostom) is most purely represented in codices 54, 59, 75, with which group 44, 82, 84, 106, 134 are frequently jointed.[2] For the books of the Pentateuch, Hautsch found no overwhelmingly clear distribution of manuscripts that had previously been considered to be Lucianic; indeed, the most assured conclusion he could draw is that certain manuscripts which had been previously thought to be Lucianic (e.g., b, w, 108) do not in fact represent this recension. Procksch continued the research on the history of the Septuagint text of the Prophets.[3] He concluded that in Isaiah the Lucianic text is represented in manuscripts 22, 36, 48, 51, 93, 144, 308; that in Jeremiah it is in manuscripts 22, 36, 48, 51, 96, 144, 229, 231; that in Ezekiel it is in manuscripts 36, 48, 51, 231; and that in the Minor Prophets it is in 22, 36, 48, 51, 93, 95, 96, 114, 130, 153, 185, 240, 308, 311.

The most vigorous and thorough-going investigation of the Septuagint text during the twentieth century was that undertaken by Alfred Rahlfs. His aim, like that of his master, Lagarde, was to distinguish among the mass of manuscripts the three principal recensions (those of Origen, Hesychius, and Lucian), and, from the agreements among these, to recover the original pre-hexaplaric Septuagint text. In the first of his *Septuaginta-Studien* he examines in minute detail Theodoret's quotations from the Books of Kings and from II Chronicles.[4] Though in general his findings confirm the

---

[1] "Textkritische Studien," *Zeitschrift für die alttestamentliche Wissenschaft*, XXVIII (1908), 1-21, 161-173.

[2] *Der Lukiantext des Oktateuch* [= Mitteilungen des Septuaginta-Unternehmens der königlichen Gesellschaft der Wissenschaften zu Göttingen, vol. I] (Berlin, 1909).

[3] O. Procksch, *Studien zur Geschichte der Septuaginta: Die Propheten* (Leipzig, 1910).

[4] *Septuaginda-Studien*; Heft I, *Studien zu den Königsbüchern* (Göttingen, 1904).

view of previous critics (namely, that Theodoret commonly quoted a text of the type represented in Lagarde's edition), Rahlfs discovered that in a considerable number of passages Theodoret's text does not agree with that of Lucian. In answer to the question of the nature of the text underlying the recension of Lucian, he found that it stands closest to Vaticanus (13) and to the Ethiopic version in the older and purer form represented by Dillmann's codices S and A. Thus Lucian is sometimes, especially in I Kings, an important witness to this old, "pre-hexaplaric" form of text.

Rahlfs gave attention next to an examination of the text of the Greek Psalter.[1] With rigorous and scrupulously careful weighing of evidence, his research is a model of patient and exact scholarship. In the chapter devoted to Lucian's text,[2] beginning with the hint given in Jerome's letter to the Gothic churchmen Sunnias and Fretela,[3] Rahlfs examines the quotations from the Psalter in Jerome, Theodoret, and Chrysostom, and concludes that the Lucianic Psalter was widely used throughout the East, where it, indeed, had obtained the status of the "official" text of the Greek Church. This text also circulated, in more or less pure form, even in the West, and at Milan influenced a revision of the Old Latin Psalter. As it happens, however, no manuscript is extant today which contains a pure Lucianic text of the Psalter (codex Alexandrinus, for example, presents a mixed text).

In a subsequent part of *Septuaginta-Studien*, Rahlfs criticizes Lagarde's edition of the Lucianic text of the books of Samuel and Kings.[4] Nowhere in his edition did Lagarde set forth the principles which he had followed in constructing the text. From Lagarde's *Nachlese*, Rahlfs shows that in the Books of Kings Lagarde depended primarily on codex 93, but here and there introduced into a transcript of this manuscript readings from other witnesses, besides making certain changes in proper names and in grammatical details without support in any manuscript whatever. Moreover, several inadvertent and arbitrary departures from the tradition also found their way into his text. The value of Lagarde's edition, therefore, as

---

[1] *Septuaginta-Studien*; Heft II, *Der Text des Septuaginta-Psalters* (Göttingen, 1907).

[2] *Op. cit.*, pp. 169-182.

[3] See p. 5 above.

[4] *Septuaginta-Studien*; Heft III, *Lucian's Rezension der Königsbücher* (Göttingen, 1911); the substance of this monograph was awarded a prize by the Göttingen Academy.

Rahlfs points out, is that it gives in convenient form a general view of the character of the recension which it represents, but for the detailed study of the Lucianic text it is quite inadequate.

Using Lagarde's collations, checked by Holmes and Parsons, Rahlfs found that in the Books of Kings four manuscripts, which fall into two sub-groups, preserve the Lucianic text; they are codices 19, 108, and 82, 93. Tested by internal probability of readings, the second of these sub-groups proves itself to be markedly superior to the other group. (It will be recalled that 108 played a considerable part in the construction of the Greek text in the Complutensian Polyglot, while Lagarde's text was based largely on 93). Rahlfs added as a major Lucianic witness codex 127. Related manuscripts are 56, 158, 245.

In subsequent publications Rahlfs continued to investigate the tangled history of the transmission of the Septuagint. In what is one of the most searching contributions ever made to the textual criticism of the Septuagint, in 1922 Rahlfs published 117 pages devoted to the textual history of the little Book of Ruth.[1] In the same year he issued in pamphlet form a *Probe-Ausgabe* of the Greek text of Ruth,[2] which opened a new era in the century-long work on the Septuagint. Rahlfs found the Lucianic recension to be preserved in codices 54, 59, 75, 82, 93, 314, and (from 4.11 to the end of the book) in 19 and 108.

Four years later the text of Genesis was published, being the first of a proposed sixteen-volume edition of the Septuagint.[3] Here the enormous mass of material and, more particularly, the lack of distinct lines of text-type prevented the editor from assigning in clear-cut fashion any codices to the Lucianic recension. The most that he was able to say is that in Genesis codex 75 is a representative of the text of Lucian, but that it contains strands of other text-types as well.[4] Rahlfs turned next to the task of editing the Psalms, and

---

[1] *Studie über den griechischen Text des Buches Ruth* (= *Mitteilungen des Septuaginta-Unternehmens*, III, 2-3).

[2] *Das Buch Ruth griechisch, als Probe einer kritischen Handausgabe der Septuaginta* (Stuttgart, 1922).

[3] *Septuaginta*; Societatis Scientiarum Gottingensis auctoritate edidit Alfred Rahlfs; I, *Genesis* (Stuttgart, 1926). For a discerning essay on the proposed edition see P. L. Hedley in *HTR*, xxvi (1933), 57-72.

[4] It is instructive that in his Preface to the edition of Genesis Rahlfs makes the statement that, though Lagarde's program of first reconstructing the three great ancient recensions of the Septuagint is correct in principle, yet in practice the enormous magnitude of the task prevents the attainment of

in 1931, as part X of the large edition, his *Psalmi cum Odis* appeared. The volume contains an extensive introduction, in which the author supplements and modifies the second part of his *Septuaginta-Studien* (1907). The great bulk of witnesses fall into the category of the Lucianic recension, which, as has been mentioned earlier, was extremely widespread and which, in fact, became the authoritative text of the Psalter for the Greek Church.

Subsequent fascicles of the Göttingen Septuagint were prepared by Werner Kappler, Joseph Ziegler, and Robert Hanhart. The manuscripts which they found to be Lucianic in the several books thus far edited are as follows:

> In I Maccabees (ed. Kappler, 1936) the Lucianic manuscripts are 64, 236, 381, 536, 728. A sub-group of Lucianic manuscripts includes 19, 62, 93, 542.
> In the XII Prophets (ed. Ziegler, 1943) the Lucianic manuscripts are 22, 36, 48, 51, 231 (only a fragment), 719, 763. Two sub-groups of Lucianic manuscripts are: (1) 62, 147, and (2) 46, 86, 711.
> In Isaiah (ed. Ziegler, 1939) the Lucianic manuscripts are 22, 48, 51, 231, 763. Three sub-groups of Lucianic manuscripts are (1) 62, 142; (2) 90, 130, 311; (3) 36, 93, 96. Other manuscripts show sporadic Lucianic readings, e.g. 46, 233, 456, and 926.
> In Ezekiel (ed. Ziegler, 1952) the Lucianic manuscripts are 22, 36, 48, 51, 96, 231, 763. Two sub-groups of Lucianic manuscripts are (1) 311, 538, and (2) V, 46, 449.
> In Susanna, Daniel, Bel and the Dragon (ed. Ziegler, 1954), the Lucianic manuscripts are 22, 36, 48, 51, 96, 231, 763. Two sub-groups of Lucianic manuscripts are (1) 311, 538, and (2) 88, 449.
> In Jeremiah, Baruch, Lamentations, and the Epistle of Jeremiah (ed. Ziegler, 1957), the Lucianic manuscripts are 22, 36, 48, 51, 96, 231, 311, 763. A sub-group of Lucianic manuscripts includes 62, 198, 407, 449.
> In II Maccabees (ed. Kappler and Hanhart, 1959), the Lucianic

that ideal. For discussions of the problems by two scholars who are critical of the Lagardian program, see Alexander Sperber's "Probleme einer Edition der Septuaginta," in *Studien zur Geschichte und Kultur ... Paul Kahle* (Leiden, 1935), pp. 39-46; the same author's study of "The Problems of the Septuagint Recensions," *JBL*, LIV (1935), 73-92; as well as Paul Kahle in *The Cairo Geniza* (London, 1947), pp. 154 ff.; 2nd ed. (1959), pp. 231 ff. For a criticism of Kahle's position, see the article by Peter Katz, "Septuagintal Studies in the Mid-Century," in *The Background of the New Testament and its Eschatology*, edited by W. D. Davies and D. Daube (Cambridge, 1956), especially pp. 205-208.

manuscripts are 64, 236, 381, 534, 728. A sub-group of Lucianic manuscripts includes 19, 62, 93, 542.

In III Maccabees (ed. Hanhart, 1960) the Lucianic manuscripts are 64, 236, 381, 534, 728. A sub-group of Lucianic manuscripts includes 19, 62, 93, 347 (1.1-2.19), 542.

The above survey of scholarly attempts to identify and study the Lucianic text suggests something of the magnitude and complexity of the problem. It will be understood that the Septuagint is not a unified version of the Old Testament, but a collection of independent translations of the several books or groups of books made at different times and places. Of some books there was more than one translation, and even in the case of individual books the hand of more than one translator can be discerned.[1] It was inevitable that during the centuries these translations should have been corrected, one by another, and all of them occasionally by the Hebrew—which may or may not have been the same form of Hebrew text as that from which the book was originally translated. Possibilities for additional contamination were accelerated by the publication in the second Christian century of three new Jewish translations, those of Aquila, Theodotion, and Symmachus.[2] Furthermore, the three recensions of the Septuagint prepared by Christian scholars—Origen, Lucian, and Hesychius—in the third century, so far from putting an end to the confusion, gave it a new impulse. It is therefore not surprising that today the manuscripts of the Greek Old Testament present a mixed form of text. Nor should the investigator imagine that it will be possible in every case to distinguish neatly ordered families of witnesses; in his search for the Lucianic text he must be prepared to acknowledge that for some of the books of the Old Testament it has left no recognizable trace among extant manuscripts.[3]

[1] See, e.g., H. St. J. Thackeray in *JTS*, IV (1902/03), 245-266, 398-411, 578-585; VIII (1906/07), 262-278; IX (1908), 88-98.

[2] According to Samuel Krauss two other Jewish translations into Greek were prepared by Ben La'ana and by Ben Tilga (see "Two Hitherto Unknown Bible Versions in Greek," *Bulletin of the John Rylands Library*, XXVII [1942-43], 97-105).

[3] For the difficulties involved in the contamination of recensional and non-recensional manuscripts, see the incisive comments of Heinrich Dörrie in his monograph, "Zur Geschichte der Septuaginta im Jahrhundert Konstantins," *ZNW*, XXXIX (1940), 57-110. Raymond Thornhill, in his discussion of "Six or Seven Nations; a Pointer to the Lucianic Text in the Heptateuch with Special Reference to the Old Latin Version" (*JTS*, N.S. x [1959], 233-246), finds that on the whole the Lucianic text of the Pentateuch has been preserved in relatively few manuscripts.

B. *The New Testament*

The first scholar to propound the critical principle of classifying New Testament manuscripts by families was the eighteenth century Pietist, Johann Albrecht Bengel, Superintendent of the Evangelical Lutheran Church of Württemberg. With the view of reducing extant witnesses to the text into "companies, families, tribes, and nations" and thus to simplify the task of evaluating the merits of variant readings, he divided the documents first into two "nations"; these were, he held, the Asiatic, chiefly those written in Constantinople and its neighborhood, and the African, which were more ancient and therefore more valuable than those of the Asiatic group, which he tended to disparage.[1]

Apparently the first scholar to use the term "recensions" in referring to groups of New Testament manuscripts, as well as the first to identify one of these recensions with the work of Lucian of Antioch, was Johann Salomo Semler, the pioneer of Biblical criticism at Halle. Though his work today is chiefly remembered for his part in pursuing the free investigation of the Canon of the Scriptures, it was Semler who, taking up Bengel's ideas, classified New Testament manuscripts into two recensions, which he called the Oriental, or that of Lucian, and the Western or Egypto-Palestinian, which Origen produced.[2] A modification of this division of manuscripts was proposed by Semler's pupil, Johann Jakob Griesbach. In what Westcott and Hort acknowledged to be an important antecedent of their own position, Griesbach divided the witnesses of the New Testament into the Western, Alexandrian, and Constantinopolitan groups.

At the beginning of the nineteenth century Johann Leonhard Hug, a Roman Catholic Biblical scholar at Freiburg im Breisgau, elaborated the theory that Lucian was responsible for one of the early recensions of the New Testament.[3] According to Hug, by the

[1] J. A. Bengel, "Prodromus Novi Testamenti Graeci recte cauteque adornandi," which is prefaced to his edition of Chrysostom's *de Sacerdotio libri sex graece et latine* (Stuttgart, 1725), and in which he sets forth his program for his edition which appeared at Tübingen in 1734.

[2] See Semler's edition of *Joh. Jac. Wetstenii libelli ad crisin atque interpretationem Novi Testamenti* (1766), to which he appended (pp. 167-206) his own "Spicilegium observationum de variantibus Novi Testamenti lectionibus in quo praecipua etiam ex Joh. Alb. Bengelii ... recensentur."

[3] J. L. Hug, *Einleitung in die Schriften des Neuen Testaments* (Stuttgart und Tübingen, 1808), § 38.

middle of the third century the text of the New Testament in the general mass of codices had degenerated into the form exhibited by codex Bezae, the Old Latin, minuscules 1, 13, 69, 124, the Sahidic, and several other witnesses. This uncorrected text, to which he gave the name κοινὴ ἔκδοσις ("common edition"), was then separately revised, he thought, by three scholars of the ancient Church, Origen, Hesychius, and Lucian. The Lucianic recension spread from Antioch to Constantinople, and from there to many other places, including Thrace, where it was quoted by Theophylact.

According to Hug's textual investigations in the Gospels, Lucian's recension is contained in the later uncial manuscripts E F G H S V and in lectionaries l 47 and l 50, as well as in the great majority of minuscule manuscripts. Making a comparison in Mark 4 of the readings of the Lucianic recension with the readings of the Hesychian recension (represented chiefly by manuscripts B C L), Hug showed the distinctive nature of each of these two recensions, as well as the relationship of the Lucianic text with the Peshitta Syriac. In the Acts of the Apostles Hug found that the Antiochian text is less close to the Peshitta than in the Gospels, and is contained in codices 101, 102, 103, 241, 464, and l^a 59, as well as in many other minuscules. In the Pauline and Catholic Epistles, besides D E F G the principal manuscript of this class is the beautifully written uncial codex K, along with many minuscules. In the Apocalypse this recension is found in codices 29, 241, 242, 2023, 2039, 2040.

Though Hug's enthusiasm for pressing the evidence into the neat categories of three recensions led him to make statements which a more cautious scholar could challenge (as was done, for example, by S. P. Tregelles),[1] it remains true that in certain respects Hug was ahead of his time, perceiving, as he did, the antiquity of many readings preserved in the later minuscule codices 1, 13, 69, 124.

The next stage, which was partly one of retrogression, was dominated by the work of Johann Martin Augustin Scholz,[2] the

---

[1] In vol. IV of T. H. Horne's *Introduction to the . . . critical Study and Knowledge of the Holy Scriptures*, 13th edition (London, 1872), pp. 78 f.

[2] J. M. A. Scholz, *Novum Testamentum graece . . .* I (Leipzig, 1830), pp. xv-xxi. Unlike Streeter, however, Scholz placed his chief emphasis upon certain external signs of provenance, such as details of palaeography, iconography, marginal notes, colophons, and evidence regarding local saints who were honored in menologia.

Roman Catholic Dean of Theology at Bonn and a former pupil of Hug. It must be said to his credit that he was the first to stress the importance of seeking to ascertain the geographical localities represented by the several manuscripts, a point which B. H. Streeter was to elaborate in the twentieth century in his theory of "local texts." After some tentative attempts at classifying manuscripts, Scholz came to adopt essentially Bengel's classification into two families, which he called the Alexandrian and the Constantinopolitan. Being impressed by the large number of manuscripts which preserve the Constantinopolitan text, he unwisely preferred this to the earlier Alexandrian type of text. In his discussion of the textual scholars in the early Church, Scholz sought to neutralize the force of the condemnation of Lucian's works, mentioned in the *Decretum Gelasianum,* by observing that only such books are put on the Roman Index of Prohibited Books as have circulated far and wide (*longe lateque*), and that therefore this adverse notice of Lucian's work is in reality a testimony to the wide diffusion of his critical labors on the New Testament text.[1]

Later in the nineteenth century the distinguished English textual critics, B. F. Westcott and F. J. A. Hort, adopted and slightly modified Griesbach's theory of three major ancient types of text of the New Testament. As is well known, they gave the name "Syrian" to the type of text which was formed about the beginning of the fourth century, and they tentatively associated Lucian with the production of this recension.[2] Since the Syrian text displays signs of having been produced by conflation of earlier texts, Westcott and Hort rejected its testimony in seeking to recover the earliest form of the text of the New Testament.[3] Though they did not supply lists of manuscripts which, in their judgment, present more or less purely the Antiochian type of text, they discussed the method of deciding whether a reading is pre-Syrian or not.[4] Readings which have little or no support in such uncials as ℵ B C D L P

---

[1] *Op. cit.,* vol. i, p. xxiv.

[2] *The New Testament in the Original Greek,* [Vol. ii], *Introduction [and] Appendix* (Cambridge, 1881), pp. 137 ff.

[3] It is significant that Bishop John W. Burgon, who ardently and, at times, acrimoniously opposed Hort's estimate of the secondary character of the Syrian text, nevertheless acknowledged that Lucian revised the text of the New Testament; see his volume, *The Revision Revised* (London, 1883), p. 29.

[4] *Op. cit.,* pp. 163 f.

Q R T Z (Δ in Mark) Ξ (also 33) for the Gospels (and similar lists
for other parts of the New Testament), are probably Syrian, and
therefore are to be rejected. The isolation and rejection of this type
of text, according to the judgment of James Hardy Ropes, "constitute the most important abiding result of nineteenth century
textual criticism."[1]

During the twentieth century by far the most thorough investigation of the Antiochian text was undertaken by Hermann von
Soden. Designating it the K (Κοινή) text, von Soden divided it into
about seventeen groups which present a progressive modification
of the text in minor details, mostly stylistic in nature. The chief
groups representing the gradual corruption of the K-text, according
to von Soden, are:

(1) K^1, which is found in Ω S V and about fifty minuscule codices.
(2) K^i (that is, K with a mixture of the I-form of text), which is
found in E F G H, etc., etc.
(3) K^x, which is found in the great mass of minuscule codices of
the eleventh and twelfth centuries.
(4) K^r, the latest form of the K-text, an officially prepared text,
which is found especially in manuscripts of the thirteenth and
later centuries, and which is furnished with a full apparatus
for lectionary purposes.

In addition to these principal groups, von Soden also distinguished a K^a-text, which is preserved in more than one hundred
manuscripts, the oldest of which is Codex Alexandrinus. Characteristic readings of this text are often found in various codices of the
I-text;[2] it is related to the texts used by the translators of the
Peshitta and by Chrysostom, the Cappadocians, and Theodoret
of Cyros.[3]

Von Soden had no hesitation in identifying the K^1 group, which
is the oldest form of the K-text, with the recension of Lucian.[4] He
also isolated the manuscripts which are provided with commentaries written by members of the Antiochian school.[5] Though von

[1] *The Text of Acts* (= *The Beginnings of Christianity*, ed. J. F. Foakes
Jackson and Kirsopp Lake, vol. III; London, 1926), p. cclxxvi.
[2] *Die Schriften des Neuen Testaments in ihrer ältesten erreichbaren Text-
gestalt*, I (Berlin, 1902), 850-893, 1160-1170, and 1460-1468. Von Soden
believed that the K^a-text was used by Victor of Antioch in his commentary
on Mark.
[3] *Ibid.*, p. 1471. For a detailed list of its characteristics, see pp. 1456-1459.
[4] *Ibid.*, pp. 718-721 and 765-774; cf. 1459-1469.
[5] *Ibid.*, pp. 249-257; cf. 535 ff.

Soden assigned several small fragments which date from the (fifth or) sixth century to the *K*-type of text, the earliest codex which contains this text complete dates from the eighth century (codex Ω).[1]

As is well known, in his textual evaluation of variant readings von Soden gave equal weight to evidence from each of his three main text types (the I H K texts), and therefore his critical edition is closer to the Textus Receptus than is true of the previous great critical texts, such as those of Tregelles, Tischendorf, Westcott and Hort, Weiss. To a greater or less extent, von Soden's methodology has influenced the textual labors of several Roman Catholic editors of the Greek Testament, notably H. J. Vogels, M. J. Bover, and August Merk.[2]

In the field of textual criticism the name of B. H. Streeter is linked to the development of the theory of "local texts" of the New Testament. Though not the first to suggest the idea (Scholz, as was mentioned above, had thrown out suggestions which may be regarded as anticipatory in certain respects, and early in the twentieth century Kirsopp Lake[3] had specifically called attention to the desirability of such investigations), Streeter was the first who systematically collected evidence for the localizing of text-types at the great Sees of the ancient church, and was the first also to isolate the so-called Caesarean text.[4] In connection with his discussion of "The Revised Versions of Antiquity"[5] Streeter declared that "nothing that has been discovered since [Westcott and Hort's work]

---

[1] *Ibid.*, p. 713.

[2] For an analysis of the textual complexion of these editions, see K. W. Clark's contribution to *The Background of the New Testament and its Eschatology*, edited by W. D. Davies and D. Daube (Cambridge, 1956), pp. 29-42, and Kurt Aland's discussion of "The Position of New Testament Textual Criticism," in *Studia Evangelica* (= *TU*, LXXIII; Berlin, 1959), pp. 717-731, especially pp. 719 ff.

[3] Referring to the use of von Soden's *apparatus criticus*, Lake wrote that it would be profitable "to see whether it does not really point to the existence of several local texts in the second and third centuries" (*Review of Theology and Philosophy*, IV [1908/09], 295); see also Lake's remarks about the possibility that fam. 1 and fam. 13 were "one ancient local text, which has suffered different degrees of corruption from mixture with the Antiochian text," *Codex 1 of the Gospels and Its Allies* (= *Texts and Studies*, VII; Cambridge, 1902), p. li.

[4] Though here again he was anticipated as to terminology by Burkitt, who pointed out that "for St. Mark, at least, Dr. Hort's categories are too few ....We have ... an Alexandrian-Caesarean group" etc.; so F. C. Burkitt in Edward A. Hutton's *Atlas of Textual Criticism* (Cambridge, 1911), p. 65.

[5] Burnett Hillman Streeter, *The Four Gospels, a Study of Origins* (London, 1924; revised, 1930), pp. 111-127.

appears to me to have weakened their case, so far as the main issue is concerned," namely, that "the Byzantine text is an essentially revised text—following sometimes one, sometimes another of the earlier texts."[1]

Streeter, however, pointed out that there are some important respects in which Hort's view of the constituent elements in the Lucianic revision must be modified in the light of subsequent discovery. The newly found Sinaitic Syriac manuscript of the Gospels, as F. C. Burkitt observed in the Additional Notes which he contributed to the second edition (1896) of Hort's volume of *Introduction [and] Appendix*,[2] reveals still more plainly than did the Curetonian Syriac manuscript that there once existed an old text of Antioch, related to the Western type of text, and that therefore agreements between the Sy^s and the Byzantine text deserve very careful scrutiny as to the possibility of their being original (a notable example is the reading εὐδοκίας of Luke 2.14, which Burkitt, Streeter, and Ropes held to be preferable to εὐδοκίας of B ℵ D).[3]

In an Excursus to the notable monograph on "The Caesarean Text of the Gospel of Mark,"[4] Kirsopp Lake gave attention to the Ecclesiastical Text of the New Testament. On the basis of a collation of 19 manuscripts, a test was made of the validity of von Soden's analysis of the sub-groups within the K-text. Among Lake's findings the following are of primary importance:

"We cannot at present distinguish anything which can be identified with von Soden's K^r, nor do we feel any confidence in his K^1-text as a really distinct text."[5]

"More important is the case of von Soden's K^a-family .... His general position is that K^a represents a revision of an I-text by K^1. The reviser chose always the variant which had a parallel in the gospels. In details of spelling and the like he followed K^1."[6]

"The most important observation made by von Soden is that the K^a-text was used by Theodoret, and in Luke and John by Chrysostom. He thinks that in Matthew and Mark Chrysostom preferred a K^1-text, though he is inclined to ascribe to him the creation of the

---

[1] *Ibid.*, p. 114.

[2] P. 330.

[3] Burkitt, *op. cit.*; Streeter, *op. cit.*, p. 115; Ropes, *HTR*, x (1917), 52-56 (see also p. 36 below).

[4] *HTR*, xxi (1928), 238-257.

[5] *Ibid.*, p. 341.

[6] *Ibid.*, p. 342.

K^a-text .... If it be true that K^a is the text of Theodoret, there is a presumption that it, as distinct from the Ecclesiastical, is the Antiochian text of the fifth century."[1]

The results of these investigations, are, as Lake observes, both instructive and disconcerting, "because they substantiate fully only two of von Soden's subdivisions of the K-text. Of course, the others may prove to be realities, but one would have supposed that the differences between K^1, K^x, and K^r would have been plain in a collation of over one hundred MSS for any chapter. It is impossible to repress a doubt whether von Soden's analysis of the K-text is not as incorrect as his classification of the I-codices,"[2] The most significant of Lake's findings, so far as the present survey is concerned,[3] is that K^a is the Lucianic recension and was used as the chief basis of the Ecclesiastical text (thus reversing von Soden's theory).

The most important uncial witnesses of the K^a group, according to von Soden, are codices A K Π. Using the consensus of two out of these three manuscripts to determine roughly the readings of the K^a-text where it differs from the Ecclesiastical text and the Textus Receptus, Lake found that the following manuscripts present a relatively pure K^a-text: 1318, 1313, 1219, 1220, 1223, 1346 (these are given in descending order of purity of text).[4]

It has often been stated by textual scholars that Chrysostom was one of the first Fathers to use the Antiochian text.[5] This opinion was examined by Jacob Geerlings and Silva New in a study based on evidence which, in default of a critical edition, was taken from Migne's edition of Chrysostom's *opera*.[6] Their conclusions are that "Chrysostom's text of Mark is not that of any group of manuscripts so far discovered and classified.... His text of Mark, or rather the

---

[1] *Ibid.*, pp. 344-345.   [2] *Ibid.*, pp. 347-348.

[3] One of the general conclusions which Lake draws is concerned with the almost total absence of evidence of direct genealogy in extant codices. Except for Family 1 and Family 13, "there seem to be no groups of manuscripts which are conceivably descendants of a single lost codex. There are cognate groups—families of distant cousins—but the manuscripts which we have are almost all orphan children without brothers or sisters ... It is hard to resist the conclusion that the scribes usually destroyed their exemplars when they had copied the sacred books," *ibid.*, pp. 348-349.

[4] *Ibid.*, p. 344.

[5] For example, Alexander Souter, *The Text and Canon of the New Testament* (New York, 1913), p. 85, "Chrysostom was the first great writer to use the fully developed ecclesiastical text" (this sentence is retained unchanged in the second edition, revised by Williams, p. 77).

[6] "Chrysostom's Text of the Gospel of Mark," *HTR*, XXIV (1931), 121-142.

text which can faintly be perceived through his quotations, is a 'mixed text,' combining some of the elements of each of the types which had flourished before the end of the fourth century."[1] Recognizing that this statement is open to misunderstanding, the authors emphasize that Chrysostom must not be linked with any one manuscript which is said to have a "mixed text." "The only similarity is the fact of being mixed, not the mixture which results."[2] In other words, "Chrysostom's text of Mark is first of all one peculiar to himself and full of unattested variants."[3] In another of the Gospels, that according to Matthew, Chrysostom seems to have followed a type of text which is preserved in the K^a group of witnesses.[4] In the Pauline Epistles an earlier study by C. K. Gifford revealed that Chrysostom preserves not a few Western readings.[5] More recently Joachim Förster, on the basis of an examination of 1043 quotations found in 88 of Chrysostom's Homilies, found that they involve "eine nicht kleine Zahl von Lesarten des westlichen Textes und der Koridethi-Familie (Θ)."[6]

In a subsequent study of one part of the Byzantine text, Mrs. Lake[7] found that K^a (i.e., family Π) does not include codex Alexandrinus, as von Soden thought, but that both had "a common ancestor which differed very little from the text which is found today in Π, rather more from that of A." She continues: "The reconstructed text of Family Π, therefore, represents a manuscript older than the Codex Alexandrinus and affords another witness to a text which must have existed in the early part of the fifth century, if not before. Moreover, both the text of Family Π and the Codex Alexandrinus were elements in the formation of the Ecclesiastical text,—the more

---

[1] *Ibid.*, 141-142.

[2] *Ibid.*, 142.

[3] *Ibid.* The authors, as will have been observed, are careful in each case to indicate that their conclusions refer only to Chrysostom's text of Mark. Though von Soden thought that in Matthew Chrysostom had used the K^1-text (Ω V etc.), he could not find material sufficient for defining the type of K-text used in Mark (*op. cit.*, i, ii, 1460 f.).

[4] Claude D. Dicks, "The Matthean Text of Chrysostom in his Homilies on Matthew," *JBL*, LXVII (1948), 365-376. This corrects von Soden's view that Chrysostom used a K^1-text in Matthew.

[5] C. K. Gifford, *Pauli epistolas qua forma legerit Johannes Chrysostomus* (Halle Diss., 1902), p. 77.

[6] Joachim Förster, "Gerechtigkeit für Lucian und die antiochenischer Text," *Monatschrift für Pastoraltheologie*, XLV (1956), 267-272.

[7] *Family Π and the Codex Alexandrinus, the Text according to Mark* (SD, vol. v; London, 1937).

or less standard text of the Middle Ages,—since it differs from each about equally and to the same extent that Π differs from A."[1]

What is the nature of the text represented in A and Π? Mrs. Lake indicates that perhaps the most important result of her investigation is the emphasis which it lays on the process of mixture. "The Caesarean text was described as a 'mixed' text, primarily a mixture of Neutral and Western. A and Π are now found to be mixed texts. The mixture varies in detail but is about the same in kind."[2] The most immediate descendents of codex Π, she found, are minuscules 114, 1079, 1219, 1500; while a descendent of 1219 was an ancestor of 489, 1346, 1816.[3]

What was the provenance of the common ancestor of Family Π and A? Without feeling any great confidence, Mrs. Lake hazarded the conjecture that this, and not the K^1-text (as von Soden thought), is to be identified with the Lucianic recension.[4]

Several other scholars have given serious attention to the great amount of mixture of text types in the Byzantine text. In an article entitled, "The Complex Character of the Late Byzantine Text of the Gospels," Ernest Cadman Colwell analyzes the text of a thirteenth century codex, Gregory 574, named the Four Gospels of Karahissar. Colwell speaks of "the almost incredibly confused

[1] *Ibid.*, p. ix.

[2] *Ibid.*, p. 71. Mrs. Lake continues as follows: "The question becomes: What texts are not mixed? The answer must be,—none of those now known. The degree of mixture varies. The mixture was made at different periods ... The whole question is: which manuscript influenced which? The solution rests upon patristic evidence if there be any. The only certainly unmixed text of each Gospel was its original text. There must once have been such an original, but only the vaguest guesses can be made as to its character."

[3] *Ibid.*, p. 29. It will be recalled that Wilhelm Bousset discovered the close relationship of K Π and 489; see his *Textkritische Studien zum Neuen Testament* (= *TU*, xi, 4; Leipzig, 1894), p. 134.

[4] *Fam.* II, pp. ix-x. In a subsequent article, Kirsopp and Silva Lake indulge in several other conjectures, which are stimulating in themselves, but for which there is no proof. Regarding the origin of the K^1 text, "We suggest that it may be linked with the renaissance of calligraphy which either started in, or found one of its chief centers in, the Monastery of the Stoudion [at Constantinople] in the ninth and tenth centuries ... If our suggestion has any validity, the K^1 text might perhaps be called the 'Macedonian' text,— for Basil the Macedonian and his successors were the great encouragers of the Stoudion and of the movement which it inaugurated. In the same way, K^x may have been the fashionable text of the Comneni, and K^r that of the Palaeologi" ("The Byzantine Text of the Gospels," *Mémorial Lagrange* [Paris, 1940], p. 255). For a study of the K^r text, see also David O. Voss, "Is von Soden's K^r a Distinct Type of Text?" *JBL*, LVII (1938), 311-316. Voss answers the question in the title of his article with a decided affirmative.

relationships of this one MS of the Gospels.... The most striking feature of the text of 574 is variety. A very close relationship has been established between its text and that of more than a dozen other MSS. But it never agrees with all twelve at once, nor does it agree with any one MS for more than half a gospel."[1] According to the author "the two most astounding results of this study were (1) the remarkably large number of variants from the *textus receptus*, and (2) the absence of one clear-cut dominant group."[2]

Two other studies of the Greek text in late witnesses also suggest its heterogeneous character. Ernest W. Saunders discovered half a dozen singular variants in a thirteenth century tetraevangelium at Duke University which agree with readings in the Commentaries of Theophylact of Bulgaria.[3] In a series of articles on the text used by Photius, the Patriarch of Constantinople, J. N. Birdsall refers to a most unexpected textual situation. Photius "knew and habitually quoted ... texts akin to those isolated by von Soden and classified in his various *I*-groups, and denominated 'mixed texts' by Ropes in his study of the text of Acts."[4] Indeed, Birdsall goes so far as to assert that "in Photius' time the Byzantine text was not the dominant text-type in Greek Christendom, and it was either unknown to him or not approved by him."[5]

C. *Charateristics of the Lucianic Text*

Since the time of Field it has been customary for Septuagint scholars to characterize Lucian's work as follows:[6]

---

[1] *JBL*, LIV (1935), 214.

[2] *Ibid.*, p. 213.

[3] Ernest W. Saunders, "Studies in Doctrinal Influences on the Byzantine Text of the Gospels," *JBL*, LXXI (1952), 85-92.

[4] J. N. Birdsall, "The Text of the Acts and the Epistles in Photius," *JTS*, n.s. IX (1958), 278-291. The quotation is from p. 290.

[5] *Idem*, "The Text of the Gospels in Photius," *JTS*, n.s. VII (1956), 42-56, 190-198. The quotation is from p. 198.

[6] Field, *op. cit.*, pp. lxxxix ff.; for other discussions of the characteristics of the Lucianic recension of various Old Testament books, see W. O. E. Oesterley, *Studies in the Greek and Latin Versions of the Book of Amos* (London, 1902), pp. 61-67; Rahlfs, *Der Text des Septuaginta-Psalters* (Göttingen, (1907), p. 231; C. C .Torrey, *Ezra Studies* (Chicago, 1910), pp. 106-109; O. Procksch, *Studien zur Geschichte der Septuaginta: Die Propheten* (Leipzig, 1910), pp. 79-87; Rahlfs, *Lucians Rezension der Königsbücher* (Göttingen, 1911), pp. 171-183, 239-288, 294; Rahlfs, *Studie über den griechischen Text des Buches Ruth* (Berlin, 1922), pp. 83-90; and J. Ziegler, "Hat Lukian den griechischen Sirach rezensiert?" *B*, XL (1959), 210-229, especially p. 229.

(1) Lucian filled up omissions in the Septuagint, showing a certain amount of freedom in handling the text. For example, in Isaiah 40.7-8 he supplied the deficiency in the Septuagint with the rendering of Symmachus and Theodotion, but with certain small changes. In Jeremiah 44.18, he inserted material from Aquila, again with small verbal changes in the Greek.

(2) He produced a large number of double, or conflate, readings; i.e. while retaining the Septuagintal reading he added a rendering that presumably expresses more closely the Hebrew text current in Antioch, which may well have differed from that current in Alexandria several centuries earlier. Thus, in I Sam. 12.2 the Hebrew has "I am old and grayheaded," which the Septuagint, adopting another pointing of the same consonants, renders "I am old and will sit down" (γεγήρακα καὶ καθήσομαι). Here Lucian kept the Septuagint and inserted (perhaps from Aquila) καὶ πεπολίωμαι to render the Hebrew. Another instance is found in Isaiah 24.23 where the Hebrew has "the moon shall be confounded, and the sun ashamed," while the Septuagint renders "the brick shall waste away and the wall shall fall." Lucian kept the latter reading and added from Symmachus a literal translation of the Hebrew. Again, in II Kings 20.3, where the Septuagint renders the phrase בֶּאֱמֶת with ἐν ἀληθείᾳ, Lucian, retaining this rendering, added καὶ ἐν πίστει, which is probably to be regarded as an alternative translation of the pregnant Hebrew phrase.

(3) He introduced a number of interpolations to serve as explanations (e.g. proper names are substituted for pronouns), or to make the connection clearer, or to smooth out instances of grammatical harshness. Thus, in II Samuel 12.1 Nathan begins his parable to David simply, "There were two men," but Lucian inserted the words—"Tell me this judgment: there were two men." Again in I Kings 15.23 the Septuagint (with the Hebrew) says of Asa, "in the time of his old age, he was diseased in his feet," which in Lucian appears in the form, "in the time of his old age Asa *did wickedly and was diseased in his feet.*" In the Book of Ruth, Lucian added the proper name Νοεμμείν in 1.7; 2.2, 3, 10, 17; 3.6, 7, 14, 16.

(4) He substituted synonyms for many words employed by the Septuagint. In some of these cases it is difficult to discover the reason for the alteration, as φρόνησις for σοφία, ἐγένετο for ἦν, διέβη for παρῆλθεν, δοῦλοι for παῖδες, ἐξείλατο for ἐρύσατο, etc., etc., etc. In other cases it appears that Lucian, acting under the influence of

the Atticizing tendency of grammarians of the time, replaced Hellenistic forms of the Septuagint (such as ἐλάβοσαν, εἶπαν, τὸ ἔλεος, ἐγενήθη) with those of Attic usage (ἔλαβον, εἶπον, ὁ ἔλεος, ἐγένετο).[1]

The critical principles and methods which Lucian followed in making his recension of the Old Testament are plainly observable in the Antiochian text of the New Testament. Indeed, Ropes declares, "There is not one of the well-known characteristics of the Antiochian New Testament which cannot be illustrated from the Old Testament of Lucian."[2] Hort's comprehensive and elegant summary of these characteristics is a classic description:

"The qualities which the authors of the Syrian text seem to have most desired to impress on it are lucidity and completeness. They were evidently anxious to remove all stumbling-blocks out of the way of the ordinary reader, so far as this could be done without recourse to violent measures. They were apparently equally desirous that he should have the benefit of instructive matter contained in all the existing texts, provided it did not confuse the context or introduce seeming contradictions. New omissions accordingly are rare, and where they occur are usually found to contribute to apparent simplicity. New interpolations on the other hand are abundant, most of them being due to harmonistic or other assimilation, fortunately capricious and incomplete. Both in matter and in diction the Syrian text is conspicuously a full text. It delights in pronouns, conjuctions, and expletives and supplied links of all kinds, as well as in more considerable additions. As distinguished from the bold vigour of the 'Western' scribes, and the refined scholarship of the Alexandrians, the spirit of its own corrections is at once sensible and feeble. Entirely blameless on either literary or religious grounds as regards vulgarised or unworthy diction, yet shewing no marks of either critical or spiritual insight, it presents the New Testament in a form smooth and attractive, but appreciably impoverished in sense and force, more fitted for cursory perusal or recitation than for repeated and diligent study."[3]

It is scarcely necessary to set forth here examples which illustrate these types of editoral revision; von Soden assembled a large num-

---

[1] Rahlfs, *Lucians Rezension der Königsbücher* (Göttingen, 1911), p. 294; and *Das Buch Ruth griechisch* (1922), p. 13.

[2] James Hardy Ropes, *The Text of Acts* (Cambridge, 1926), p. cclxxxiii.

[3] Westcott and Hort, *Introduction [and] Appendix*, pp. 134 f.

ber in order to describe the Koine text.[1] It will be sufficient to observe that, to judge by the pains which the reviser or the revisers obviously took in performing their task, their aim was not merely to bring an old manuscript up-to-date, but to prepare an exemplar from which semi-official copies could be made.

III. THE INFLUENCE OF THE ANTIOCHIAN TEXT OUTSIDE THE GREEK CHURCH

The influence of Lucian of Antioch as textual editor was felt far beyond his native country of Syria. As has been indicated in the previous pages, his recension of the New Testament was adopted at Constantinople and from there it spread widely throughout Greek speaking lands. Portions of his work on the Old Testament (notably the Psalter) became the official text of the Orthodox Church, and manuscripts of his recension of the rest of the Old Testament circulated alongside other forms of the Septuagint. But even beyond the limits of the Greek Orthodox Church, Lucian influenced the form of the New Testament and parts of the Old Testament which were used, and are still used, by millions who never heard of his name.

The first translation of the Bible into a Teutonic language dates from the second half of the fourth century and was made, as is well known, by Ulfilas, the apostle to the Goths. When one considers that it was probably at Antioch in Syria that he was consecrated bishop (about A.D. 341),[2] and that in A.D. 360 he was present at the synod of Constantinople,[3] one is not surprised that the basis of his version should have been the Antiochian-Constantinopolitan type of text. This was proved by Kauffmann, who, in a thorough textual analysis of the very fragmentary remains of the Gothic Old Testament, showed that Ulfilas followed a Greek text which at some points was in close agreement with Lucian's recension of the Septuagint text.[4] Thus in Neh. 7.24 and 35 the Gothic version agrees with two manuscripts of the Lucianic recension (Holmes and Parsons 93, 108) in

[1] *Op. cit.*, I, ii, 1456-1459 (cf. 1361-1400), 1784-1787.
[2] See C. A. A. Scott, *Ulfilas, the Apostle of the Goths* (Cambridge, 1885), pp. 47 f., and 115.
[3] See Lagarde, *Mitteilungen*, IV (Göttingen, 1891), 21-23; and *Librorum Veteris Testamenti canonicorum pars prior* (Göttingen, 1883), pp. viii ff.
[4] Friederich Kauffmann, "Beiträge zur Quellenkritik der gotischen Bibel-übersetzung," *Zeitschrift für deutsche Philologie*, XXIX (1897), 306-337.

the names Ἀσσομ and Ἡραμ, agreements found in no other known manuscripts of the Septuagint.[1]

On the other hand Kauffmann also collected instances in which the Gothic departs from Lucian and agrees with the B-text of the Septuagint. He concluded, therefore, that the Gothic does not preserve the original Lucianic text, but one derived from it. This conclusion, however, was modified in 1912, when through the cleaning of certain Gothic fragments it became possible to read more precisely the script of a fragment (codex D) which preserves some verses of Neh. 7. It was discovered that no fewer than sixteen new readings could be deciphered, and that all of them agree with the Lucianic text. Thus, both as to number and significance, this new evidence resulted in a reassessment of Kauffmann's evaluation of the textual character of the Gothic fragments of the Old Testament, which are now seen to be more thoroughly Lucianic than had been previously suspected.[2]

As regards the New Testament, scholars generally agree that the type of text represented in the Gothic version is basically the Antiochian or Syrian form of text with a certain number of Western and non-Western readings embedded in it.[3] Von Soden was unable to find in Greek a precisely similar mixture of K and I readings, but he observed that its affinities seemed closest to his K^a-type.[4] The Gothic version, therefore, appears to be the oldest extant representative of the Lucianic recension, despite subsequent infiltration of readings from the Old Latin version.[5]

---

[1] Kauffmann thought that the text of the brief fragments from Genesis in the Gothic version were also Lucianic, but the subsequent research by Hautsch (see p. 10 above) proving that Lagarde was in error in his reconstruction of the Lucianic recension of the book of Genesis necessitates that a new analysis be made of the Gothic version for this book.

[2] Wilhelm Streitberg, *Die gotische Bibel*, 3te aufl., 1 (Heidelberg, 1950), pp. xxxiv f.

[3] E.g. Westcott and Hort, *op. cit.*, p. 158; Friederich Kauffmann, "Beiträge zur Quellenkritik der gotischen Übersetzung," *Zeitschrift für deutsche Philologie*, xxx (1898), 144-183; xxxi (1898-99), 178-194; Paul Odefey, *Das gotische Lucas-Evangelium. Ein Beitrag zur Quellenkritik und Textgeschichte* (Flensburg, 1908); G. W. S. Friedrichsen, *The Gothic Version of the Gospels, a Study of its Style and Textual History* (Oxford, 1939); Streitberg, *op. cit.*, pp. xxxv-xl; and H. Steubing, "Miscellen zur gotischer Bibelübersetzung des Ulfilas," *Zeitschrift für Kirchengeschichte*, LXIV (1952-53), 137-165. On the difficulties of analyzing the Gothic text, see Friedrichsen, "The Gothic Text and the Fourth Century Byzantine Text," *JTS*, xxxix (1938), 42-44.

[4] Von Soden, *op. cit.*, 1, ii, 1469.

[5] See, now, Friedrichsen, *Gothic Studies* (Oxford, 1961), pp. 63 f. and 67 ff.

Besides influencing the Gothic version, the Lucianic recension made itself felt also on the first translation of the Scriptures into a Slavic language, that of Sts. Cyril and Methodius in Old Church Slavonic. In view of the contacts which these two apostles to the Slavs had with Constantinople, such dependence is not unexpected.[1] Those who have examined the question as regards the Old Testament report that the amount of Lucianic influence on the Slavonic text varies in different books. On the basis of a limited number of passages, the author of an unsigned article in the *Church Quarterly Review*[2] found that in the books of Kings the version commonly agrees with Lucian against manuscripts A and B, while for other books it agrees with A and B against Lucian. A definitive examination of the textual complexion of the Old Slavonic Psalter was made by Josef Vajs. On the basis of a critical analysis of 529 passages Vajs discovered that in 449 instances the Old Slavonic version is purely Lucianic in character, while the remaining 80 variants show influence from the Latin Vulgate text (as is not uncommon in Croatian manuscripts).[3]

In the case of the New Testament, several scholars have examined the textual relations of the Old Slavonic version.[4] Though they differ somewhat as to details, the consensus of their findings seems to be that the predominant character of the Old Slavonic New Testament is derived from the Antiochian or Byzantine text, with a certain number of readings from other families of texts. On the basis of an examination of about 2500 variant readings in the Slavonic tetraevangelium, Vajs concluded that almost one half of them belong to the Antiochian recension, about a fifth to the Western, and an even smaller proportion to the Alexandrian.

The Old Church Slavonic Bible formed, as is well known, the basis for other translations into several Slavic languages of the

---

[1] Lagarde remarks in the preface to his edition of Lucian, "Ni omnia fallunt, Slavos nihil aliud vertit nisi Luciani recensionem," p. xv, and in his *Mitteilungen*, II (Göttingen, 1887), 53, he expresses the need for further examination of the relation of the Slavonic version to Lucian.

[2] "Lucian's Recension of the Septuagint," *CQR*, LI, (1900-1901), 388 f.

[3] "Které recense byla řecká předloha staroslověnského překladu žaltáře," (with a French résumé), *Byz.*, VIII (1939-1946), 55-86. In the case of the Book of Ruth, however, Vajs discovered that its text goes back, not to the Lucianic recension but apparently to the Hesychian; Josef Vajs, *Kniha Rut v překladě staroslovanském* (= *Kritické studie staroslovanskeho texta biblického*, II; Prague, 1926); cf. Alfons Marguliés in *Archiv für slavische Philologie*, XLII (1928), 52.

[4] For a survey of this research, see pp. 79 ff. below.

past and present.[1] Thus in modified form the Antiochian or Constantinopolitan recension has formed the basis of the New Testament and the Psalter for millions of Slavic peoples.

As regards the history of the printed form of the Greek New Testament, the so-called *Textus Receptus*, which was based chiefly on manuscripts of the Antiochian recension, has been reprinted, with only minor modifications, in almost one thousand editions from 1514 down to the twentieth century.[2] When one considers how many translations into the vernaculars of Europe, Asia, Africa, and South America have been based on the Greek Textus Receptus, or on a translation which in turn was rendered from the Textus Receptus of the New Testament (such as the King James version or Luther's translation), it will be appreciated how enormous has been the influence of Lucian's recension, made in Antioch about the turn of the third and fourth centuries of the Christian era.

IV. The Critical Value of the Lucianic Recension

Westcott and Hort's view that the Syrian text of the New Testament is worthless for the recovery of the original text has left its mark, not only on their own edition, but on much subsequent textual analysis. As regards the Old Testament Eberhard Nestle declared flatly, "The recension of Lucian is quite the most useless for those objects for which we use and need the Septuagint most."[3]

---

[1] For a list of these, see T. H. Darlow and H. F. Moule, *Historical Catalogue of the Printed Editions of Holy Scripture in the Library of the British and Foreign Bible Society*, 2 vols in 4 parts (London, 1903-1908), and *British Museum General Catalogue of Printed Books*, vols. XVI-XVIII (London, 1936-37).

[2] For a classified list of printed editions of the Greek New Testament, see Eduard Reuss, *Bibliotheca Novi Testamenti Graeci* (Brunsvigae, 1872). This list is supplemented by Isaac H. Hall in Philip Schaff, *A Companion to the Greek New Testament and the English Version*, 3rd ed. (New York, 1889), pp. 497-524. For a scathing indictment of British scholarship which acquiesced to using an outdated Greek text, see Eberhard Nestle, "The Present Greek Testaments of the Clarendon Press, Oxford," *JTS*, V (1904), 274-279, with a weak defense by W[illiam] S[anday], *ibid.*, pp. 279 f. For a summary of a series of articles against modern critical editions of the New Testament and in favor of the Ecclesiastical Greek text, written by Prof. Ivanov of the Moscow Theological Academy and published in *Zhurnal Moskovskoi Patriarchii* (1954-1956), see Robert P. Casey, "A Russian Orthodox View of New Testament Textual Criticism," *Theology*, LX (1957), 50-54.

[3] Nestle made the statement first in his *Septuagintastudien*, I (Ulm, 1886), 9. He repeated it (*ibid.*, II [Ulm, 1896], 12) with a comment of approval from Franz Delitzsch, and explained his meaning more fully in "Zur Rekonstruktion der Septuaginta," *Philologus*, LVIII (1899), 121-131.

It appears to the present writer, however, that these unfavorable estimates of the value of the Antiochian text must be at least partially revised in the light of critical study of what may be called (for the want of a better name) the Ur-Lucianic text. Let us begin first with the Old Testament.

A. *The Old Testament*

It is a curious fact that certain readings which have been generally regarded as typical of Lucian's recension of the Greek Old Testament occur in texts and authors that are earlier than Lucian. The following is a list of seven such pre-Lucianic witnesses to a form of text which, at least in part, resembles the Lucianic recension.

(1) Although not all scholars who have investigated the subject are in agreement as to how to explain the data, there seems to be substantial evidence to prove that various parts of the Old Latin version of the Old Testament contain Lucianic readings. This was noticed first by Ceriani in connection with Lamentations,[1] and then by Vercellone,[2] who observed that when the glosses in the margin of the Leon manuscript depart from the ordinary Septuagint text they agree with the readings of the Lucianic group 19-82-93-108. Other scholars have called attention to the same type of text in other parts of the Old Latin Bible. Thus, Burkitt found that "the Old Latin in the Prophets sometimes supports 'Lucianic' readings. This fact proves that among the constituents of the eclectic text most used by the Antiochene Fathers of the fourth century there was an ancient element akin to the Old Latin, but quite independent of our leading MSS codd. A ℵ B."[3] For the Books of Samuel, S. R. Driver wrote, "The Old Latin is a version made, or revised, on the basis of manuscripts agreeing closely with those which were followed by Lucian in framing his recension. The Old Latin must date from the second century A.D.; hence it cannot be based on the recension of Lucian as such; its peculiar interest lies in the fact that it affords independent evidence of the existence of MSS. containing Lucian's characteristic readings (or renderings), considerably before

---

[1] A. M. Ceriani, *Monumenta sacra et profana*, i, i (Milan, 1861), p. xvi (addenda).

[2] Carlo Vercellone, *Variae lectiones Vulgatae latinae Bibliorum editionis*, ii (Rome, 1864), xxi-xxii, 179; cf. i, pp. xciii-xcv.

[3] F. C. Burkitt, *The Book of Rules of Tyconius* (= *TS*, iii, 1; Cambridge, 1895), p. cxvii.

the time of Lucian himself."[1] The Belgian scholar, Dieu, sought to explain these parallels in terms of scribal activity in replacing the original form of the Old Latin quotations with a form that resembles the text of Lucian.[2] Although a certain number of Lucianic glosses may have been introduced here and there into one or more Old Latin witnesses, the wide variety of evidence makes it difficult to explain all the data in this way. According to the investigation of Montgomery,[3] the Old Latin text of Daniel likewise displays Lucianic readings, and Haupert, one of Montgomery's students, found that the situation is similar for the Books of Kings.[4]

These phenomena in Old Latin manuscripts appear to be corroborated by quotations of the Bible made by Latin authors who lived prior to Lucian. Although Rahlfs had concluded that no Latin author before Lucifer of Cagliari (died 371) cited characteristic Lucianic readings in the Books of Kings,[5] Capelle, in a monograph on the text of the Latin Psalter in Africa, discovered that both Tertullian and Cyprian show a certain amount of acquaintance with a pre-Lucianic form of text of the Psalms.[6] In a recent analysis of Cyprian's citations from the four Books of Kings, Fischer[7] found that Cyprian agrees with Lucian in those readings which are linguistic corrections or which otherwise improve the Greek text according to the Hebrew, but that, quite understandably, he does not agree with Lucian when the latter takes over hexaplaric variants. Furthermore, in many cases where Cyprian agrees with Lucian, other Old Latin witnesses are corrected to the Septuagint.

---

[1] S. R. Driver, *Notes on the Hebrew Text and the Topography of the Books of Samuel*, 2nd ed. (Oxford, 1931), p. lxxvi.

[2] L. Dieu, "Retouches Lucianiques sur quelques textes de la vieille version latine (I et II Samuel)," *RB*, n.s., XVI (1919), 372-403.

[3] James A. Montgomery, *A Critical and Exegetical Commentary on the Book of Daniel* (New York, 1927), pp. 54-55.

[4] R. S. Haupert, *The Relation of Codex Vaticanus and the Lucianic Text in the Books of the Kings from the Viewpoint of the Old Latin and the Ethiopic Versions* (Univ. of Penna. Diss., 1930), pp. 36 f. Whether these data prove that the Old Latin Version was made originally at Antioch in Syria, as some have thought, need not be examined here; for a classic discussion of the problem, see H. A. A. Kennedy, "Latin Versions, the Old," Hastings' *Dictionary of the Bible*, III (New York, 1900), p. 54.

[5] *Lucians Rezension der Königsbücher* (Göttingen, 1911), pp. 158 ff.

[6] Paul Capelle, *Le texte du Psautier latin en Afrique* (= *Collectanae biblica latina*, IV; Rome, 1913), p. 204.

[7] Bonifatius Fischer, "Lukian-Lesarten in der Vetus Latina der vier Königsbücher," *Miscellanea biblica et orientalia R. P. Athanasio Miller ... oblata* (= *Studia Anselmiana*, XXVII-XXVIII; Rome, 1951), 169-177.

The wide distribution of Old Latin evidence and the general consensus among scholars that the origin of the Old Latin version of the Old Testament dates from about the second century A.D. make the conclusion inevitable that the Greek text lying behind the Old Latin was one element, and perhaps one of the more important elements, from which the composite Lucianic text was constructed.

(2) The Peshitta version of the Old Testament also exhibits numerous readings which find a parallel in the recension associated with Lucian. At the end of the last century Stockmayer[1] found more than a score of readings in I Samuel where Lucian agrees with the Peshitta against the Masoretic text and the current Septuagint text. Although the exact date of the translation of the Old Testament Peshitta is not known, most scholars believe that it was made in the second or third century of the Christian era. Thus, at least in the Books of Samuel, it too affords evidence of Ur-Lucianic readings.

One is not limited, however, to versional evidence testifying to the existence of an Ur-Lucianic text. Several pieces of Greek evidence point in the same direction; they are the following:

(3) A papyrus fragment (Rahlfs' no. 2054),[2] dating from the third (or possibly the second) Christian century, contains the Greek text of Psalm 77.1-18 in a form which exhibits several significant agreements with the Lucianic text, some of which are against all other witnesses cited by Rahlfs in his edition of *Psalmi cum Odis*. In other words, fully half a century before Lucian made his recension in Syria, a Greek text circulated in Egypt which anticipated certain of Lucian's characteristic readings.

(4) At the middle of the second century Justin Martyr cited the Old Testament in a form which Bousset found to agree frequently with the Lucianic recension; moreover, this agreement, Bousset declared, is "nicht nur in einzelnen Stellen, sondern in weiterem Umfange."[3] Puzzled as to how to explain the apparent anachronism, Bousset felt compelled to suppose that scribes in transmitting Justin's works brought his quotations into harmony with the pre-

---

[1] Theodor Stockmayer, "Hat Lucian zu seiner Septuagintrevision die Peschito benützt?" *Zeitschrift für die alttestamentliche Wissenschaft*, XII (1892), 218-223.

[2] The fragment, which is 240 in the Greek and Roman Museum in Alexandria, was edited by M. Norsa in *Bulletin de la Société royale d'archéologie d'Alexandrie*, XXII (1926), 162-164.

[3] Wilhelm Bousset, *Die Evangeliencitate Justins des Märtyrers in ihrem Wert für die Evangelienkritik* (Göttingen, 1891), p. 20.

vailing Antiochian text of the Old Testament. Schürer, however, in his review of Bousset's monograph pointed out that not every reading which is found in Lucianic manuscripts is later than Justin.[1]

(5) At the end of the first Christian century Josephus had before him a Greek copy of the Books of Samuel which, according to the research of Mez, diverged widely from codices A and B and habitually agreed with the text of Lucian, following this text even against the Hebrew.[2] Rahlfs re-examined with great care the evidence presented by Mez, extending the scope of the investigation to Josephus's text of the Books of Kings. His conclusion was that Mez exaggerated the measure and significance of the agreement between Josephus and Lucian, but that, particularly in the Books of Samuel, some readings which appear in the Lucianic recension were current at a much earlier time.[3] Going far beyond this cautious evaluation, Thackeray (who showed no acquaintance with Rahlfs's monograph) asserted roundly: "The Josephan Biblical text is *uniformly* of this Lucianic type from I Samuel to I Maccabees."[4]

(6) In an analysis of the Old Testament quotations in the New Testament, Staerk discovered that here and there New Testament citations diverge from all the major codices of the Septuagint and agree with the Lucianic text.[5] It must be admitted, however, that this evidence is not conclusive, for we can never be sure on which side the borrowing may lie (i.e., the Byzantine scribe of the Lucianic codices may have conformed the Old Testament text to the Antiochian form with which he was familiar in the New Testament quotations). Nevertheless, it is pertinent to observe that the very widespread interpolation of the Pauline catena in Romans 3.13-18

---

[1] *Theologische Literaturzeitung*, XVI (1891), 67.

[2] Adam Mez, *Die Bibel des Josephus untersucht für Buch V-VII der Archäologie* (Basel, 1895), p. 80.

[3] Rahlfs, *Lucians Rezension der Königsbücher*, pp. 80-111.

[4] Henry St. John Thackeray, *Josephus, the Man and the Historian* (New York, 1929), p. 85. In the Preface to the Cambridge edition of the Septuagint text of the Books of Samuel, Thackeray declares that from I Sam. 8 onwards "Josephus becomes a witness of first-importance for the text of the Greek Bible ... His main source is a Greek Bible containing a text closely allied to that of the 'Lucianic' group of MSS., but anterior by more than two centuries to the date of Lucian" (p. ix).

[5] W. Staerk, "Die alttestamentlichen Citate bei den Schriftstellern des Neuen Testaments," *Zeitschrift für wissenschaftliche Theologie*, XXXV (1892), 464-485; XXXVI, 1 (1893), 70-98.

after Psalm 13 (14).3, an addition which Jerome says[1] was current in the widely-used text of his day and which Rahlfs even prints as part of the Septuagint text, did not appear in the Lucianic recension, nor did the scribes of these manuscripts succumb to the temptation to add it.

(7) In the John Rylands Library at Manchester there are fragmentary remains of a papyrus scroll containing Deuteronomy 23.25; 25.2-3; and 26.18 in Greek.[2] The text of these tiny fragments, which date from about the middle of the second century B.C., appears to be related to the Lucianic form of the Greek Bible.[3]

From these seven items it can be seen that various texts and authors earlier than Lucian of Antioch present readings which agree with what is believed to be the Lucianic recension of the Greek Old Testament.[4] The conclusion which one must draw is that, despite the numerous secondary features which Lucian introduced into his recension of the Old Testament, one may expect to find here and there in it certain readings, not extant in the other forms of the Septuagint, which will be useful in ascertaining the most ancient form of the Hebrew text.

B. *The New Testament*

In evaluating the critical worth of the Antiochian text of the

---

[1] For a discussion of the correct text of Jerome's comment on this interpolation, see E. F. Sutcliffe, "The κοινή, 'diversa' or 'dispersa'? St. Jerome, P.L. 24, 548 B," *B*, xxxv (1955), 213-222. It is curious that elsewhere Jerome calls the Lucianic recension the κοινή text; see p. 5 above.

[2] It was edited by C. H. Roberts, *Two Biblical Papyri in the John Rylands Library, Manchester* (Manchester, 1936).

[3] So Albert Vaccari, "Fragmentum Biblicum saeculi II ante Christum," *B*, xvii (1936), 501-504; compare P. E. Kahle, "Problems of the Septuagint," in *Studia Patristica*, ed. by Kurt Aland and F. L. Cross, I (= *Texte und Untersuchungen*, LXIII; Berlin, 1957), 328-338.

[4] It may be mentioned here that Paul Wendland's careful examination of the Old Testament quotations in one of Philo's tractates and his conclusion that in a large proportion of cases the text of Philo agrees with Lucian and seldom joins other manuscripts against Lucian, cannot be accepted without being re-examined ("Zu Philos Schrift *de posteritate Caini*. Nebst Bemerkungen zur Rekonstruktion der Septuaginta," *Philologus*, LVII [1898], 248-288). Wendland naturally made use of Lagarde's edition of the Lucianic text, but since this begins to be Lucianic only on p. 259, line 3, with Ruth 4.11 (so Rahlfs, *Studie ... Ruth*, pp. 77 f.), a comparison of Philo's Pentateuchal quotations with this edition counts for nothing. See Peter Katz, "Das Problem des Urtextes der Septuaginta," *Theologische Zeitschrift*, v (1949), 19 f., and his monograph, *Philo's Bible* (Cambridge, 1950), p. 12, note 1.

New Testament, one finds a general disposition among scholars (except a few who have been influenced by von Soden's methodology) to disregard readings in the New Testament which are supported solely or chiefly by this recension. The poor opinion which Westcott and Hort had of the Syrian text is shared by many, and doubtless there is much to justify such an evaluation. On the other hand, however, what was said above regarding the presence of ancient readings in the Lucianic recension of the Old Testament ought to make one cautious about rejecting off-handedly and as a matter of course every Antiochian reading in the New Testament. In fact, since the time of Westcott and Hort, the acquisition of several new witnesses has tended to put the matter in a new light.

Already in the second edition of Westcott and Hort's volume of *Introduction [and] Appendix* (1896), F. C. Burkitt proposed several minor modifications of their estimate of the Syrian text. In characterizing the text of the newly discovered Sinaitic manuscript, Burkitt wrote:

> "This Eastern text, which does not survive in an approximately pure form in any known Greek MS, has thus affinities with both the great Pre-Antiochian groups headed by ℵ B and D respectively; it also stands in places against ℵ B D united, entering not unfrequently as an independent constituent element into the Antiochian (Syrian) text. Most of the Antiochian readings which contain interesting matter and which are witnessed by neither ℵ B nor D latt are found in the Old Syriac; and while there is no trace in the Old Syriac of the distinctively Antiochian conflations, there are several instances where the Antiochian text has been composed out of the mutually exclusive variants of ℵ B D and the Latins on the one hand, and the Old Syriac, supported perhaps by a few cursives, on the other."[1]

As examples of Antiochian readings which contain interesting material, and are not supported by ℵ B or D latt, Burkitt cited the omission of οὐδὲ ὁ υἱός in Matthew 24.36; the addition of καὶ ταραχαί in Mark 13.8; εὐδοκία in Luke 2.14; and ἔδει substituted for γέγραπται in Luke 24.46.[2] While perhaps Burkitt would not have gone so far as to accept the Antiochian form of all of these examples as the original text, he saw clearly that one must not reject a Syrian reading out of hand merely because it is not supported by either ℵ B or D latt.

---

[1] Westcott and Hort, *The New Testament in the Original Greek*, [vol. ii] *Introduction [and] Appendix*, 2nd ed. (London, 1896), p. 330.
[2] *Ibid.*

A few years later, in his discussion of the relation of the Old Syriac and the Antiochian text, Burkitt again pointed out that, while in general the Textus Receptus "has but little affinity with the Old Syriac Version," yet "in a few cases, some of them of considerable importance, the Old Syriac does agree with the later Greek MSS against the early Western and Alexandrian evidence."[1] He cited three examples to illustrate his point, εὐδοκία of Luke 2.14, ἄριστον in Luke 14.15, and ἀναβοήσας of Mark 15.8. Of these three, the last seemed to him to have the greatest possibility of being the original.

Since, however, the Syr[s] and Syr[c] are both incomplete, and since they would supply, even if they were complete, but slender evidence for the Ur-Lucianic text at Antioch, it is not unreasonable to suppose that some of the readings of the Lucianic text which do not appear in the Old Syriac may have been derived from the old text of Antioch. Concerning the possibility of detecting pre-Lucianic elements, Streeter wrote: "We have no means of identifying those readings of the old text of Antioch, which survive in the Byzantine text, but which do not happen to occur in the Old Syriac, except internal probability. That criterion is, as a matter of fact, unfavourable to most characteristically Byzantine readings; but there are some few which I think are deserving of more serious consideration than was accorded by Hort. For the old Alexandrian text we have MS. evidence not substantially inferior to that possessed by Lucian, and we know how to use it better; but for the various types of Eastern text Lucian must have had MSS. of a greater variety and better quality than any we possess. Hence, though the principles on which he made use of them may have been the reverse of critical, to say offhand that he has never preserved an ancient reading for which we have no other authority seems over-bold."[2]

In a similar vein, and with characteristic caution, Ropes declared: "We may assume that the revisers worked, in part at least, on the basis of Greek MSS. preserved at Antioch that represented such a text as had long been used in this great, rich, and active church, but no literary monuments from Antioch earlier than the time of Lucian are capable of aiding our inquiry. It may well happen, therefore, that readings now found only in the Antiochian recension, or in texts dependent upon it, had been current in Antioch from the

---

[1] *Evangelion da-Mepharreshe*, II (Cambridge, 1904), 224 f.
[2] B. H. Streeter, *The Four Gospels* (London, 1924), p. 119.

earliest times. Any reading, however, which is to be accepted as of this sort, must possess very strong internal credentials of genuineness."[1]

During the past decades several papyri have come to light which tend to increase one's uneasiness over Hort's reluctance to acknowledge the possibility that an ancient reading may have been preserved in the Antiochian text even though it be absent from all the great uncial manuscripts. Since the discovery of the Chester Beatty Papyri (particularly P[45] and P[46]) and the Bodmer Papyrus II (P[66]), proof is available that occasionally the later Byzantine text preserves a reading that dates from the second or third century and for which there had been no other early witness. A few examples selected from a large number will serve to illustrate this changed situation in the textual evaluation of the New Testament (the first variant is that adopted by Westcott and Hort, while the second variant is that found in the Textus Receptus):

Luke 11.33 for φῶς in א B D Θ fam 1 fam 13 *pm*, φέγγος is read by P[45] 𝔖 33 *al.*

John 10.29 for ὃ ... μεῖζον in B latt bo, ὅς ... μείζων is read by P[66] 𝔖 fam 1 fam 13 *al.*

John 11.32 for πρός in א B C* D L X, εἰς is read by P[66] 𝔖 Θ *pm.*

John 13.26 for βάψας οὖν in א B C L X 33, καὶ ἐμβάψας is read by P[66c]A Θ *al.*

Acts 17.13 καὶ ταράσσοντες is omitted by P[45] 𝔖 E *al.*

I Cor. 9.7 for τὸν καρπόν in א* A B D* G P, ἐκ τοῦ καρποῦ is read by P[46] 𝔖 *pl.*

Eph. 5.9 for φωτός in א A B D* G P, πνεύματος is read by P[46] 𝔖 *pm.*

Though this list could be expanded,[2] enough examples have been cited to suggest that some of the roots of the Antiochian text go back to a very early date, antedating Lucian by several generations. It does not follow, of course, that the Textus Receptus should be rehabilitated *en bloc*,[3] or even that in the examples cited

---

[1] Ropes, *The Text of Acts*, 1926, pp. cclxxxiv f. Referring to the text of Acts, Ropes says, "Apart from the 'Western' readings found in the Antiochian recension, the Old Uncial base which the revisers used was evidently an excellent text," *ibid.*, p. cclxxxvii.

[2] For further examples of distinctively Byzantine readings which are also found in P[66], consult Jn. 1.32; 3.24; 4.14, 51; 5.8; 6.10, 57; 7.3, 39; 8.41, 51, 55; 9.23; 10.38; 12.36; 14.17.

[3] Despite Edward F. Hills's valiant attempt to do so in his essay "Dean Burgon in the Light of Recent Research" prefixed to the 1959 reprinting of Burgon's *The Last Twelve Verses of the Gospel according to S. Mark*, pp. 44-67.

above the Antiochian text is necessarily the original text. The lesson to be drawn from such evidence, however, is that the general neglect of the Antiochian readings which has been so common among many textual critics is quite unjustified.[1] It is equally unsatisfactory to utilize the evidence of the Koine text in a purely mechanical fashion, as von Soden did. On the contrary, the only proper methodology is to examine the evidence for each variant impartially, with no predilections for or against any one type of text. In the case of the Antiochian recension, very many readings will no doubt continue to be judged to be the result of the editorial labors of Lucian and those who shared his preference for a smooth and often composite reading, but here and there a discriminating criticism will discover ancient and perhaps original readings which the Antiochian revisers took from the texts on which they worked. The possibility should even be left open that a reading which happens to be preserved in only the Lucianic recension may commend itself as the original.[2]

V. Problems Relating to the Lucianic Recension

In the course of his discussion of "The Antiochian Recension of the Septuagint," George Foot Moore declared, "Every serious bit of investigation in any spot in the Greek Bible reveals in some new way the immense variety and baffling complexity of the problems it presents."[3] A few of the problems and tasks which clamor for attention from both Old Testament and New Testament scholars include the following.

(1) The text of Codex Y (Cod. Macedonianus, Gregory 034, von Soden ε 073), a manuscript dating from the ninth century and containing the Four Gospels (with lacunae), deserves to be studied

---

[1] Compare G. Zuntz, "The Byzantine Text in New Testament Criticism," *JTS*, XLIII (1942), 25-30; and *The Text of the Epistles; a Disquisition upon the Corpus Paulinum* (London, 1953), pp. 49-57 and 150 f.

[2] For several examples of readings peculiar to Lucian, which nevertheless so sober a critic as Ropes was disposed to accept as original, see his discussion in *The Text of Acts*, p. cclxxxv. For an attempt to prove the originality of six Antiochian variants in Matthew, see J. M. Bover, "Variantes semíticas del texto antioqueno en san Mateo," in *Miscellanea biblica B. Ubach*, curante Dom Romualdo M.ª Días (*Scripta et documenta*, 1; Montisserrati, 1953), pp. 323-327. H. Greeven argues cogently for the originality of ἱερεῖς in Lk. 20.1. which is supported by the Koine text alone (*NTS*, VI [1960], 295 f.).

[3] *American Journal of Semitic Languages and Literatures*, XXIX (1912-1913), 50.

more thorougly than has hitherto been the case.[1] It is inadequately cited by Tischendorf, while a collation made by Gregory is buried in the "Nachträge" to his *Textkritik*.[2] According to von Soden, the manuscript belongs to his K^a-text.[3] Mrs. Lake found that this manuscript shares with Fam. Π and A some readings not preserved elsewhere.[4]

(2) According to Mrs. Lake, in both Testaments codex Alexandrinus contains a large number of misspellings or itacisms of a consistent character. A thorough study of these by a Greek philologist would no doubt lead to worthwhile and interesting results.

(3) It is generally believed that John of Damascus used the Ecclesiastical text, but this has never been either proved or refuted.

(4) Though it is commonly said that Chrysostom's New Testament text was Antiochian, partial studies of the problem suggest that further analysis of his text is much to be desired.

(5) It is not to the credit of textual critics of the Greek Bible that they have been so slow in utilizing information derived from the iconography of Byzantine manuscripts in determining their date, provenance, and textual relationships.[5]

(6) What principles, if any, controlled the formation of the texts of those manuscripts (such as B, ℵ, A, etc.) which contain both Old and New Testament?

(7) Is it possible on palaeographic or iconographical grounds to prove that this or that New Testament manuscript belongs to this or that Old Testament manuscript of Lucianic derivation and that both were originally one and the same complete Bible? (It does not necessarily follow, of course, that the textual complexion of both Testaments would be the same or even similar.)

(8) In view of the research published by the Lakes on certain

---

[1] For relatively brief accounts of this manuscript see W. C. Braithwaite, "A New Uncial of the Gospels," *Expository Times*, XIII (1901-02), 114-117, and "The Lection-System of the Codex Macedonianus," *JTS*, V (1904), 265-274.

[2] Vol. III (Leipzig, 1909), pp. 1028-1037.

[3] *Op. cit.*, I, ii, 1161.

[4] *Family* Π, p. 57, note 5.

[5] Cf. Kurt Weitzmann, "The Relation between Text Criticism and Picture Criticism," in *Illustrations in Roll and Codex, a Study of the Origin and Method of Text-Illustration* (Princeton, 1947), pp. 182 ff., and also "Die Illustration der Septuaginta," *Münchner Jahrbuch der bildenden Kunst*, Dritte Folge, III/IV (1952/53), 96-120, especially pp. 113-114.

parts of the Byzantine text, precisely how far is von Soden's classification of the Koine text in need of correction?

(9) Why did the Lucianic Old Testament fail to gain the same
acceptance as the corresponding Antiochian text of the New
Testament?

(10) What precisely was the textual basis of the Lucianic recension, and to what extent can readings of that recension be
accepted as probably inherited, and not produced, by Lucian and
his fellow-workers?

CHAPTER TWO

THE CAESAREAN TEXT OF THE GOSPELS

Of all the thousands of Greek manuscripts of the New Testament, the immediate and exact parentage of only a very few is known. Even those manuscripts which were written in the same *scriptorium* manifest few if any signs of direct relationship.[1] But although the overwhelming majority of manuscripts have thus far resisted all efforts to discover immediate filiation, New Testament textual critics have succeeded in establishing with some degree of confidence the more remote relationship of certain groups of witnesses. These groups of manuscripts, in accord with the degree of affinity of relationship, may be called families or texts. A family of manuscripts is ordinarily more limited in extent than is a text and discloses much closer affinity among its members than is expected of a text. Consequently it is usually possible to reconstruct the common archetype of a family with but a slight margin of error. To reconstruct the archetype of a text, however, involves far greater difficulties, and the common ancestor which lay behind its known descendents can often be determined only approximately, particularly when the extant manuscripts have been corrected against one another. There are, of course, many intermediate stages between the extremes of family and text, but the distinction between the two, though at times apparently only academic, is none the less a valid and helpful one.[2]

Over the past century the combined efforts of many scholars have succeeded in isolating and analyzing several families of New Testament manuscripts which together constitute, so it has been held, a certain type of text, the so-called Caesarean text. In view of a new turn which this investigation has recently taken, it seems both profitable and necessary first to review the several stages in the isolation of the component parts of this text of the Gospels, then to summarize the more important discussions and debate regarding the interpretation of the evidence, and finally to indicate several of the tasks and problems which remain to be investigated.

[1] See p. 21, n. 3, above.

[2] For a discussion of the distinction between a text and a family of manuscripts, see E. C. Colwell, "The Significance of Grouping of New Testament Manuscripts," *NTS*, IV (1958), 73-92, especially pp. 79 ff.

I. THE BEGINNINGS: FAMILY 13

As long ago as 1868 a professor of Latin at Trinity College, Dublin, W. H. Ferrar, discovered that four mediaeval Greek Gospel manuscripts, those known as 13, 69, 124, and 346, were closely related textually. His collations were published posthumously in 1877 by his friend and colleague, Professor T. K. Abbott.[1] It was their opinion that these four minuscule manuscripts were descendents of a not very distant uncial ancestor of good character.

It was not long before the interest of other scholars was aroused. F. H. A. Scrivener noticed that codex 543 is related to the group and prepared a careful collation of the document.[2] The Abbé J. P. P. Martin pointed out that at least three of the four manuscripts (namely 13, 124, 346) were written in Calabria in southern Italy, and concluded that this was the home of the archetype. He was also of the opinion that codex 348, whose Calabrian origin he thought he had demonstrated, was also a member of the Ferrar group.[3]

At about the same time a British scholar, J. Rendel Harris, while teaching at Haverford College in Pennsylvania, published several pieces of investigation concerning this family of manuscripts. First of all, he observed that manuscript 713 is related to the Ferrar group,[4] and further research has proved him to be correct at least for Matthew.[5] Of much more significance was his

---

[1] *A Collation of Four Manuscripts of the Gospels* (Dublin and London, 1877).

[2] *A Plain Introduction to the Criticism of the New Testament*, 3rd ed. (London, 1883), p. 236. The collation was published posthumously in *Adversaria Critica Sacra* (Cambridge, 1893).

[3] *Quatre manuscrits importants du Nouveau Testament, auxquels on peut ajouter un cinquième* (Paris, 1886), a reprint of his article of the same title in *Revue des sciences ecclésiastiques*, sixième série, tome III, no. 313 (Jan. 1886), 5-33.

[4] "Cod. Ev. 561—Codex Algerinae Peckover," *JBL*, 1886, 79-89; and "An Important Uncollated Manuscript of the New Testament," *The Sunday School Times* (Philadelphia), XXVIII (Nov. 6, 1886), 707.

[5] A. Pott (*Der griechisch-syrische Text des Matthäus, ε 351 im Verhältnis zu Tatian, S^{se}, Ferrar* [Leipzig, 1912], p. 41) concluded that this manuscript is closely related to the Ferrar group but not so closely as the four Ferrar manuscripts are related to each other. Later Harris defended his opinion concerning the textual affinities of this manuscript (*Expositor*, Eighth ser., XXIII [1922], 120-129) against what he termed misrepresentation on the part of Kenyon (*A Handbook to the Textual Criticism of the New Testament* [2nd ed., London, 1912], p. 139).

thorough investigation of the origin of 69.[1] He also sought, on the basis of certain affinities with the Old Syriac version, to establish a Syriac origin for the most characteristic readings of the group,[2] while in a subsequent study[3] he argued that this Syriac influence had been transmitted via an Arabic medium. More important, however, was his discovery that most of the Ferrar manuscripts are provided with much the same selection of various "helps for the reader," that is, with a menology, the lives of the apostles, a list of the patriarchates, the appearances of the risen Christ, the symbols of the evangelists, and so on.[4]

Meantime, while serving as curate of St. Mary's church in Oxford, Kirsopp Lake examined a number of Greek manuscripts from Italy which had been suspected of being related to the Ferrar group and added two more members to the group, codices 826 and 828.[5]

The next great advance was made by Hermann von Soden, who discovered that the Ferrar group, to which he had added other members, falls into three sub-groups: (a) 983 and 1689; (b) 69, 124, 174 (only in Matthew), and 788; (c) 13, 230, 346, 543, 826, and 828.[6]

A British vicar, the Reverend E. A. Hutton, in what he entitled *An Atlas of Textual Criticism*,[7] devoted an excursus to an examination of several manuscripts of the Ferrar group and concluded that, of the five at his disposal,[8] 69 and 124 are the two best representatives of the group. Mr. Hutton's analyses, important though they were of the time, were later superseded by the definitive work of Professor and Mrs. Lake, who printed the Greek text of Mark according to what they regarded as the archetype of the group.[9] The stemma which they worked out is as follows:

---

[1] J. Rendel Harris, *The Origin of the Leicester Codex of the New Testament* (Cambridge, 1887).

[2] *On the Origin of the Ferrar Group* (Cambridge, 1893).

[3] *Further Researches into the History of the Ferrar Group* (Cambridge, 1900).

[4] *Ibid.*

[5] *JTS*, I (1899-1900), 117-120.

[6] *Die Schriften des Neuen Testaments*, I, ii (Leipzig, 1906), 1066 ff.

[7] Cambridge, 1911.

[8] Namely codices 13, 69, 124, 346, and 543.

[9] Kirsopp and Silva Lake, *Family 13 (The Ferrar Group); the Text According to Mark (SD*, xi; London and Philadelphia, 1941). It may be added here that, while the present volume was passing through the press, Jacob Geerlings of the University of Utah published three fascicles on *Family 13—The Ferrar Group*; their sub-titles are *The Text According to Matthew (SD*, xix; Salt Lake City, 1961), *The Text According to Luke (SD*, xx; Salt Lake City, 1961), and *The Text According to John (SD*, xxi; Salt Lake City, 1962).

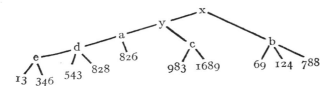

In their discussion of the date and provenance of the manuscripts they inclined to a slightly earlier date (eleventh century) than that ordinarily assigned (twelfth century, so Gregory and von Soden) to the majority of the documents. Many of their notes on the textual variants are invaluable, and the whole monograph will remain a landmark in the history of the investigation of the Ferrar group.

II. Further Advances: Family 1, etc.

Four other Byzantine manuscripts (dating from the twelfth to the fourteenth century) were discovered by Lake to be related to one another in a family which manifests many of the characteristics of family 13. These are manuscripts 1, 118, 131, and 209.[1] Later, manuscript 1582 (tenth century) was recognized by Lake as likewise belonging to this group.[2] Von Soden also regarded certain others[3] as weak representatives of the same family. In view, however, of the inaccurate collation of at least one of these manuscripts (codex 22)[4] which von Soden used, other scholars are not inclined to put much reliance upon the trustworthiness of his

[1] *Codex 1 and its Allies* (*TS* VII, 1; Cambridge, 1902). Subsequently the Lakes conjectured that the perpetuation of the form of Caesarean text found in family 1 may have been due to Arethas, Bishop of Caesarea in Cappodocia ("The Scribe Ephraim," *JBL*, LXII [1943], 267).

[2] K. Lake, *The Text of the New Testament*, 6th ed. revised by Silva New (London, 1928), pp. 20f.; and *JBL*, LXII (1943), 264 and 266.

[3] Namely 22, 205, 206, 697, 872^Mk, 924, 1005, 1192, 1210, 1278, and 2193 (*op. cit.*, I, ii, 1042 ff.). Still another member of family 1 is 1542, whose kinship with the rest, though recognized by von Soden (it is his ε1337; *op. cit.*, I, ii, 1289 f.), was obscured by his grouping and seems to have been generally overlooked by other investigators. The merit of calling renewed attention to its affinities belongs to C. A. Phillips, who drew up a list of the readings it shares with other Caesarean witnesses (*BBC*, x [Leyden, 1935], 12-19).

[4] Kirsopp Lake, *The Text of the New Testament*, 6th ed., p. 21; and H. A. Sanders, "A New Collation of Codex 22" (*JBL*, XXXIII [1914], 91-117). On von Soden's accuracy in general, see Hoskier's damaging evidence in *JTS*, xv (1914), 307-326.

opinion either in this case or in other cases where they are unable to check his material.

With these two families of manuscripts, family 1 and family 13, subsequent study has identified certain other individual codices which possess texts more or less closely related. The full and accurate edition of the Koridethi Gospels (Θ), published by Gustav Beermann and C. R. Gregory in 1913, enabled scholars to examine its textual affinities with much more precision than von Soden's earlier (1906) notices of this manuscript had permitted. The most elaborate of such examinations was the careful study by K. Lake and R. P. Blake in 1923 which showed that in Mark Θ is closely connected with families 1 and 13 as well as with 28, 565, and 700.[1]

Another group which von Soden isolated (the I^{φ} group) exhibits certain affinities with the manuscripts just mentioned. In Matthew and Mark the sub-divisions of this group are, according to von Soden, (a) 349, 517, 954, 1424, and 1675; (b) 7, 115, 179, 267, 659, 827, 1082, 1391, 1402, 1606, and 2191; (c) 160, 945, 990, 1010, 1207, 1223, and 1293; (r) M, 27, 71, 692, and 1194. In Luke and John they are (a) 349, 517, 954, 1188, 1424, and 1675; (b) 7, 185, 267, 659, 1391, and 1606; (c) 945, 1010, 1207, 1223, and 1293; (r) M, 27, 71, and 1194.[2]

[1] "The Text of the Gospels and the Koridethi Codex" (*HTR*, xvi [1923], 267-286). The collation of 28 was supplied privately by H. C. Hoskier. This has been newly collated by the Lakes in Appendix I of their *Family 13*. A full collation of 565 (which is Tischendorf's 2^{pe} and Westcott and Hort's 81) is available only for Mark: J. Belsheim, *Das Evangelium des Marcus nach dem griechischen Codex aureus Theodorae Imperatricis purpureus Petropolitanus aus dem 9ten Jahrhundert* in *Forhandlinger i Videnskabs-Selskabet i Christiania*, 1885, no. 9 (Christiania, 1886). Belsheim was a notoriously inaccurate collator; his collation of Mark was corrected by H. S. Cronin (appendix to *TS*, v, 4) and his partial collation of (Luke and) John by I. A. Moir (*TS*, n.s. II, pp. 113-114). Codex 700 is available in H. C. Hoskier, *Collation of Codex Ev. 604* (London, 1890). Von Soden had, indeed, included many other diverse manuscripts in the same group. With D, W, and Θ he associates 21,28, 79, 279, 372, 399, 406, 544, 565, 700, 1515, 1542, and 1654. But practically all subsequent investigators have regarded these as far too heterogeneous to be brought under the same *vinculum*. On the other hand, however, H. C. Hoskier maintained that "it is not correct to divide Θ and these cursives [family 1, family 13, 28, 565, and 700] from the Dd text" ("A Note on 'Eastern' and 'Caesarean' Texts," *BBC*, v [1928], 14). See also Hoskier's *Codex B and its Allies; a Study and an Indictment*, I (London, 1914), 136-39, where he cites numerous instances throughout Mark where W, 28, 565, and 700 are supported by Old Latin witnesses; his article "Some Study of P^{45} with Special Reference to the Bezan Text" (*BBC*, xii [1937], 51-57) makes no direct reference to the matter.

[2] *Op. cit.*, I, ii, 1109-1147.

In 1924 Burnett Hillman Streeter published a brilliant volume on *The Four Gospels* in which, *inter alia*, he came independently to the same conclusion as Lake and Blake regarding family Θ and went beyond it in showing that this text group is not confined to Mark but applies also to the other Gospels. To the already expanding family he added several other witnesses more or less closely related. The primary authorities of this text, according to Streeter, are Θ and 565[Mk]; the secondary authorities, family 1, family 13, 28, 700, (W[Mk]),[1] and the Old Georgian; the tertiary authorities, family 1424,[2] 544, N-Σ-O, Φ, and 157; and the supplementary authorities, U, Λ, 1071, 1604, and the Old Armenian.

Streeter's research suggested to him a name for the text. He believed that he had proved that Origen used a Neutral type of text of Mark at Alexandria but another type, very like Θ, after moving to Caesarea. Streeter felt justified, therefore, in calling this type of text Caesarean and thought that Origen found this text first in Caesarea of Palestine.[3]

This opinion, however, was modified slightly by a joint publication entitled, "The Caesarean Text of the Gospel of Mark," by Kirsopp Lake, R. P. Blake, and Silva New.[4] These scholars corrected Streeter's theory by showing that Origen possibly used a Caesarean text before leaving Alexandria, and that at Caesarea he at first used an Alexandrian text but soon reverted permanently to a Caesarean type of text. In other details their investigation corroborated Streeter's analyses, confirming and supplementing his work. At the conclusion of the monograph they printed their reconstruction of the Caesarean text of three sample chapters of Mark, namely chapters 1, 6, and 11.

In the estimation of these three scholars the most significant new contribution to a knowledge of the Caesarean text was the

---

[1] Streeter discovered later, in time to add an appendix to the second impression of his book (1926), that in Mark two-thirds of W is Caesarean in character (from Mark 5.31 to 16.8). See also Streeter's article in *HTR*, XIX (1926), 165-172; and C. A. Phillips' remarks on Streeter's discovery (*BBC*, V [1928], 9-12).

[2] Streeter's family 1424 is von Soden's I^φ group.

[3] Kirsopp Lake had, indeed, so long ago as 1900, thrown out the suggestion that one ought to localize the text of some of these minuscules at Caesarea; see the first ed. of his *The Text of the New Testament*, p. 21. He removed the statement from the following editions, restoring it in the last—the 6th, revised by his student, Miss Silva New, 1928—after Streeter had confirmed the guess.

[4] *HTR*, XXI (1928), 207-404.

publication in 1924 of a small vellum fragment of Mark 11.11-17.
It is Berlin Mus., äg. Abt., P. 13416, which was assigned the
Gregory-Dobschütz number 0188.[1] Its editor, A. H. Salonius of
Helsingfors, found that it goes with E, G, H, 565, certain early
versions, and Origen;[2] and Lake, Blake, and New, refining his
textual analyses, discovered that this short section comes from a
codex strongly marked by Caesarean readings.[3] "The fragment,"
they write, "contains an unusual number of singular readings [four
out of 17 variant readings which they cite], and suggests either
that the variations within the Caesarean text may have geen greater
than the existing evidence would indicate, or that the correction
of manuscripts to the standard of the Ecclesiastical Text went even
further than we had thought."[4]

Another fragment, a papyrus leaf containing Matthew 26.19-52,
was assigned by Père M.-J. Lagrange and others to this same
textual stock. The original editor, indeed, had concluded that the
text of the fragment belongs to the Western text,[5] but Lagrange
had little difficulty in pointing out that his conclusions were based
on presuppositions which beg the question regarding the relation
of the Western text to other texts.[6] Lagrange showed that the
papyrus, designated P[37], oscillates between B and D and agrees
with Θ as many times as with B; he therefore classified this early
fragment as a witness to the Caesarean type of text.[7]

III. ORIENTAL VERSIONS AND THE CAESAREAN TEXT

Not the least valuable part of the monograph on the Caesarean
text of Mark by Lake, Blake, and New is the attention given to

---

[1] *ZNW*, XXIII (1924), 252; and XXVII (1928), 219.

[2] *ZNW*, XXVII (1928), 98. Salonius dated the fragment in the seventh
century, but von Dobschütz (*ZNW*, XXVII [1928], 219) dated it in the fourth
century.

[3] *HTR*, XXI (1928), 212.

[4] *Ibid.* It may be mentioned that Henry A. Sanders reopened the question
of the legitimacy of regarding 0188 as evidence for the Caesarean text,
arguing that it is basically Western (*HTR*, XXVI [1933], 83-87).

[5] Henry A. Sanders, "An Early Papyrus Fragment of the Gospel of
Matthew in the Michigan Collection" (*HTR*, XIX [1926], 215-226). He dates
it between A.D. 200 and 350.

[6] *RB*, XXXVIII (1929), 161-177; and *Critique textuelle*; II, *La critique rationnelle* (Paris, 1935), pp. 157 f.

[7] Compare J. M. Bover's earlier analysis of P[37] in "Dos papiros egipcios del
N. T. recientemente publicados" (*EE*, IX [1930], 289-320, especially 290-306),
where he points out the decided Caesarean affinities of this papyrus.

certain oriental versions, namely, the Old Armenian, the Old Georgian, and the Palestinian Syriac. They regard the Caesarean text as the basis of all three versions. The relationship is traced from the Caesarean Greek text through a postulated Syriac text to the Palestinian Syriac version on the one hand and to the Old Armenian (no longer extant) on the other.[1] The Old Georgian is held to be based on the latter. All extant manuscripts of the current Armenian version and almost all extant manuscript of the Georgian version have been corrected to a Byzantine standard.[2]

It will be appropriate to mention at this point other investigations concerning these oriental versions. In 1919 Frédéric Macler[3] claimed for the Armenian version certain textual affinities with D and Θ, regarding it, in fact, as a weak representative of that type of text which was later to be called Caesarean. Macler was also impressed by a very considerable amount of Greek influence still observable in the Armenian and denied the existence of any Syriac stratum whatsoever in the Armenian, asserting categorically that the Armenian was translated directly from the Greek text.

[1] F. C. Conybeare was the first to observe that quotations by ecclesiastical writers seem to indicate the existence of an Armenian version whose text differed from that of extant Armenian manuscripts and editions. In the last article he wrote before his death, he advanced tentatively the suggestion that this early Armenian version of the Gospels was in the form of a diatessaron (*JTS*, xxv [1924], 232-245). This hypothesis was investigated with greater thoroughness by Paul Essabalian (*Le Diatessaron de Tatien et la première traduction des Évangiles arméniens* [Vienna, 1937]), in modern Armenian with a substantial résumé in French; see the review by R. P. Casey (*JBL*, lvii [1938], 95-101). Essabalian and Stanislas Lyonnet ("La première version arménienne des Évangiles," *RB*, xlvii [1938], 355-382) conclude that there really was an Armenian diatessaron such as Conybeare suggested, based on a Syriac model either identical with or analogous to Tatian's Diatessaron. According to Lyonnet, when it was found desirable to have separate Gospels, the primitive Armenian version was worked over by several revisers who used Greek texts of a decidedly Caesarean character and thus introduced into all extant manuscripts of the Armenian version a Caesarean strain (see also Lyonnet in Lagrange, *Critique textuelle*, ii, 354, 361, and 386). Lyonnet strengthened his argument by an important article in *B*, xix (1938), 121-150, entitled "Vestiges d'un diatessaron arménien," in which he showed that the *Rituale Armenorum*, published by the Mekhitarists of Vienna, preserves traces of an Armenian diatessaron which was colored by certain Caesarean readings. See also p. 102, n. 3, below.

[2] *HTR*, xxi (1928), 324 ff., and Kirsopp Lake, *The Text of the New Testament*, 6th ed., pp. 44 f.

[3] *Le text arménien de l'Évangile d'après Matthieu et Marc (Annales du Musée Guimet*, xxciii; Paris, 1919), pp. 569-637.

Merk[1] and Blake,[2] however, took issue with the latter position and pointed out Syriacisms which can have come from neither the Evangelion da-Mepharreshe nor the Peshitta, but which (according to Blake) can be explained only by postulating the existence of a third Syriac text akin to the Caesarean.

Concerning Macler's former point, that the Armenian version is only a weak representative of the Caesarean text, Stanislas Lyonnet had little trouble in showing that Macler's textual analyses were much too rough. A more refined and discriminating analysis discloses, Lyonnet maintained, that the Armenian text of Matthew agrees little if any with D, but does show a very decided affinity with Θ and its family.[3] Likewise in Mark the Armenian text is, according to the same scholar, an important witness of the Caesarean text.[4] Indeed, Lyonnet believed that he had sufficient evidence to prove that not only in Matthew and Mark but also in Luke and John, as far as one can speak of a Caesarean text in these Gospels, the Armenian version is definitely Caesarean in character, "maintaining a happy equilibrium between the Western and Neutral texts."[5]

Another important study of the Caesarean content of the extant Armenian text disclosed that, far from having lost its specific Caesarean coloring (as Lake, Blake, and New held), the text of

---

[1] *B*, VII (1926), 40-71 (especially 63-68).

[2] *PO*, XX (1929), 448.

[3] "La version arménienne des Évangiles et son modèle grec: l'Évangile selon saint Matthieu" (*RB*, XLIII [1934], 69-87). As can be seen from the title, Lyonnet agrees with Macler against Merk regarding the direct dependence of the Armenian version upon the Greek and not upon any form of Syriac. C. S. C. Williams, "Syriasms in the Armenian Text of the Gospels" (*JTS*, XLIII [1942], 161-167), examines afresh fourteen of the sixteen passages from the Gospels that J. Armitage Robinson cited (*Euthaliana* [= *TS*, III, 3; 1894], 76 ff.) "in which the Armenian Version offers us a rendering which is not easily accounted for by supposing it to a direct translation of any known reading of the Greek text." Williams finds only two of the fourteen instances to be convincing, and concludes that, "while it is probable that there was an early translation from Syriac into Armenian, as opposed to the later revision with Greek manuscripts, the Syriac element remaining is not strong" (p. 167). See also Mariès, "Le texte arménien de l'Évangile d'après Matthieu et Marc" (*Recherches de science religieuse*, X [1920], 28-54).

[4] "Un important témoin du texte césaréen de saint Marc: le version arménienne" (*Mélanges de l'université saint-Joseph*, Beyrouth, XIX; 1935). See the reviews by Mahler (*Orientalist. Literaturzeitung*, XLI [1938], 631 f.) and by Baumstark (*OC*, 3te Serie, XI [1936], 245-252). The latter strongly opposed Lyonnet.

[5] Lyonnet, in Lagrange, *Critique textuelle*, II, 365.

Armenian manuscripts still preserves a very considerable proportion of the typically Caesarean readings. E. C. Colwell tested the amount of Caesarean influence in the text of Mark chaps. 1, 6, and 11 in six Armenian manuscripts and discovered that "the large majority of these Caesarean readings are supported by all the Armenian sources studied. The list included about 235 readings; of these 179 are found in all the Armenians .... Each of the Mss reads about 205 Caesarean variants; the American Bible Society text contains about 200."[1] Colwell found that the Armenian text agrees most often with Θ, 565, 700; less often with family 1, family 13, 28, and W. He concluded, therefore, that "extant Armenian Mss (and printed texts) contain a text of Mark that is strongly Caesarean in type."[2]

The investigation of the Georgian version is restricted to an even smaller number of scholars than the Armenian. F. C. Conybeare's[3] preliminary work on its textual affinities was largely superseded by the investigations of R. P. Blake, who first called Streeter's attention to the significance of a collation of Mark 1 in certain Old Georgian manuscripts. With Lake and New in the Harvard article already referred to as well as in his edition of the Georgian version of Matthew and Mark,[4] Blake found its text to be definitely of the Caesarean pattern,[5] and held that it is a better witness of the Old

[1] "The Caesarean Readings of Armenian Gospel MSS" (*ATR*, XVI [1934], 125). In the following year Lyonnet published in *Handes Amsorya*, XLIX (1935), cols. 596-603, a discussion of "Le tétraévangile de Moscou et son importance pour l'établissement du texte critique de la version arménienne," in which, on the basis of an examination of selected readings in Mark chaps. 1 and 6 in Etchmiadzin ms. 229, he concluded that this Armenian ms. manifests decided Caesarean affinities.

[2] *Ibid.*, p. 132. See also Colwell's article in *JR*, XVII (1937), 48-61, "Slandered or Ignored: the Armenian Gospels," where he argues that "the Armenian version is one of the strongest witnesses to the Caesarean text" (p. 59).

[3] See his brief account in Scrivener's *Plain Introduction*, 4th ed. (1894), II, 156-158, and his article in the *American Journal of Theology*, I (1897), 883-912.

[4] *PO*, XX, 3 (Paris, 1929), and XXIV, 1 (Paris, 1933). Regarding Blake's work in *HTR* for 1928, Baumstark thought that it was far from being the last word on the subject; see his criticism in "Zum georgischen Evangelien-text" (*OC*, 3te Serie, III/IV [1928-29], 117-124). Cf. also G. Peradse's general discussion of "Die Probleme der georgischen Evangelienübersetzung" (*ZNW*, XXIX [1930], 304-309), and Blake, "Notes on the Text of the Georgian and Armenian Gospels" (*Quantulacumque*, ed. R. P. Casey *et al.* [London, 1937], pp. 355-363).

[5] "The Adysh ms. [dated 897] is closely related to the group Θ, 565, 700, and in spite of all translational loss is almost as good a representative of the

Armenian, from which it was translated and which is no longer extant, than are any of the extant Armenian manuscripts.

Colwell, followed by Lyonnet,[1] agreed with Blake in regarding the Georgian version as Caesarean, but took exception to ranking it above the extant Armenian version as the better witness to the Caesarean text.[2] Anton Baumstark, on the other hand, would not admit that the Georgian version is Caesarean at all. He characterized it as harmonistic, and traced it back through the Armenian (which, in his opinion, is no more Caesarean than its daughter version, the Georgian) to a Syriac model, the Diatessaron.[3]

The Palestinian Syriac version, according to Lake, Blake, and New, discloses the presence of the Caesarean text, and is thought by these scholars to be derived from a postulated Syriac version of the fourth century no longer extant.[4]

IV. The Caesarean Text in Greek Lectionaries

As is well known, the several parts of the Greek Gospel lectionary are far from homogeneous in textual complexion.[5] It is necessary, therefore, to analyze separately the text of each constituent section of the lectionary system. Of the various sections which have been thus far examined, several show signs of Caesarean affinities. The Marcan week-day lections, according to Paul Schubert, are akin to von Soden's I^{φ} group, a tertiary authority of the Caesarean

clan as the best mss. A and B, however [A = Opiza ms, written 913; B = Tbet' ms, written 995], contain a considerable amount of Caesarean material which has been revised out of the Adysh, and in particular they manifest special affinities to family 1 (1, 118, 209), and to the Ferrar group. If one rejects the different K variants found in the three mss., the residuum of readings when combined affords a very pure Caesarean text" (PO, xx, 3 [Paris, 1929], 447).

[1] In Lagrange's Critique textuelle, ii, 384 and 386.

[2] ATR, xvi (1934), 129.

[3] OC, 3te Serie, iii/iv (1929), 117-124; and ibid., xi (1936), 246-252 (see also p. 49, n. 1, above).

[4] Simultaneously with the publication of the study in HTR, Lake advanced several considerations which, he thought, mitigated somewhat the strangeness of the hypothesis that a Syriac version which existed in the fourth century should have disappeared so completely; see his article, "The Text of the Gospels," in Studies in Early Christianity, ed. S. J. Case (New York, 1928), pp. 41 f. Colwell offered some trenchant criticisms of this "postulated" Syriac version in his article, "Slandered or Ignored: the Armenian Gospels" (JR, xvii [1937], 56).

[5] See, e.g., Colwell in E. C. Colwell and D. W. Riddle, edd., Prolegomena to the Study of the Lectionary Text of the Gospels (Chicago, 1933), p. 15.

text.[1] The Lucan Saturday and Sunday lessons, according to the investigations of the present writer, are much closer to the text of family 1 and family 13 than to any other text group.[2] A subsequent study by Bray of the week day lessons from Luke revealed that in general the same textual complexion prevails also in this area of the lectionary text.[3]

In a thoughtful and thought-provoking analysis of the Johannine Lessons in the lectionaries, Harry M. Buck argued that "the lectionaries—at least in John—are a connecting link between the 'Caesarean' text-type and the Byzantine recension which dominated the middle ages."[4] Put in another way, Buck found that "the lectionaries had their origin in the Caesarean textual tradition, and that gradually more and more important readings were conformed to a Byzantine standard. Readings which were allowed to stand unchanged—probably because they were not regarded as important—betray the Caesarean ancestry of the lectionaries."[5]

The so-called Ferrar Lectionary (l. 547), discovered years ago by Cardinal Mercati, has at last found an editor, Jacob Geerlings. In an analysis of its textual affinities, Geerlings concludes that it belongs to the branch of the Ferrar group designated "b" in the stemma given on p. 45 above.[6]

---

[1] In Colwell and Riddle's *Prolegomena*, pp. 43-56. Streeter classified von Soden's *I*φ group as the most important of what Streeter terms the "poor relations" of the Caesarean text (*The Four Gospels*, p. 84 and pp. 575 ff.).

[2] *The Saturday and Sunday Lessons from Luke in the Greek Gospel Lectionary* (Chicago, 1944), pp. 66-67.

[3] See William D. Bray, *The Week Day Lessons from Luke in the Greek Gospel Lectionary* (Chicago, 1955), pp. 23 and 30.

[4] Harry M. Buck, *The Johannine Lessons in the Greek Gospel Lectionary* (Chicago, 1958), p. 76. Quite independently of Buck, Bernard Botte discovered that in John lectionary 253 (a manuscript copied in A.D. 1020 at Salerno whose readings are reported in Tischendorf) is a strong witness to the Caesarean text, closely associated with fam. 13 ("Un témoin du texte césaréen du quatrième évangile: *l.* 253," *Mélanges bibliques rédigés en l'honneur de André Robert* [Paris, n.d.], pp. 466-469).

[5] *Op. cit.*, p. 58.

[6] Jacob Geerlings, *The Ferrar Lectionary (Cod. Vat. Gr. 1217, Greg. 547)* (*SD*, XVIII; Salt Lake City, 1959), p. 5. Perhaps it may be mentioned here that Geerlings also investigated the inter-relations of the members of the branch of the Ferrar group designated "a" in the stemma given above (p. 45) and concluded that ms. 826 is its archetype; see his article, "Is Ms. 826 the Archetype of Fam 13a?" *JBL*, LXVII (1948), 357-363.

V. Debate

Canon Streeter formulated four main conclusions concerning the characteristics of the Caesarean text. He believed that (1) as far as minor variants are concerned, the text of family Θ is almost equidistant from both the Alexandrian (Neutral) and the Western texts; the balance inclines slightly, but only slightly, to the Western side. (2) In family Θ are found certain striking additions to the Textus Receptus which the Old Syriac shares with D and the Old Latin, besides others found only in the Old Syriac or the Armenian. (3) As regards the longer omissions from the Textus Receptus found in B and the Sinaitic Syriac, family Θ nearly always supports the shorter text. (4) Family Θ is nearer to the Old Syriac than is any other surviving Greek text, but it is by no means identical; it is frequently supported by the Armenian against the Syriac. Most frequently of all it is supported by the oldest manuscripts of the Georgian version.[1]

F. C. Burkitt, however, was not convinced that it is correct to speak of a Caesarean text at all. "My chief objection," he wrote in an extensive review of Streeter's book, "to speaking of 'the Caesarean text' is that this term gives apparent definiteness and consistence to a set of 'various readings' that remain to me obstinately disparate and amorphous."[2] He likened the unity underlying family Θ to a unity of undenominationalism, as if a man should combine the peculiarities of the Baptist, Congregationalist, and other Protestant bodies into a sect marked by complete dissent from common catholicity.[3] Nevertheless, Burkitt admitted that the sub-groups within the Caesarean family (he dubbed it the "Caesarean crowd") do exhibit individuality, and he thought that the ancestors of family 1 and family 13 could be reconstructed.[4]

Streeter replied to Burkitt's review in an article entitled, "The Caesarean Text of the Gospels,"[5] in the course of which he explains the sense in which he used the word "text" (in "Caesarean *text*"). By it he did not mean "recension" (i.e., *one definite* manuscript), but the majority of readings which are either peculiar to, or only rarely found outside, this group of authorities. That is, most of

[1] *The Four Gospels*, pp. 84 f.
[2] *JTS*, xxvi (1924-25), 284.
[3] *Ibid.*, pp. 286 f.
[4] *Ibid.*, p. 286
[5] *JTS*, xxvi (1924-25), 373-378.

these readings would have been found in an *average* manuscript used at Caesarea, while of the rest of these characteristic variants, some would have been found in one, some in another manuscript in that locality.[1]

To this reply by Streeter, Burkitt added a note in rejoinder, the gist of which amounts to objecting to dividing the testimony of the Eastern group of witnesses into the Antiochian and Caesarean families. He regarded the Sinaitic Syriac as an integral element of the Eastern group, and held that when "the attestation of any reading of this group does not include syr. S. there is a strong presumption that the reading in question is a later corruption inside the group, not an original feature of it."[2]

The debate, though apparently ended, was carried on indirectly in an article entitled, "The Washington MS. and the Caesarean Text of the Gospels," where Streeter urged that the point on which he and Burkitt differed is small compared with those on which they were agreed.[3] He concluded by turning against Burkitt what the latter had written ten years before in an article entitled, "W and Θ."[4] In this article Burkitt had (rightly, says Streeter) argued for the general superiority of the Bℵ text. "But, if so, are we to say that the larger number of readings in which the Θ family supports Bℵ against Syr. S. are 'later corruptions'; or are they evidence that the family is not only independent of, but at times superior to, the text found in Syr. S.?"[5]

A few years later in an extended notice of the Lake, Blake, and New monograph, Burkitt reiterated his view that, whereas the task of reconstructing the text of the Ferrar group is feasible and practicable, the attempt to reconstruct the Caesarean text is impossible because it was and is non-existent.[6]

---

[1] *Ibid.*, p. 375. Lake, Blake, and New admitted, also, that "the Caesarean text was never a definite single entity like the Vulgate or the Peshitto, but is analogous to the European Latin .... The MSS. of the European Latin can be easily recognized as neither African nor Vulgate; they were used at one period in one place, but they are full of variations" (*HTR*, XXI [1928], 326).

[2] *JTS*, XXVI (1924-25), 380; so too he had expressed himself much earlier in *Evangelion da-Mepharreshe*, II (Cambridge, 1904), 246.

[3] *JTS*, XXVII (1925-26), 144-147.

[4] *JTS*, XVII (1915-15), 1-21, 139-152.

[5] *JTS*, XXVII (1925-26), 147.

[6] *JTS*, XXX (1928-29), 347-358. Burkitt subsequently modified this extreme position, allowing the existence of such a text but observing that "it is

Similar to Burkitt's position was that of another British scholar, P. L. Hedley, who had studied under Burkitt at Cambridge. In his survey of "The Egyptian Texts of the Gospels and Acts" he had occasion to express his opinion concerning whether it is legitimate to speak of a Caesarean family. He asked the question, "Is it probable that every single important Greek MS. of the Gospels with a non-β text (except D) should be descended from a 'Caesarean' ancestor?"[1] The Caesarean family, so Hedley maintained, is really an artificial amalgamation formed by textual critics from diverse texts which "are not descended from any one source, but represent the general treatment of the Gospel text in the East during the first two or three centuries."[2]

At about the same time Henry A. Sanders of the University of Michigan argued that as far as fragments of papyri are concerned,[3] the dominant complexion of the Egyptian text of the Gospels and Acts is Western. The Caesarean text, in his opinion, had no great influence on the Egyptian New Testament,[4] being, he was inclined to think, a revision of that type of the Western text which circulated in Palestine.[5]

An unexpected development in textual studies came in 1935 when R. V. G. Tasker, of King's College, London, apparently overturned the "assured results" of textual criticism. In that year he published two brief articles dealing with "The Quotations from the Synoptic Gospels in Origen's *Exhortation to Martyrdom*"[6] and "The Text Used by Eusebius in *Demonstratio Evangelica* in Quoting from Matthew and Luke."[7] The conclusions which Tasker drew in these two studies were, from Streeter's point of view, most disconcerting. In the former Tasker argued that because he had shown that "in no case does a member of family Θ support Origen's reading to the exclusion of support from the Neutral Text.... [therefore] ... No clearly 'Caesarean' text emerges in

easier, from some points of view, to reconstruct the original than some halfway house like the 'neutral' or the 'Caesarean' text that contains some corruptions but not all" (*JTS*, xxxiv [1933], 367).

[1] *CQR*, cxviii (1934), 224.
[2] *Ibid.*, p. 38, note 6.
[3] "The Egyptian Text of the Four Gospels and Acts," *HTR*, xxvi (1933), 77-98.
[4] *Ibid.*, p. 95.
[5] *Ibid.*, p. 94.
[6] *JTS*, xxxvi (1935), 60-65.
[7] *HTR*, xxviii (1935), 61-69.

Matthew and Luke."[1] In the latter article he concluded that "the text of אB has more right to be called the Caesarean text used by Eusebius than Family Θ."[2]

These statements did not go unchallenged. In the same year Canon Streeter contributed to each journal a refutation of Tasker's conclusions.[3] While praising Tasker for his industry in collecting and publishing textual data, he condemned him for methodological errors in interpreting these data. The gist of Streeter's articles is that precisely the same textual phenomena are found in the citations of Origen and Eusebius from Matthew and Luke as from Mark, and since Tasker admitted that in Mark these Fathers used a Caesarean text, the same conclusion ought to be drawn regarding the other two Synoptic Gospels. Streeter's characterization of the present state of the Caesarean text is as follows: "All the MSS. which preserve this [Caesarean] text have been heavily corrected to accord with what Griesbach called the 'Byzantine', what Hort and others the 'Syrian' or 'Antiochian' text; but the different MSS. have been so corrected in different places. Accordingly it is only when MSS. of this family differ from the Byzantine text that we can identify their readings as authentically representing the characteristic family Text."[4]

What explanation did Streeter have for the fact that Origen's and Eusebius's readings are supported by Neutral as well as Caesarean manuscripts? He acknowledged that "the great majority of 'Caesarean' readings are to be found either in Hort's 'Neutral' or in his 'Alexandrian' texts or in the 'Western' (D and the Old Latin). The same thing holds for the Byzantine text. The majority of its readings are to be found either in the 'Neutral' or in the 'Alexandrian' or in the 'Western' text. But the particular selection of Neutral, Alexandrian, and Western readings in the Byzantine text is totally different from the selection in the Caesarean text. What constitutes the characteristic feature of both these texts is not so much the relatively small proportion of readings peculiar to themselves as the specific pattern, so to speak, in which Neutral, Alexandrian and Western readings are found combined."[5]

---

[1] *JTS*, xxxvi (1935), 64 f.

[2] *HTR*, xxviii (1935), 67.

[3] "Origen, א and the Caesarean Text," *JTS*, xxxvi (1935), 178-180; "The Caesarean Text of Matthew and Luke," *HTR*, xxviii (1935), 231-235.

[4] *HTR*, xxviii (1935), 232.

[5] *Ibid.*, p. 233; and, to the same effect, Lake, Blake, and New, *HTR*, xxi (1928), 257.

Streeter concluded his article by appealing to the Chester Beatty Papyrus as a "dramatic vindication of the critical methods by which it is attempted to reconstruct this [Caesarean] text."[1]

Evidently Streeter convinced (or intimidated) Tasker, for in a subsequent publication on "The Chester Beatty Papyrus and the Caesarean Text of Luke,"[2] he indicated that Streeter "read my original draft of this article and made valuable suggestions, which I have incorporated, for the treatment of the evidence."[3] He concluded that the text of the papyrus in Luke "is akin to, though not identical with, that found in members of fam Θ." Moreover, "there are in proportion more Neutral readings preserved in members of family Θ of Luke than in Mark. In other words, the distinction between the Neutral and Caesarean text in Luke is less than it is in Mark."[4]

In two subsequent articles Tasker examined "The Text of St. Matthew Used by Origen in his Commentary on St. Matthew"[5] and "The Chester Beatty Papyrus and the Caesarean Text of John."[6] His conclusion in the former is that "the text used by Origen while writing this portion of his Commentary on St. Matthew at Caesarea was that of family Θ."[7] His conclusion in the latter is that "the remarkable thing about the text [of P45 in John] is its mixed character, which is similar to the mixed character of the text of family Θ."[8]

Both Streeter and Tasker—as well as other textual critics—overlooked what is without doubt a most significant analysis of the textual complexion of the Caesarean text. In 1936 James E. McA. Baikie was awarded a M.Litt. degree by the Faculty of Divinity at Cambridge University for a dissertation entitled, "The Caesarean Text *Inter Pares.*" Baikie sought to determine whether or not the Caesarean text is a unity, basing his investigation on analyses of Caesarean agreements with Western, Syrian, and Neutral readings in three test chapters, Matt. 3, Mark 12, and Luke

[1] *HTR*, XXVIII (1935), 234.
[2] *HTR*, XXIX (1936), 345-352.
[3] *Ibid.*, p. 345, note 1.
[4] *Ibid.*, p. 350.
[5] *JTS*, XXXVIII (1937), 60-64.
[6] *HTR*, XXX (1937), 157-164.
[7] *JTS*, XXXVIII (1937), 64.
[8] *HTR*, XXX (1937), 162.

12. The author's succinct summary of his dissertation is as follows:[1]

Statistical tables of agreements for Mark 12 show "that the Caesarean witnesses (1) did not agree in one family preference for types of variant; (2) did not agree in one family order of domestic preferences; (3) in agreement with the Latins, under certain types of variant, showed almost complete unanimity of preference, but, under others, diversity; (4) in agreement with the Syriac, had, some, an almost constantly high place, others, a uniformly low one, the remainder, a variable one; (5) in agreement with Neutral comparative to Western, displayed, some, a consistent preference for Western, one, a less consistent preference for Neutral, part of the remainder, an almost consistent preference for Western, the rest of the remainder, a varying preference between Western and Neutral.

"From a co-ordination of these tables it was observed that in most cases the Caesareans were in greater absolute agreement with outsiders than with the majority of their fellows.

"Further evidence of Caesarean diversity was afforded by Inter-Familiar Variation, i.e. cases where, when two or more variants occur, the family witnesses are divided against themselves and united with those of other families.

"The Caesarean witness of Origen and Eusebius sometimes agreed with other Caesareans, at times had isolated agreements with outsiders, and also took part in Inter-Familiar Variation. Both are thus typical Caesareans.

"Two explanations of the problem, not mutually exclusive, can be offered. The above divergences are due, either to later and irregular correction, or to varying textual influences. Inter-Familiar Variation would seem to demand the latter, thus denying the Caesarean unity, while the Caesarean 'self-consciousness' observed in agreement with the Latins and the lack of continuity in grouping observed in cases of Inter-Familiar Variation favour the former.

"A final suggestion is made that the Caesarean unity is one of influences rather than origin, and that the Caesarean text, in a measure at least, is really a Textual Process."

Meanwhile, the Caesarean group was assigned not a few additional members. Just before Canon Streeter's tragic death in an airplane accident in the Alps he wrote a brief study for Lake's *Festschrift* (*Quantulacumque* [London, 1937]) in which he expressed his belief that most, if not all, of the minuscules which von Soden had assigned to his *I* text are really Caesarean. These manuscripts, it is true,

[1] See *Abstracts of Dissertations Approved for the Ph. D., M. Sc. and M. Litt. Degrees in the University of Cambridge during the Academic Year 1935-1936* (Cambridge, 1936), pp. 53 f.

have a much larger Byzantine element than do the authorities on
which Lake based his reconstruction; but—so he argued—"the value
of these 'weak' supporters to the 'Caesarean' text, including *fam* 1424,
is that they appear occasionally to preserve a 'Caesarean' reading
which has been revised out of the more important authorities
for that text... That some of the readings in the inferior authorities
are authentically 'Caesarean' is shown by the fact that they appear
in quotations by Origen and Eusebius."[1]

Another investigator of the affinities of P[45] with the Caesarean
text, C. C. Tarelli, struck out in a different direction.[2] Tarelli
alleged that Kenyon's analysis of P[45] was vitiated by two errors
of methodology. In the first place, Kenyon had unfairly cited,
Tarelli claimed, agreements of P[45] with members of the Caesarean
group even when they agree with Byzantine text. But in this
regard it is no doubt Tarelli's judgment and not Kenyon's which
is at fault. For if the Byzantine text (which, for most purposes,
may be identified with the Textus Receptus) disagrees with, say,
the Neutral and Western texts while agreeing with the Caesarean,
the evidence of P[45] in agreeing with the Caesarean text may quite
fairly be presumed to be significant, and the agreement of the
Textus Receptus may be explained on the hypothesis that the
Textus Receptus, an eclectic text, has absorbed a Caesarean
reading.

The other charge of error in methodology which Tarelli leveled
against Kenyon is more serious. He pointed out that in Kenyon's
statistics "the 323 agreements [of P[45]] with the [Caesarean] group
are obtained by adding together the agreements with its individual
members, so that an agreement with W and Θ counts as two,
an agreement with Θ, fam. 1 and fam. 13 as three, and an agreement with all four as four agreements. The total number of agreements with the group is in fact more than twice as many as the
total number of variants noted. This is an obvious oversight, and
the question of the Caesarean affinities of the papyrus evidence
requires reconsideration. As, moreover, 28, 565, and 700 are equally
regarded as belonging to the family, their agreements should also
be taken into account, and the agreements of the whole group

---

[1] "Codices 157, 1071 and the Caesarean Text," *Quantulacumque*, ed. R. P.
Casey *et al.*, p. 150.
[2] "The Chester Beatty Papyrus and the Caesarean Text," *JTS*, XL (1939)
46-55.

and its various combinations should be properly weighed."[1]

Nevertheless, even after making necessary adjustments in the evaluation of the textual affinities of P[45], Tarelli confessed: "It must be frankly admitted that the papyrus falls very readily into Streeter's pattern, at least so far as it has extremely few agreements with ℵ, B, or A, and none at all with D, which are not supported by some members of the WΘ group. This does not mean, however, that the P[45] text is identical with 'the text which results from the purely objective process of deducting Byzantine readings from members of Family Θ.' The text resulting from that process in Prof. Lake's tables (*Harvard Theological Review*, 21 [1928] 216-246) is so uncertain that it is necessary in many cases to assume 2, 3, 4, and sometimes even 5 possible family readings, and, as we have seen, there are only two non-Byzantine readings in P[45] which do not find the family in conflict, nor are the opposing members of the family invariable in agreement with the Byzantine text."[2] Yet, "P[45] has no Byzantine reading which is not supported by some members of the Caesarean group, and all but 14 of such readings are supported by family 13, and all but 17 of these by W also."[3]

After raising many important issues regarding the Caesarean text and asking not a few questions difficult to answer, Tarelli concluded that "what underlies P[45] and its supporters is not a local text but rather such a text as von Soden imagined under the name *IHK*, containing elements of all later texts 'in their pregnant causes mixed'. No doubt actual mixture of different lines of transmission took place at all periods of the MS. tradition, but it is highly probable that the fundamental cause of the 'mixed' texts of which P[45] is our earliest example is the fact that the original text itself was 'mixed' in this sense of combining elements found in all of its descendants."[4] In a later study Hollis W. Huston re-opened

---

[1] *Ibid.*, pp. 46 f. Tarelli failed to mention, however, that Kenyon employed exactly the same procedure in evaluating the non-Caesarean, pre-Byzantine elements of P[45]. This circumstance largely counterbalances the otherwise excessive weight which would be allowed the Caesarean witnesses by Kenyon's method of counting variants.

[2] *Ibid.*, p. 50.

[3] *Ibid.*, p. 52.

[4] *Ibid.*, p. 55. In two other articles dealing with P[45], Tarelli touched upon but did not deal explicitly with the problems of the Caesarean text; the articles are "The Chester Beatty Papyrus and the Western and Byzantine Texts" (*JTS*, XLI [1940], 253-260), and "Some Linguistic Aspects of the Chester Beatty Papyrus of the Gospels" (*JTS*, XLIII [1942], 19-25).

the problem of the analysis of "Mark 6 and 11 in P[45] and in the Caesarean Text."[1] His conclusion is that "P[45] in these chapters cannot be classed as a strong supporter of any text."[2]

VI. A New Orientation

In 1933 Sir Frederic G. Kenyon published a papyrus of the Gospels which, like an acid, was to dissolve the unity of the elaborately constructed Caesarean text.[3] At first sight the text of the papyrus seemed to confirm all that had been accomplished in the isolation of the several parts of this text. Both its editor and Streeter[4] hailed it as possessing strong affinities with the Caesarean group. But then gradually the realization began to dawn on scholars that if this papyrus, which its editor dated in the first half of the third century, agrees with the Caesarean text, that text can scarcely be called the Caesarean text. In other words, the text which had been localized at Caesarea in Palestine is now discovered to antedate its introduction there; its origins must be traced to Egypt.

It is interesting to observe the slowly shifting opinion. In 1924 Streeter was confident that the Caesarean text was found by Origen when he moved from Alexandria to Caesarea in Palestine. But the investigations of Lake, Blake, and New cast doubt upon the certainty of this opinion, showing that Origen may possibly have known it in Alexandria. They could find, however, no unequivocal answer to give to the question they raise, "Was it found by Origen in Caesarea or brought thither by him? On that question we have no firm convictions."[5]

It was Père Lagrange who spoke with more assurance on this matter. As early as 1929 (that is, four years before the publication of P[45]) he wrote, "The [Caesarean] family is not necessarily the type of a recension made at Caesarea. It is certainly not the work of Origen.... Its origin in Egypt appears to us to be more probable

---

[1] *JBL*, LXXIV (1955), 262-271.

[2] *Ibid.*, p. 269.

[3] *The Chester Beatty Papyrus I* (London, 1933).

[4] Streeter's concurrence is to be found in the preface to the fifth impression of his *The Four Gospels*, dated 1936. See also his enthusiastic remarks in *HTR*, XXVIII (1935), 234, quoted at the top of p. 58 above.

[5] *HTR*, XXI (1928), 324.

[than its origin in Caesarea]."[1] Similar too was the tenor of Lagrange's brief notice of the discovery of the Chester Beatty papyrus,[2] and in his subsequent article, "Les papyrus Chester Beatty
pour les Évangiles,"[3] he asserted with great positiveness: "Nothing
prevents the recognizing in this type [of text] a product of Alexandrian criticism, as we have suggested earlier." These same con-
clusons were likewise embodied by Lagrange in his comprehensive
treatise on textual criticism.[4]

There were, as one would have expected, other estimates of
the significance of P[45]. Leon Vaganay, believing that the Western
text was the prevailing type of primitive text, regarded P[45] as a
witness to this primitive text which was current in much the same
form in Alexandria as well as in Caesarea prior to the time when
revisers began methodically to work upon it.[5] He proposed, furthermore, another term for the group ordinarily designated "Caesarean."
Since he thought that the textual characteristics of the several
members of the group (he did not include P[45] in the group) derive
from the recension of Pamphilus, i.e. the Palestinian text, he proposed
calling the text the Palestinian or Pamphilus Recension.[6]

But none of these generalized statements can be compared with
the methodical and painstaking study which Teófilo Ayuso, professor in the Roman Catholic Seminary at Segovia, published under
the title, " ¿Texto cesariense o precesariense ?"[7] He came to the
following conclusions: (1) At Caesarea Origen and Eusebius used a
"Caesarean" text. (2) This text did not originate at Caesarea but
was carried there from Egypt. It did not, however, come from
Alexandria, where a Neutral text was in use. (3) It originated in
a locality off the beaten track as far as scholarship was concerned;
it came from the region of Gizeh and the Fayyum. Evidence for

---

[1] "Le groupe dit césaréen des manuscrits des Évangiles," RB, xxxviii
(1929), 507.
[2] RB, xli (1932), 453 f.
[3] RB, xliii (1934), 23.
[4] Critique textuelle, ii, 166, "There is no reason to say that the Caesarean
text is Caesarean in origin."
[5] Initiation à la critique textuelle néotestamentaire (Paris, 1934), p. 101
(Eng. trans. [London, 1937], p. 119). See too, P. L. Hedley, CQR, cxviii
(1934), 224, note 35.
[6] Op. cit., pp. 86 f. (Eng. trans., pp. 114 f.).
[7] B, xvi (1935), 369-415; the subtitle is "su realidad y su trascendencia
en la crítica textual del Nuevo Testamento." For a discussion of this article
in another setting, see pp. 125 ff. below.

localizing it here is to be found in W (which Charles L. Freer bought of an Arab dealer in Gizeh in 1906), in P³⁷, Berlin P. 13416, and especially P⁴⁵, all of which came from the Fayyum, or nearby, and all of which exhibit a "Caesarean" type of text.

On the basis of elaborate analyses of variant readings, Ayuso divided the "Caesarean" witnesses into two groups: P⁴⁵, W, fam 1, 28, and fam 13, calling this group primitive and pre-Caesarean; and Θ, 565, 700, Origen, Eusebius, Sinaitic Syriac, Old Georgian, and Old Armenian, calling this group recensional and Caesarean proper. The former was localized in Fayyum-Gizeh and belongs to the "subgrupo occidental"; the latter was localized in Caesarea and represents the "subgrupo oriental."

Slowly a few other investigators began to sense that a new phase had been reached, but these scholars were apparently unaware of Ayuso's studies. One of Kirsopp Lake's students, Norman Huffman, published part of his doctoral dissertation in which he suggested a pre-Caesarean stage of the Caesarean text. He observed that "Caesarean readings are very frequently found also in other texts which are perhaps older than the Caesarean.... There may have been in Egypt in the second and third centuries a text, as yet unidentified, which was the ancestor of the old Syriac version, of the Caesarean text, and of the type of text found in Pap.⁴⁵ and W—in short, an 'Egyptian text'—antedating the earliest texts which we know."[1]

In a tribute to the memory of Père Lagrange, who died in 1938, Kirsopp and Silva Lake found occasion to publish their revised views regarding the Caesarean text.[2] Without referring to Ayuso (and therefore, one can assume, with independent confirmation of his studies) they expressed themselves in terms similar to his regarding the bipartite division of the Caesarean family. They recognized that with the acquisition of the evidence in P⁴⁵ the textual critic must separate Θ, 565, and 700 (the text of which accords closely with the citations in Origen and Eusebius) from W and fam 13 (with which P⁴⁵ is in close agreement). Obviously, too, the text of an Egyptian papyrus which antedates Origen's hegira to Caesarea

---

[1] "Suggestions from the Gospel of Mark for a New Textual Theory," *JBL*, LVI (1937), 356.

[2] "De Westcott et Hort au Père Lagrange et au-delà," *RB*, XLVIII (1939), 497-505. A similarly orientated discussion by the same authors had appeared in *Religion in Life*, V (1936), 90-95.

cannot be called Caesarean. This term, therefore, must be reserved for the text identified by the citations of Origen and Eusebius and for the text of 700. On the other hand, P⁴⁵, W, and fam 13 may be regarded as witnesses of a text on which the "Caesarean" was to be established, and P⁴⁵ and W suggest that this more ancient text was Egyptian before it was Caesarean. It is from P⁴⁵ that something of the nature of this pre-Origenian, Egyptian text can be learned. Here the Lakes left the matter to take it up again in the fascicle entitled *Family 13 (The Ferrar Group)*.[1]

In this study of one part of the Caesarean text the Lakes reconstructed the Marcan text of family 13 as a preliminary step in the reconstruction of the Caesarean text of Mark, a task which they had contemplated since about 1924.[2] In their discussion of the textual affinities of family 13 they acknowledge that readings of W, family 1, family 13, and 28 must not be considered (as both Streeter and they had done) to be witnesses of a bad Caesarean text. They are not Caesarean at all, but, as the discovery of P⁴⁵ (with which they agree so closely) made plain, they represent "a pre-Origenian text which was revised into the true 'Caesarean.'"[3]

More recently several younger scholars have given attention to the type of text represented in the quotations of Church Fathers of the third and fourth centuries. In an analysis of representative works of Origen, K. W. Kim concludes that "the Matthean text of Origen [in his commentary on Matthew] is neither 'Caesarean' nor 'Neutral'; it is a distinct text-type which is represented by Codex 1 and 1582."[4] In a study of Origen's treatises *On Prayer*, *Commentary on Matthew*, and *Against Celsus*, Kim declares that "the term 'Caesarean text' should not be used with reference to

[1] See also Mrs. Lake's monograph on *Family II and the Codex Alexandrinus* (SD, v [London, 1937]), p. 4, note 5; p. 55; pp. 61 ff.

[2] *HTR*, xxi (1928), 210.

[3] *Family 13*, p. 7. This statement represents no doubt the real opinion of the authors. The statement on p. ix ("Fam 13 is associated with Θ, W, fam 1, 28, 565, 700 and the Georgian version, as a representative of the type of text used by Origen in Caesarea in Palestine") contradicts the one cited above. In a subsequent article the Lakes suggested that the type of text found in family 1 should be called either pre-Caesarean or Old Egyptian ("The Scribe Ephraim," *JBL*, lxii [1943], 267).

[4] "The Matthean Text of Origen in his Commentary on Matthew," *JBL*, lxxviii (1949), 125-139. The quotation is from p. 139. According to Kim the same conditions are true as regards "Origen's Text of Matthew in his *Against Celsus*," *JTS*, n.s. iv (1953), 42-49.

Origen's text of John; it should be confined to his text of Mark."[1]

Several studies of Eusebius's New Testament text suggest that his "text stands between the Western and Alexandrian texts, but somewhat closer to the Western."[2] At the same time, "No one of the 'Great Texts' can be claimed as Eusebius' text.... [In fact,] there is a marked tendency in Eusebius to reject the 'eccentricities' of each of the 'Great Texts'.... The chief witnesses for the Matthean text of Eusebius are 'Caesarean' and 'Western,' with 'Western' witnesses slightly in the ascendency."[3] In an article entitled "Eusebius' New Testament Text in the *Demonstratio Evangelica*," H. R. Murphy presents the following summary: "The text of the *Demonstratio* in the Gospels is supported most frequently by the witnesses of fam Θ with the Neutrals and/or Westerns; the few variants from Acts find their strongest support from the Neutral witnesses; and the text of the Pauline Corpus is attested to most strongly by P^{46}, the Neutrals, and 1739, with moderately strong support by the Westerns."[4]

Prior to 1955 no one, it appears, had given systematic attention to the Gospel text of Cyril of Jerusalem (who flourished during the first half of the fourth century). In that year J. Harold Greenlee published his doctoral dissertation done at Harvard University, in which he characterizes Cyril's text of Mark as "Caesarean..., more closely related to the Neutral than to the Western text, more closely related to ℵ than to B, and strongly supported by the Georgian (and, to a less degree, by the Armenian) version."[5] Cyril's text of the other Gospels, according to Greenlee, is also Caesarean, though in John it appears to have somewhat closer affinity to the Western than to the Neutral text.[6] In a discussion of the significance of these textual data Greenlee pointed out that

---

[1] "Origen's Text of John in his *On Prayer, Commentary on Matthew*, and *Against Celsus*," *JTS*, n.s. 1 (1950), 74-84. The quotation is from p. 84.

[2] So M. Jack Suggs, "Eusebius' Text of John in the Writings Against Marcellus," *JBL*, LXXV (1956), 137-142. The quotation is from p. 140.

[3] M. Jack Suggs, "The Eusebian Text of Matthew," *Novum Testamentum*, I (1956), 233-245. The quotations are from pp. 243 and 244. In an article entitled, "Eusebius and the Gospel Text" (*HTR*, L [1957], 307-310), Suggs corrects D. S. Wallace-Hadrill, who had concluded that in Matthew and Luke Eusebius's text was predominately Alexandrian ("Eusebius and the Gospel Text of Caesarea," *HTR*, XLIX [1956], 105-114).

[4] *JBL*, LXXXIII (1954), 167.

[5] *The Gospel Text of Cyril of Jerusalem* (*SD*, XVII; Copenhagen, 1955), p. 94.

[6] *Ibid.*, p. 84.

they do not support a theory which had been broached by Edward F. Hills a few years earlier. Hills had suggested that, since "in Mark the variants of the Caesarean MSS from the TR agree in far greater proportion with the other Gospels than do the variants of the other MSS from the TR," ..."it would seem that the Caesarean text is a harmonistic text...."[1] Though Hills was at first reluctant to attribute this alleged harmonistic element to Tatian,[2] in a later study he declares, "The Caesarean MSS seem to be connected in some way with the Diatessaron of Tatian."[3] But, as Greenlee rightly observes, since the data which Hills collected pertain only to Mark, it is hazardous to rest such a sweeping generalization upon so narrow a base.[4]

By way of summary, it must be acknowledged that at present the Caesarean text is disintegrating.[5] There still remain several families—such as family 1, family 13, the Armenian and Georgian versions—each of which exhibits certain characteristic features. But it is no longer possible to gather all these several families and individual manuscripts under one *vinculum* such as the Caesarean text. The evidence of P[45] clearly demonstrates that henceforth scholars must speak of a pre-Caesarean text as differentiated from the Caesarean text proper. Future investigators must take into account two hitherto neglected studies, namely Ayuso's significant contribution to *Biblica* in 1935, in which he sets forth fully the compelling reasons for bifurcating the Caesarean text, and Baikie's M. Litt. dissertation in 1936, the implications of which suggest that the Caesarean text is really a textual process.

[1] "Harmonizations in the Caesarean Text of Mark," *JBL*, LXVI (1947), 135-152. The quotations are from pp. 140 and 144.

[2] *Ibid.*, p. 144.

[3] "A New Approach to the Old Egyptian Text," *JBL*, LXIX (1950), 345-362. The quotation is from p. 357.

[4] *Op. cit.*, p. 96.

[5] See A. H. White, "The Problem of the Caesarean Text," *Journal of the Manchester University Egypt and Oriental Society*, XXIV (1942-1945; published in 1947), 39-59, especially pp. 51 ff., for a vigorous discussion of what he calls the decline of the reputation of the Caesarean text. For the sake of completeness of bibliographical record two rather general articles may be mentioned here: Francesco Russo, "I manoscritti del gruppo 'Ferrar,'" *Bollettino della badia greca di Grottaferrata*, n.s. III (1949), 76-90; and Lars-Olov Almgren, "Diskussionen om den caesarensiska texttypen," *Svensk exegetisk årsbok*, XV (1950), 81-100.

VII. Tasks and Problems

Although no little time and energy have been expended in investigating the Caesarean text, many more tasks and analyses remain for future scholars. The following are some of the problems —not all of the same magnitude—which clamor for attention.[1]

1. Manuscript 565, which agrees so frequently in Mark with Θ, ought to be collated carefully in the other Gospels as well. Its editor, J. Belsheim, thought it good to cite only the more weighty variants from the Textus Receptus in Matthew, Luke, and John.[2]

2. The Caesarean text of Mark has been investigated with some care in three sample chapters (chapters 1, 6, and 11). Similar investigations should be undertaken in the rest of the Gospel as well as in the other three Gospels.[3]

3. Lake, Blake, and New reported that the Palestinian Syriac version is Caesarean in its textual affinities, and thought that it derived its Caesarean coloring from a Syriac version of which no trace remains. According to Lagrange[4] and Colwell[5] this hypothetical Syriac version was postulated without adequate reason. The grounds for assuming such a Syriac intermediary between the Caesarean Greek text and the Palestinian Syriac version need to be reviewed.

[1] It goes without saying that a perennial task is the textual analysis of hitherto uncollated or imperfectly analyzed manuscripts; e.g. Ian A. Moir has recently found that in Mark Codex Climaci Rescriptus Graeci has a connection with the Caesarean group (TS, n.s. II [1956], p. 20), and J. N. Birdsall concludes that in Mark, chaps, 1, 6, and 11, manuscript 406 possesses a considerable number of strong Caesarean readings (TU, LXXIII [1959], pp. 732-736).

[2] Moir corrected those sections of Belsheim's collation of Luke and John which find parallels in Codex Climaci Rescriptus Graecus; see p. 46, n. 1, above.

[3] In looking further afield one could wish that someone would do for the Pauline corpus what Streeter did for the Gospels (though here perhaps some of the necessary materials are lacking; there is no Θ and no ante-Nicene Syriac version); see W. Arndt, "A Definite Need in the Field of New Testament Textual Criticism" (Concordia Theological Monthly, XVI [1945], 180-186). It would no doubt be profitable to investigate more completely the textual affinities of codex 1739, a tenth century manuscript of the Acts and Pauline Epistles whose text is connected with Origen (Six Collations of New Testament Manuscripts, edd. Kirsopp Lake and Silva New [Cambridge, 1932], pp. 141-219; cf. K. and S. Lake, JBL, LXII [1943], 263 ff.) but is not Caesarean (so Lagrange, Critique textuelle, II, 470). See also Heinrich Seesemann, "Die Bedeutung des Chester-Beatty Papyrus für die Textkritik der Paulus-briefe" (Theologische Blätter, XVI [1937], cols. 92-97).

[4] Critique textuelle, II, 167, note 4.   [5] JR., XVII (1937), 56.

4. In an article on "Syriasms in the Washington Text of Mark,"[1] C. S. C. Williams concluded that there is "a strong streak of Syriac in the Caesarean texts, and they and Sy^s are more closely affiliated than even the diagram in *Harvard Theological Review*, 1928, 324 f. would suggest." Detailed reasearch in this field would almost certainly be fruitful.

5. In Kirsopp Lake's volume, *The Text of the New Testament* (6th ed.), the hint is thrown out that the text of the Persian version may be Caesarean in character. This hint should be explored.

The preceding five problems presuppose that the methods of textual criticism employed heretofore are valid. But certain other problems concerning basic methodology clamor for attention. Embarrassing questions rise; questions for which there are no satisfactory answers.

6. The discovery of P^{45} revealed that what had been accounted as one text must, in fact, be divided into a pre-Caesarean text and a Caesarean text proper. Suppose P^{45} had not been found; scholars would no doubt have continued to combine diverse families which ought to be separated. Was there a fundamental flaw in the previous investigation which tolerated so erroneous a grouping? It may be, of course, that in the nature of the case scholars could not have been expected to make allowances for evidence only subsequently brought to light. But on the other hand one wonders why textual critics could not have distinguished the presence of two groups of manuscripts even before the discovery of P^{45}, as astronomers were able to predict the existence of another planet before they had a telescope powerful enough to see it.

7. A glance at the apparatus in Kenyon's edition of P^{45} reveals how very frequently fam 1 and fam 13 are opposed to each other. Why should this be so? In the same vein, when Origen and Eusebius differ, which is to be regarded as presenting the Caesarean text? Or if, as not infrequently is the case, Origen and Eusebius are on one side and the oriental versions (Armenian, Georgian, and Palestinian Syriac) are on the other, with the Greek manuscripts of the families divided between them, what explanation are we to give? The only answer Lake, Blake, and New could offer is the suggestion that the Caesarean text was never a definite single entity like the Vulgate or the Peshitta but is analogous to the

---

[1] *JTS*, XLII (1941), 177 f. See also a similar view expressed by A. H. White on pp. 56-59 of his article mentioned in n. 5, p. 67, above.

European Latin.[1] Is this a legitimate and helpful analogy or an evasion of a disturbing question?

8. Is it licit to reconstruct the ancient Caesarean text from what are frequently late documents merely by pooling the non-Byzantine variants? Lake, Blake, and New, for instance, included in the Caesarean text of Mark chaps. 1, 6, and 11, 168 variants from the Textus Receptus which are read by only one of eight Caesarean witnesses.[2] Is it reasonable to maintain that originally most or all of the witnesses had the Caesarean reading but that this common reading was supplanted by the Textus Receptus in all but one Caesarean witness? In very many of these 168 instances the variant read by only one Caesarean witness is found also in Neutral or Western witnesses. Why should not such readings be called simply Neutral or Western? Moreover, the accepted method of determining the Caesarean text cannot but fail to discover all Caesarean readings, for certain Caesarean readings have undoubtedly passed into the Byzantine text and therefore are not disclosed when Caesarean manuscripts are collated against a Byzantine text. On the other hand, however, must it not be acknowledged that we have but Hobson's choice in the matter; is any other more satisfactory method for determining the Caesarean text at our disposal?[3]

9. Is it possible to determine whether the Caesarean text is a correction of the Western text by the Neutral (as the Lakes,[4] H. A. Sanders,[5] and, with certain reservations, P. L. Hedley [6] be-

---

[1] *HTR*, XXI (1928), 326. (Quoted above, p. 55, n. 1.)

[2] That is, by one of these eight: Θ, fam 1, fam 13, 28, 565, 700, W, and the Georgian.

[3] In his article entitled, "The Inter-Relationship of the Caesarean Manuscripts" (*JBL*, LXVIII [1949], 141-160), Edward F. Hills discusses the merits of various methodologies which have been used in isolating the Caesarean text; he concludes that the best method is to use the variants from the TR, comparing pairs of Caesarean manuscripts with each other and pairs of other manuscripts with each other. On the other hand, Harold S. Murphy (*JBL*, LXXXIII [1954] 167-168) gives three reasons why this method inevitably overlooks significant data.

[4] *The Text of the New Testament*, 6th ed., p. 84; also "The Text of the Gospels" in *Studies in Early Christianity*, ed. S. J. Case (New York, 1928), pp. 30 f. Yet compare their letter (with R. P. Blake) to *The Times* (London), Dec. 29, 1931, p. 13, just after Kenyon's preliminary announcement of the discovery of the Chester Beatty papyri (*ibid.*, Nov. 19, 1931), in which they pose the question of whether the Neutral text is not rather to be explained as a revision of the Caesarean (so too Silva New in *JBL*, LI [1932], 73 f.).

[5] *HTR*, XXVI (1933), 94.

[6] *CQR*, CXVIII (1934), 225.

lieved), or a correction of the Neutral text by the Western (as Lagrange[1] maintained), or an independent text, co-ordinate in value with the Western and Neutral texts (as Streeter[2] and apparently Kenyon[3] held)? The answer given to this question will determine one's attitude toward the usefulness of the Caesarean text in discovering the elusive text of the autographs. For if the Caesarean text is a correction of the Western text by the Neutral, or a correction of the Neutral by the Western, it obviously is secondary to both the Neutral and the Western.

10. Finally—and to swing into a much wider orbit—is it possible to analyze the textual complexion of a given document by utilizing all variants, large and small? Is the principle, employed with such persuasive force by Hort,[4] that "Identity of reading implies identity of origin," really applicable in analyzing the affinities of the Caesarean text on the basis of often very minor variations from the Textus Receptus?

On the one hand, if it is licit to employ all variants in determining family consanguinity, the full possibilities of the method have been largely neglected. The proper method of determining the relation of a hitherto unknown manuscript to the Neutral, Western, Caesarean, and Byzantine families is not merely to count how many of its variants from the Textus Receptus (or from any given norm) agree with B, ℵ, D, Θ, W, etc. Such a procedure is indeed necessary and not uninstructive, but the only really satisfactory method is to reconstruct the text of each of the major families and to determine precisely what proportion of variants from the Textus Receptus in such a reconstructed text is also present in the manuscript to be analyzed. For obviously it is of slight value in determining family relationship to know only that in a certain area a given manuscript agrees with, say, B and ℵ ten times in differing from Textus Receptus. If B and ℵ should differ from the Textus Receptus in ninety other instances, the Neutral element in the given manuscript would be slight indeed. It is necessary, therefore,

---

[1] *Critique textuelle*, II, 165.

[2] *The Four Gospels*, p. 106.

[3] *Recent Developments in the Textual Criticism of the Greek Bible* (The Schweich Lectures of the British Academy, 1932; London, 1933), pp. 70 f. and 85; "The Bible Text and Recent Discoveries," *University of Toronto Quarterly*, V (1936), 315; *The Text of the Greek Bible* (London, 1937), pp. 210 ff.

[4] *The New Testament in the Original Greek*, [vol. ii] *Introduction [and] Appendix* (2nd ed., London, 1896), p. 46, § 58.

assuming that identity of reading implies identity of origin, to determine exactly what proportion of the total number of variants of each type of text (and/or of each manuscript) is present in the manuscript to be a analyzed.[1]

But, on the other hand, is it really legitimate to utilize all variants, large and small, to determine the relation between manuscripts? Manifestly a spectacular variant, such as the presence of the *pericope de adultera* after Luke 21.38 in the manuscripts of family 13, has real significance in disclosing the textual affinities of a given manuscript. But it seems to the present writer that the possibility of mere chance coincidence among manuscripts in agreeing in small variations (involving *inter alia*, word order, common synonyms, the presence or absence of the article, the aorist for the imperfect or historical present) has not been sufficiently taken into account. Is the fact, for example, that in Mark 6.27 manuscripts 565 and 700 agree in reading ἀλλά, while all the other Caesarean witnesses read καί with the Textus Receptus, prove that ἀλλά was the original family reading (as Lake *et al.* suppose)?[2] Or did the scribes of 565 and 700 just happen independently to use ἀλλά instead of καί? If one hundred people today were to transcribe independently from a common text, how often would they agree fortuitously in their errors? The point is that in many instances it is exceedingly difficult to decide with finality whether a given variant present in four or five manuscripts is significant or insignificant in determining genealogy. The conclusion which one must draw is that some of the variants which are commonly utilized to show relationship among the members of the Caesarean text (or almost any other text) are not really capable of turning the scales in either direction.

[1] This procedure was employed by the present writer in his analysis of the textual affinities of the Saturday and Sunday lessons from Luke in the Greek Gospel Lectionary; see p. 53, n. 2, above.

[2] *HTR*, XXI (1928), 230.

CHAPTER THREE

THE OLD SLAVONIC VERSION

I. Sts. Cyril and Methodius, Apostles to the Slavs

With the exception of St. Jerome, more is known of the life and work of Sts. Cyril and Methodius, the apostles to the Slavs, than of any other translator of an ancient version of the Scriptures.[1] Briefly, they were sons of a wealthy official in Salonika, and thus were probably acquainted from childhood with the Slavic dialect spoken in that district. The elder brother, Methodius, died April 6, 885; the year of his birth is unknown. The younger brother, born in 826-827, was christened Constantine; later, having become Photius's successor at the University of Constantinople (about 850-851), he came to be known as the Philosopher. Still later (about Christmas, 868), having entered a monastery at Rome, he took the monastic name Cyril. He died February 14, 869. With Ulfilas, the Bishop of the Goths, Cyril shares the distinction of being credited with the

---

[1] For problems relating to Cyril and Methodius, scholars are fortunate in having two highly useful bibliographical tools: G. A. Il'jinskij, *Opyt sistematičeskoj Kirillo-Mefodevskoj bibliografii*, edited with additions by M. G. Popruženko and St. M. Romanski (Sofia, 1934), xliii+303 pp., and M. G. Popruženko and St. M. Romanski, *Bibliografski pregled na slavjanskitě kirilski iztočnici za života i dejnost'ta na Kirila i Metodija* (Sofia, 1935), 68 pp. In the former volume there is indexed in comprehensive fashion the literature of the life, activity, and significance of the Apostles to the Slavs. Items dealing with textual criticism are listed on pp. 119-124. The magnitude of the bibliography may be appreciated from the circumstance that the compilers labored more than twenty years to collect 3385 items written in various languages and scattered in manifold publications. The second volume is a survey of the sources of the life and activity of the two saints. The authors cite Slavic sources which are written in Cyrillic, the libraries in which these manuscripts are found, as well as works which treat of these sources. For literature on Cyril and Methodius since the date of publication of these two works, reference has been made to Emil Georgiev, "Die bulgarische Literaturwissenschaft in den Jahren 1929-1939," *Zeitschrift für slavische Philologie*, XVII (1940-1941), 171-175, and to the bibliographical sections which appear regularly in *Byzantinische Zeitschrift* and *Byzantinoslavica*. Bibliographical guidance in the wider area of Slavic theological literature in general is supplied by *Slavorum litterae theologicae*, being *Acta academiae velehradensis*, I (1905), and succeeding volumes.

invention of a new alphabet,[1] which he used as the vehicle for his translation of the Scriptures.

One of the most perplexing problems in this connection arises from a passage in the legendary *Vita* of Cyril which has mystified several generations of scholars. According to chap. viii of the *Vita*, when Constantine went to Cherson (in southern Russia) "he found there [a copy of] the Gospel and the Psalter written in Russian letters and a man speaking that language."[2] Since there is no definite evidence of the previous existence of any developed Slavic script (although there may have been a runic script among certain Slavs),[3] this passage has given rise to quite diverse theories. A. A. Vasiliev argued that these letters were Gothic.[4] André Vaillant[5] suggested an emendation which was endorsed by Henri Grégoire[6] and was elaborated by Roman Jakobson,[7] namely that instead of

---

[1] Whether it was the Glagolitic or the Cyrillic or both has been a mooted question among scholars; for a summary of the problems involved see Josef Vajs, *Rukovět hlaholské paleografie* (*Manuel de paléographie glagolitique*), (Prague, 1932); David Diringer, *The Alphabet, a Key to the History of Mankind* (New York, 1948), pp. 485-487; and James G. Février, *Histoire de l'écriture* (Paris, 1948), pp. 429-432. The view which is perhaps as widely held as any among present-day scholars is that the Apostles to the Slavs invented the Glagolitic alphabet and that soon thereafter one of Cyril's disciples (probably Clement) invented the so-called Cyrillic alphabet, being an adaptation of the former to the Greek alphabet; see Roman Jakobson, *Slavic Languages*, 2nd ed. (New York, 1955), p. 11.

[2] Fr. Dvorník, *Les légendes de Constantin et de Méthode vues de Byzance* (*Byzantinoslavica supplementa*, 1; Prague, 1933), p. 359.

[3] See V. Jagić, "Vopros o runakh u Slavian," *Enciklopedija slavjanskoj filologij*, III, 1-36.

[4] *The Goths in the Crimea* (Cambridge, 1936), pp. 113 f.

[5] "Les lettres russes de la Vie de Constantin," *Revue des études slaves*, XV (1935), 75-77.

[6] *Byzantion*, X (1935), 771.

[7] "Saint Constantin et la langue syriaque," *Annuaire de l'institut de philologie et d'histoire orientales et slaves* (Université libre de Bruxelles), VII (1939-1944), 181-186. A decade later Jakobson reopened the questions whether Cyril may not have known Syriac (see also p. 88, n. 2, below) and, if so, whether "he had not looked into the Syriac *Diatessaron*" (*Harvard Slavic Studies*, II [1954], 69-70). Essentially the same point of view was taken by Karel Horálek in an article entitled, "Sv. Kirill i semitskie yazyki," which he contributed to the Festschrift, *For Roman Jakobson, Essays on the Occasion of his Sixtieth Birthday* ... Compiled by Morris Halle *et al.* (The Hague, 1956), pp. 230-234. In fact Horálek goes so far as to assert that St. Cyril knew various Semitic languages and sometimes used the Syriac and Aramaic (!) versions when translating the Gospels into Old Slavonic (see also the French summary of Horálek's article by A. Dostál in *Byz.* XIX [1958], 391). This problem, it need scarcely be mentioned, is quite different

reading **роуськымн пнсьменьι** ("Russian letters") the adjective be altered slightly to read **соурьскымн** ("Syriac"). But for various reasons, including the fact that the passage in the *Vita* goes on to declare that Constantine had no difficulty in conversing with the man who spoke the language in which the manuscript was written and that after some study he began to read the script also, it is probably best to conclude that the characters were a primitive kind of Slavic script (George Vernadsky has suggested a mixture of Armenian and Georgian characters adapted to the local Slavic dialect),[1] and that later, perhaps on the basis of a revision and adaptation of these, the Apostles to the Slavs invented the Glagolitic alphabet.

According to a subsequent statement in the *Vita* (chap. xiv), Cyril began to translate "the word of the Gospel" while still in Constantinople on the eve of his departure to Moravia (perhaps in 862-863).[2] That this version was originally in the form of a lectionary appears to be certain, not only because the singular number, "Gospel," is used here, but also because of the subsequent statements that Cyril commenced with John 1.1 (which, as is well known, opens the first pericope of the Greek lectionary system)[3] and completed a rendering of the whole "ecclesiastical cycle."[4] The *Vita* of Methodius supplies corroborative evidence by also using the singular number, "Gospel" and by indicating that a translation of selected parts

from the presence of Hebraisms in the Slavonic Old Testament; see Metropolit Dr. Ilarion [= Ivan Ohijenko], "Die Hebraismen in der altkirchenslavischen biblischen Sprache," *Münchener Beiträge zur Slavenkunde, Festgabe für Paul Diels* (1953), pp. 163-178. The present writer knows of no evidence that the Syriac Diatessaron circulated in the West in the ninth century, nor have the textual analyses embodied in this chapter revealed so much as a hint that the Apostle to the Slavs had ever seen in any language a Harmony even remotely related to Tatian's. For problems relating to the Diatessaron, see pp. 97 ff. below.

[1] *Ancient Russia* (New Haven, 1943), pp. 349-350.

[2] Dvorník, *op. cit.*, pp. 372 ff.

[3] It is true that Tatian's Diatessaron, according to Ephraem's Commentary, confirmed by the express statement of Dionysius bar Ṣalibi, also began with John 1.1, but no substantial evidence has thus far been found proving that the Diatessaron ever penetrated Slavic countries; see p. 76, n. 3, below. (Van Wijk's suggestion, mentioned in n. 5, p. 87 below, involves no more than the possibility of influence from the Diatessaron mediated through the Latin Vulgate.) With regard to divergent testimony concerning the beginning of the Diatessaron, see p. 104 below.

[4] So the *Life of Constantine* (Cyril), chap. xv (Dvorník, p. 373), according to the manuscripts of the Russo-Slavonic redaction; the manuscripts of the Serbo-Slavonic redaction read, "he accepted the ecclesiastical cycle."

preceded the translation of the whole.[1] In harmony with these inti-
mations is the circumstance that the Apocalypse, which never was
included in the Eastern system of pericopes, appears to have been
translated into Slavic first in the twelfth century.[2]

These details regarding the historical background of the earliest
Slavonic translators, generally accepted by modern scholars,[3] will
suffice as an introduction to a discussion of the nature of the
Old Slavonic version. The following pages will (1) survey previous
investigations of the Old Slavonic version of the New Testament,
and (2) analyze the prevailing text-type lying behind Josef Vajs's
edition of the Old Slavonic version of Luke.

[1] *Life of Methodius*, chap. xv (Dvorník, p. 391).
[2] V. Oblak, "Die kirchenslavische Übersetzung der Apokalypse," *Archiv
für slavische Philologie*, XIII (1891), 321-361. The oldest known manuscript
of the Apocalypse is from the twelfth or thirteenth century; see V. Peretc,
"Drevnejshij spisok slavjanskogo tolkovogo Apokalipsisa," *Slavia*, II (1923-
1924), 641-644. Apparently Peretc was unaware of Oblak's study.
[3] On the other hand, Valerij Pogorělov thought that he had found evidence
in the Old Slavonic version of the translator's ignorance of certain Greek
words, and he doubted, therefore, whether Cyril and Methodius (who are
said to have been well acquainted with Greek) were responsible for the Old
Slavonic version of the Psalter and the Gospels; see his article, "Importance
de la forme des mots grecs dans la traduction Cyrille-Méthodienne," *Studi
bizantini e neoellenici*, v (= *Atti del V congresso internazionale di studi bizantini*; Rome, 1939), 534-540.
Among those who hold that the Apostles to the Slavs were well acquainted
with both Greek and Slavonic, it will be sufficient to mention E. Berneker,
"Kyrills Übersetzungskunst," *Indogermanische Forschungen*, XXXI (1912-
1913), 399-412; V. Jagić, *Zum altkirchenslawischen Apostolus*, II, *Lexika-
lisches*, in *Sitzungsberichte der Akademie der Wissenschaften in Wien*, phil.-
hist. Kl., Band CXCIII, Abh. 1, 1919, pp. 4-5; and J. Vajs, in the articles
cited below, p. 88, n. 1. With reference to Vaillant's proposal that
the Old Slavonic fragment from the twelfth century called the leaf of
Hil'ferding, or *feuillet macédonien*, be regarded as none other than Constantine's own preface to his translation of a Gospel lectionary (André Vaillant,
"La preface de l'évangéliaire vieux-slave," *Revue des études slaves*, XXIV
[1948], 1-20), one must observe that he has not fully met the objection raised
by André Mazon (*Comptes rendus de l'académie des inscriptions et
belles lettres*, 1948, 189-191), namely that the preface may quite as well
refer to the work of one of the corps of disciples (perhaps Clement of Ohrid
or Nahum) who continued to translate various ecclesiastical books in Mace-
donia. Furthermore, Vaillant's ingenious interpretation of a quotation in
the leaf from Cyril of Alexandria as a reference to Tatian's Diatessaron is
totally gratuitous.

II. Survey of Research on the Old Slavonic Version

Apparently the first[1] editor of the Greek New Testament to cite evidence from the Slavonic version was Christian Friedrich Matthaei, a Thuringian scholar who at various times taught Classical Literature in Moscow, first in a gymnasium and later in the University. While in Russia Matthaei added considerably to the knowledge of the textual basis of the Greek Testament by collating many manuscripts hitherto unknown to Western scholarship.[2] During the course of the publication of his rambling, twelve-volume edition of the Greek New Testament, he indicates that it occurred to him to cite evidence from the Slavonic version. (The only other version represented in his edition is the Latin Vulgate, based upon a single manuscript at Moscow, codex Demidovianus.) In an appendix to his edition of the Book of Revelation, Matthaei lists ten Slavic manuscripts which he had seen in Russia. He contented himself, however, with collating the text of Revelation in the folio edition of the Slavonic Bible published at Moscow in 1762. This evidence is given in Latin, the collation having been made against the Vulgate manuscript previously mentioned.[3]

Franz Karl Alter, a Jesuit from Silesia who was professor of Greek at Vienna, was the first editor of the Greek New Testament to incorporate evidence from Slavonic manuscripts themselves. In his cumbersome and inconvenient edition of the Greek Testament, he chose to print a thirteenth century Greek manuscript in the Royal Library at Vienna (Greg. 218; von Soden δ 300), which he corrected by substituting the text of Stephanus's first edition (1546).

[1] Gregory indeed states that at an earlier date J. J. Wetstein had cited Slavic evidence (Caspar René Gregory, *Textkritik des Neuen Testamentes*, II [Leipzig, 1902], 734), but he supplies no references by which to verify this statement, nor does Wetstein discuss the Slavic version in the Prolegomena to his edition (1751-1752).

[2] It appears that Matthaei was, moreover, guilty of purloining from Russian libraries many Greek manuscripts of both the Classics and the Fathers. Some of these he kept in his own library, others he sold to various libraries in Germany and Holland. For an account of his life with incriminating evidence of his brazen thievery, see Oscar von Gebhardt, "Christian Friedrich Matthaei und seine Sammlung griechischer Handschriften," *Centralblatt für Bibliothekswesen*, XV (1898), 345-357, 393-420, 441-482, and 537-566.

[3] Christianus Fridericus Matthaei, *Ioannis apocalypsis graece et latine, ex codicibus nunquam antea examinatis editit et animadversiones criticas* (Riga, 1785), Appendix II, "De versione slavonica apocalypseos," pp. 343-388.

A list of readings thus modified is given at the end of each volume. On the basis of this oddly constructed text, Alter supplied in separate appendixes evidence from twenty-four other manuscripts in the same Library, including three Slavonic codices collated for him by Fortunatus Durich.[1] Unfortunately, however, most of the Slavonic evidence can be used only by one who is acquainted with that tongue, for the variants are cited by a transliteration of the Slavonic words with Roman letters.

The first textual critic who can be said to have made really serious use of the Slavonic version was Johann Jakob Griesbach. At his request Josef Dobrovský, the founder of Slavic philology (1753-1829), collected noteworthy readings from nearly a score of Old Slavonic manuscripts.[2] Griesbach incorporated this evidence in the second edition of his Greek New Testament,[3] which remained for several generations substantially the only source of information regarding Slavonic variants. In fact, in 1869-72 Tischendorf borrowed the fruit of Dobrovský's labors from the pages of Griesbach, and Gregory reproduced Dobrovský's catalogue of Slavonic manuscripts of the New Testament.[4]

At the close of the last century, G. N. Voskresenskij of Moscow began preliminary work in classifying Slavic manuscripts of the New Testament.[5] He divided them into four families which repre-

[1] Franciscus Carolus Alter, *Novum Testamentum ad codicem Vindobonensem graece expressum*, I (Vienna, 1787), 1122-1156, 1157-1194; II (Vienna, 1786), 968-1039. The three manuscripts are numbers 101, 355, and 356 from the fifteenth or sixteenth centuries. Alter refers to these in his Preface as follows: "Solum tres codices slavonicos eo consilio perlustravi, ut eruditos viros ad hanc utilissimam versionem (verbo venia sit, kralitzam, id est, reginam versionum appellarim) attentos redderem ..." (vol. I, p. vii).

In addition to these three manuscripts, which are completely collated in the Gospels, Alter also supplied Slavonic evidence from a fragment containing Luke 24.12-35 (vol. I, pp. 1008-1011) as well as a collation of the printed text of John 1-14 in the Slavonic edition published at Moscow in 1614 (vol. I, pp. 403-411; see also p. 1202).

[2] Cf. Josef Dobrovský, "Über den ersten Text der böhmischen Bibelübersetzung, nach den ältesten Handschriften derselben, besonders nach der Dresdener," *Neuere Abhandlungen der königlichen böhmischen Gesellschaft der Wissenschaften*, diplom.-hist.-litt. Theil, III (Prague, 1798), 260.

[3] J. J. Griesbach, *Novum Testamentum graece*, ed. sec., I (Halle and London, 1796), xc-xci, xcvii, cxxvii-cxxxii; II (Halle and London, 1806), xix-xxi and xxxii-xxxix.

[4] Gregory, *Prolegomena* (Leipzig, 1894), pp. 1113-1117, and *Textkritik des Neuen Testamentes*, II (Leipzig, 1902), 736-738.

[5] G. N. Voskresenskij, *Poslanija svjatago apostola Pavla s raznočtenijami iz pjatidesjati odnoj rukopisej Apostola xii-xvi vv.—Vypusk pervyj, Poslanie*

sent, he thought, four recensions. The oldest recension is preserved in the South Slavic manuscripts, to which group most of the famous codices belong. The second recension is preserved in the oldest Russian manuscripts, dating from the eleventh and twelfth centuries. The other two recensions belong to the fourteenth and fifteenth centuries. Voskresenskij believed that he had shown that, in the Gospels, the Old Slavonic version agrees with the type of Greek text used by Photius, Patriarch of Constantinople.

It was not until well along in the twentieth century that the Old Slavonic version began to receive more sustained attention from a text critical point of view.[1] In a painstaking study of permanent value on the translation-technique of the Old Slavonic version of the Gospels, Grünenthal devoted some attention to the textual

k Rimljanam [The Epistles of Paul, with various Readings from Fifty-one Manuscripts of the Apostle, dating from the Twelfth to the Sixteenth Centuries—Part i, The Epistle to the Romans] (Moscow, 1892); Evangelie ot Marka s raznočtenijami iz sta vos'mi rukopisej Evangelija xi-xvi vv. [The Gospel of Mark, with various Readings from a Hundred and Eight Manuscripts of the Gospel, dating from the Eleventh to the Sixteenth Centuries] (Moscow, 1894); and Kharakterističeskija čerty četyrekh redakcij slavjanskago perevoda Evangelija ot Marka [Charakteristic Features of the Four Redactions of the Old Slavic Version of St. Mark] (Moscow, 1896). For information regarding the first two of these works, cf. [Ll. J. M. Bebb], "The Russian Bible," CQR, xli (October, 1895), 203-225, and idem, Hastings' Dictionary of the Bible, iv (1902), 863-864.

According to a survey by Evsěev, there are 4101 Biblical manuscripts in a variety of Slavic dialects, dating from the eleventh to the seventeenth century found in various libraries; see I. E. Evsěev, "Rukopisnoe predanie slavjanskoj Biblii," Khristianskoe čtenie, 1911, 436-450, 644-660 (brief summary in Latin in Acta academiae velehradensis, ix [1913], 89). J. Vašica and J. Vajs have catalogued the Old Slavonic manuscripts which are in the National Museum at Prague; see their Soupis staroslovanských rukopisů národního musea v Praze (Prague, 1957).

[1] How slowly, however, this information becomes generally available is reflected in the disconcerting fact that during the present century most handbooks on the textual criticism of the New Testament either make only a passing reference to the Old Slavonic version (e.g., Dobschütz, Gregory, Lake), or more often maintain complete silence on the subject (e.g., Kenyon, Lagrange, Nestle, Robertson, Souter, Taylor, Vaganay, Vogels).

As regards a later Slavonic version, the Old Bohemian, in 1926 James Hardy Ropes lamented with some degree of justification: "A complete knowledge of the Old Bohemian Acts might yield results of much importance for the 'Western' text of Acts. Such a knowledge would not be difficult to secure, and it is not to the credit of New Testament scholarship that nearly a century and a half has passed [since Dobrovský] without any use being made of sources easily accessible in Germany and Bohemia" (The Text of Acts, being vol. iii of The Beginnings of Christianity, Part i, The Acts of the Apostles, edd. F. J. Foakes Jackson and Kirsopp Lake [London, 1926],

affiliation of the more important manuscripts of this version.[1] He found that the text of codex Marianus frequently agrees with the Constantinopolitan (or Lucianic) type of text found in the Greek manuscripts EFGHKMSUV, while the text of codex Zographensis offers more often a Western type of reading, agreeing with D, the Old Latin, and Vulgate text. Grünenthal also observed that although the Old Slavonic lectionaries, Assemanianus and Savva, may present the same Gospel pericope twice at different places in the same manuscript, yet there is occasionally in Assemanianus and frequently in Savva a different text[2] as well as a different translation-technique discernible.

A few years later the veteran Slavic philologist, Vatroslav Jagić, published a thorough study of the fourteenth century codex Matica-Apostolus, containing the Acts, the Catholic Epistles, and the Pauline Epistles.[3] Jagić found that in all its parts this manuscript shows a close dependence upon the older forms of the Byzantine text, with sporadic agreements with pre-Byzantine texts.

In 1922 Andrej Snoj, professor of Sacred Scripture at Ljubljana (Laibach), challenged the preliminary analyses made by Voskresenskij.[4] On the basis of more detailed study, Snoj discovered not a few readings which had previously been overlooked where the Old Slavonic version agrees with the Egyptian (or so-called Hesychian) text in opposition to Photius. The chief object of his brief study was to plead that the Old Slavonic version, which contains old readings, should no longer be neglected by textual critics.

The scholar in the twentieth century who, more than all others, has given the greatest amount of attention to the Old Slavonic

---

p. cxli). That a certain amount of work, however, has been accomplished on this version can be seen from the admirable surveys by Josef Vraštil, S.J., "Conspectus recentiorum de antiqua bibliorum versione bohemica litterarum et consilia," *Acta academiae velehradensis*, IX (1913), 31-44, and J. Vašica, *Staročeské Evangeliáře*, being No. 68 of the *Rozpravy české akademie věd a umění*, III (Prague, 1931).

[1] O. Grünenthal, "Die Übersetzungstechnik der altkirchenslavischen Evangelienübersetzung," *Archiv für slavische Philologie*, XXXI (1910), 321-366, 507-528; XXXII (1911), 1-48.

[2] Exactly the same phenomena occur in Greek lectionaries.

[3] Vatroslav Jagić, *Zum altkirchenslavischen Apostolus*; I, *Grammatisches und Kritisches*, in *Sitzungsberichte der Akademie der Wissenschaften in Wien*, phil.-hist. Kl., Band CXCI, Abh. 2 (1919).

[4] Andrej Snoj, "Veteroslavicae versionis evangeliorum pro critica et exegesi sacri textus momentum," *Biblica*, III (1922), 180-187. His book, *Staroslovenski Matejev evangjelij* (Ljubljana, 1922), was not available to me.

version was the late Professor Josef Vajs of Prague.[1] In considering the more significant of his many contributions to the subject one may begin with the first volume of his "Critical Studies of the Old Slavonic Biblical Text." This is an edition of the Slavonic text of Mark with the Greek *textus receptus* printed on opposite pages.[2] Vajs summarizes his research into the textual complexion of the Old Slavonic as follows:

> "An attentive examination of the Gospel of St. Mark has revealed that the Slavonic version belongs chiefly to the Syrian (or Constantinopolitan) recension, with numerous pre-Syrian readings of two kinds, Western and Alexandrian. The Greek manuscript from which it was translated was therefore a mixed manuscript; by reason of the numerous pre-Syrian elements which it contains, the Slavonic version is as worthy of attention as some other manuscripts or groups, such as the Ferrar group, Lake's fam. 1, or the manuscript 565.... Among the pre-Syrian variants, the Western readings are more numerous than the Alexandrian; but the majority of the pre-Syrian readings being common to the two groups, Western and Alexandrian, it is difficult to discover their origin."[3]

Two years later Vajs published an article[4] in which he reveals that, of about 2500 variant readings that he had found in the Old Slavonic tetraevangelium, about one half belong to the Byzantine or Antiochian recension, about a fifth to the Western, and an even smaller proportion to the Alexandrian.[5]

Continuing his study of the nature of the prevailing Byzantine element in the Old Slavonic Version, Vajs discovered that it comes

---

[1] For an appreciative survey of Vajs's work, published on the occasion of his seventieth birthday, see Josef Kurz's article in *Byz*, VI (1935-36), 221-235 (with a picture of Vajs). A bibliography of 168 items is included; very many of these deal with the Old Slavonic version. Two other Festschriften were presented to him; one in 1948 (see p. 89, n. 1, below for the title of this volume), and the other in 1957 when the articles in parts 6 to 8 (pp. 1-334) of the journal *Slovo* (Zagreb) were dedicated to him with the following citation: Zbornik posvecén Josipu Vajsu prilikom 60-te godišnjice njegova dolaska u Hrvatsku.

[2] *Evangelium sv. Marka a jeho poměr k řecké předloze* (*Kritické studie staroslovanského textu biblického*, 1; Prague, 1927), p. 127.

[3] *Ibid.*, p. 127 (French résumé).

[4] "Byzantská recense a evangelijní kodexy staroslovenské" (German résumé, "Die byzantinische Rezension und die altkirchenslavischen Evangelienkodexe"), *Byz*, I (1929), 1-9.

[5] *Ibid.*, p. 8.

closest to von Soden's K^i and K^a families, particularly the latter.[1] (According to von Soden, it will be recalled, the K^a family has manuscripts AKΠ at its head, with about one hundred others in more or less close relationship, of which A is the oldest and Π the best representative.) The Old Slavonic version, Vajs declared, "like the K^a family, (a) retains in many passages the word order of the Western text, and (b) in still more passages agrees with Western additions or even omissions."[2]

Vajs's next publications grew out of a proposal made at the meeting of the First Congress of Slavic Philologists, held at Prague in 1929, namely that the Old Slavonic text of the Gospels be reconstructed. As a preliminary step in editing such a text, Vajs published a study of certain noteworthy characteristics of the earliest manuscripts of the Old Slavonic version.[3] After classifying and assessing the relative worth of the manuscripts, Vajs concluded that "since the Old Slavonic Lectionary was certainly the first literary work of St. Constantine-Cyril, in the reconstruction of the Gospel text one must proceed from the oldest Lectionary (Assemani)."[4]

Furthermore, Vajs found that in a relatively recent manuscript of Bogomile origin, the tetraevangelium (a) monasterii s. Nicolai at Belgrade, dating from the fourteen century, "the Alexandrian and the so-called Western variants are found in much greater number than in the other mss. This circumstance leads us necessarily to the conviction that this codex is to be regarded as a fairly accurate copy of a glagolitic original, especially with reference to textual criticism."[5]

The fruits of Vajs's studies in the Old Slavonic version were published during 1935 and 1936 in four volumes.[6] In each volume

---

[1] Vajs, "Byzantská recense a evangelijní kodexy staroslověnské, II" (German résumé, "Die byzantinische Rezension und die altkirchenslavischen Evangelien-Kodexe"), *Byz*, IV (1932), 1-12.

[2] *Ibid.*, p. 11.

[3] Vajs, "K characteristice nejstarších evang. rukopisů staroslověnských" (German résumé, "Zur Characteristik der älteren altslavischen evang. Handschriften"), *Byz*, V (1933-34), 113-119.

[4] *Ibid.*, p. 119. In 1929 Vajs and Josef Kurz published a handsome photographic facsimile edition of this lectionary, *Evangeliarum Assemani, codex Vaticanus 3. slavicus glagoliticus, editio phototypica cum prolegomenis, textu litteris cyrillicis transcripto, analysi, annotationibus palaeographicis, variis lectionibus, glossario*, Tom. I (Prague, 1929). Tom. II, edited by Kurz, was published in 1955. It contains a transcription of the Old Slavic text in Cyrillic letters and a critical apparatus.

[5] *Byz*, V (1933-34), 119.

[6] Vajs, *Evangelium sv. Matouše. Text rekonstruovaný* (Prague, 1935);

he prints his reconstructed text of the Old Slavonic version on one page and on the opposite page gives the Greek which inferentially lies behind the Old Slavonic. Each text is equipped with an apparatus supplying evidence of variant readings. The Slavonic text rests upon the evidence of thirteen manuscripts dating from tenth to the thirteenth centuries. A list of these is given below (p. 91).

In the introduction to his volume on Mark, Vajs assembled statistics regarding the frequency of the Constantinopolitan (Koine) and the Western variants contained in his reconstructed Old Slavonic text.[1] These figures are as follows:

	Matt.	Mark	Luke	John
Constantinopolitan	306	291	319	169
Western	292	200	289	210

As can be seen, in each Gospel except that of John the number of Constantinopolitan readings exceeds the Western. For Matthew the percentages are: Constantinopolitan = 51.25%, Western = 48.8%; for Mark, Constantinopolitan = 57.3%, Western = 42.7%; for Luke, Constantinopolitan = 52.4%, Western = 47.6%; for John, Constantinopolitan = 44.6%, Western = 55.4%.

In answer to the question of what significance is to be seen in the circumstance that the Gospel of John has the highest percentage of pre-Syrian variant readings, while the Gospel of Mark has the highest percentage of Byzantine readings, another Slavic scholar, Josef Kurz, suggested that the answer is related to the historical background of the making of the Old Slavonic version from a lectionary text.[2] In a standard Eastern Orthodox lectionary almost the entire text of the Gospel of John is represented (90.6% of the Gospel), whereas only about one fourth of the text of Mark is included (27%). Obviously, therefore, the Greek lectionary text which lay behind the extant Old Slavonic version had proportionately more Western variants than did the non-lectionary Greek original which, probably at a somewhat later date, was used to

---

Evangelium sv. Marka. Text rekonstruovaný (Prague, 1935); *Evangelium sv. Lukáše. Text rekonstruovaný* (Prague, 1936); and *Evangelium sv. Jana. Text rekonstruovaný* (Prague 1936). These are vols. III, IV, V, and VI respectively of the series *Kritické studie staroslovanského textu biblického.*

[1] *Evangelium sv. Marka*, p. xii.

[2] Josef Kurz, *Byz*, VI (1935-36), 238 and 242. A few years earlier, on the basis of an examination of linguistic phenomena, Nicolaas van Wijk had suggested the same explanation; see his brief note, "Evangelistar und Tetra-evangelium," *Slavia*, V (1926-27), 677.

supplement all the Slavonic Gospels (but chiefly Mark) in making a non-lectionary Slavic text.

Noteworthy among the reviews of Vajs's Old Slavonic Gospels was a critique prepared by Robert P. Casey and Silva Lake.[1] After giving a helpful summary of the historical background of Sts. Constantine (Cyril) and Methodius, the authors devote their attention principally to the manuscript material and its analysis. Restricting themselves to the Gospel of Mark, they conclude that Vajs, having followed von Soden's faulty grouping of New Testament Greek manuscripts, was in error in thinking that the Old Slavonic text belongs to family K^a. On the basis of a more highly refined analysis of family relationship in two chapters of Mark (chapters 6 and 11), Casey and Mrs. Lake make "the tentative suggestion that possibly von Soden's I^π text lies behind the original Slavonic version. This is the text which he believes to have been that of the Cappadocian fathers, Basil, Gregory of Nyssa and Gregory Nazianzenus, and is extant in N, Σ, Φ, and ה. This suggestion is, however, most tentative...."[2]

Casey and Mrs. Lake comment also upon Vajs's method of reconstructing the Old Slavonic version. As a working rule, Vajs apparently favored that reading which diverges from the later Byzantine type of text. On the one hand Casey and Mrs. Lake acknowledge that "within very definite limits this method is sound,"[3] but at the same time they rightly point out that a slavish application of such a rule would produce a quite distorted "original" text. They do not, however, present evidence indicating that Vajs has in fact proceeded in such a purely mechanical fashion. They conclude their study by expressing appreciation of Vajs's preliminary work, while acknowledging that "the text of the Slavonic still remains one of the most obscure problems in the history of the text of the New Testament."[4]

After the publication of his reconstructed text, Vajs continued to give attention to various intra-versional problems unearthed

---

[1] Robert P. Casey and Silva Lake, "A New Edition of the Old Slavic Gospels," *JBL*, LV (1936), 195-209. For a briefer statement, see Casey in M. M. Parvis and A. P. Wikgren, eds., *New Testament Manuscript Studies* (Chicago, 1950), pp. 78-80.

[2] *JBL*, LV (1936), 208.

[3] *Ibid.*, p. 206.

[4] *Ibid.*, p. 209. Casey (in Parvis and Wikgren, eds., *op. cit.*, p. 79) is less satisfied with Vajs's standards of completeness and accuracy.

during his previous study. For example, continuing Grünenthal's preliminary analysis Vajs rightly concluded that, despite the superiority of codex Marianus in accidence and vocabulary, because it so frequently exhibits later (Constantinopolitan) variant readings, it can scarcely be regarded as preserving a primitive form of the Old Slavonic version.[1] On the other hand (as Vajs had pointed out in an earlier study), the late Bogomile manuscript of Nicolai preserves the older Western readings best of all.

In a subsequent brief study, Vajs rejects Snoj's view that Alexandrian influence is appreciably discernible in the Old Slavonic version, and reiterates in still more sharply defined terms his own view, namely that Cyril and Methodius used a Byzantine manuscript of their own age, containing an extraordinary number of non-Byzantine variants which were predominantly Palestinian in origin.[2] Vajs refers to von Soden's I^π group as an example of such a type of mixed text. This subdivision of the I-text contains, according to von Soden's judgment, manuscripts U, 213, 443, 1071 (except Matt.), 1321 (only in John), 1574, 2145.

The next contribution[3] chronologically marks a retrogression in reliable conclusions. Joseph Schweigl published what, at first sight, appears to be a careful and sound investigation regarding the Slavic Textus Receptus of the liturgical form of the Gospels.[4] Here he concluded that the lectionary text in common use today in Slavic lands (Bulgaria, Poland, Russia, Serbia, Slovakia, and the Ukraine), namely the Liturgical Gospel published at Moscow in 1905, "approaches closely to the H-type of text (Egyptian-Alexan-

---

[1] Vajs, "Kladné a záporné výsledky kritického bádání v staroslovaském evangelním textu" (with a German résumé), *Byz*, VII (1937-1938), 149-157.

[2] Vajs, "La recensione bizantina e la versione paleoslava dei Santi Vangeli," *Studi bizantini e neoellenici*, V (= *Atti del V congresso internazionale di studi bizantini*; Rome, 1939), 560-564.

[3] No account is taken here of the edition of the Old Slavonic Gospels published at Rome in 1943 (the first Slavic edition to receive general approval from the Holy Roman Apostolic See), inasmuch as it was professedly framed not on critical but on "practical" principles and designed for liturgical services; see Schweigl's review in *B*, XXV (1944), 240-243.

[4] Joseph Schweigl, "De textu recepto slavico evangelii liturgici," *B*, XXIV (1943), 289-303. In an earlier article on "La Biblia slava del 1751 (1756)," *B*, XVIII (1937), 51-73, Schweigl refers to several bibliographical items of historical interest. It may be mentioned also that much curious information regarding the Old Slavonic Scriptures and early Bibles printed in Russia can be found in Ebenezer Henderson's *Biblical Researches and Travels in Russia* (London, 1826), pp. 60-135.

drian), and therefore greatly excels the Old Slavonic (glagolitic) version of the ninth century, which in many passages reveals a dependence upon the Palestinian-Caesarean recension."[1] It is, however, only by a most perverse and uncritical evaluation of the significance of his evidence that Schweigl can come to this conclusion. The long lists of citations of passages which allegedly contain Alexandrian readings[2] are made up of examples such as the following.

Matt. 11.19, the official Slavonic lectionary supports τέκνων with CL Ψ 33, 892, etc., whereas ἔργων is read by B* א W 788, 2145, etc.

Mark 10.29, the Slavonic lectionary adds καὶ γυναῖκα with C Ψ 28, 33, 597, 892, etc., whereas this is lacking in B א D, etc.

Luke 22.64, the Slavonic lectionary supports ἔτυπτον αὐτοῦ τὸ πρόσωπον with Ψ 33, 579, 892, etc., whereas this is lacking in B א K L M T Π, 209, etc.

To identify these lectionary readings as Alexandrian is to display ignorance of the most elementary knowledge of textual criticism. The extraordinary number of supposed Alexandrian readings which Schweigl supposed he had discovered in the Liturgical Slavonic Gospel is gained by labeling as Alexandrian any variant that may be supported by even *one* Alexandrian manuscript, irrespective of the character of that manuscript or the weight of the evidence for the contrary reading.

Mention must also be made of the debate regarding the question of possible influence on the Old Slavic version from the Latin and the Gothic versions. So long ago as 1853, the philologist Šafařík expressed the opinion that in the Old Slavonic text of the Gospels influence from the Vulgate was perceptible.[3] In 1925 Pogorělov worked afresh on the problem and found what he believed to be additional examples of Latin influence upon the Old Slavonic version.[4] Having scrutinized Pogorělov's examples, Vajs concluded that they were insufficient to prove his thesis.[5] The noted linguist, Meillet, also weighed Pogorělov's hypothesis and found that his

[1] *B*, XXIV (1943), 294; cf. also p. 303.
[2] *Ibid.*, pp. 292-294.
[3] P. J. Šafařík, *Památky hlahoského písemnictví* (Prague, 1853), pp. xxiv, xxxvi ff. (referred to by van Wijk in *Byz*, III [1931], 89).
[4] Valerij Pogorělov, "Iz nablyudenijv oblasti drevne-slavjanskoj perevodnoj literatury; I, Latinskoe vlijanie v perevode Evangelija," *Sborník filosofické faculty University Komenského v Bratislavě*, III, 32 [6] (1925), 207-216.
[5] Vajs, "Jaký vliv měla latinská Vulgáta na staroslovanský překlad evangelní," *Slavia*, V (1926-1927), 158-162.

examples prove no more than that the Old Slavonic vocabulary which Cyril and Methodius used had already been influenced by certain Latinisms, but that these are quite insufficient to prove any influence of the Vulgate upon the Old Slavonic version as such.[1]

In the following year the Polish scholar, Słoński, in a much more detailed discussion, concluded that apparent agreements with the Vulgate text against the presumed Greek original, so far as they do not rest upon hitherto unknown Greek variants, may be explained best by postulating a certain critical independence with which the Slavonic translator executed his edition.[2]

In a subsequent article Vajs[3] made several small concessions to Pogorělov's thesis by admitting that there are a few passages which can scarcely be explained apart from reference to the corresponding Vulgate renderings. These are Matt. 23.4, which involves a misunderstanding of *colligunt* and *alligant*; John 6.23, which rests on a misinterpretation, *gratias agentes* (instead of *agente*) *Deo* (instead of *Domino*): εὐχαριστήσαντες τοῦ κυρίου; and Matt. 6.11, *nasǫštǐny*, which is a literal translation of Jerome's *supersubstantialem* for ἐπιούσιον. According to a critique by Rozov, however, each of these examples is susceptible of a different explanation which does not involve the supposition of influence from the Vulgate.[4]

Nicolaas van Wijk introduced a new element into the discussion by suggesting that the Old Slavonic rendering of συνέλεξαν in Matt. 13.48 as *izbǐrašę* ("they choose") reveals dependence upon Tatian's Diatessaron (*via* the Latin Vulgate *elegerunt*).[5]

In 1942 the Croatian scholar, Hamm, proposed the theory that the Gothic version influenced the Old Slavonic.[6] He recognized that, according to all that is known of the Goths and their literature, it is unthinkable that the Gothic Bible could have influenced Cyril and

[1] A. Meillet, "L'hypothèse d'une influence de la Vulgate sur la traduction slave de l'évangile," *Revue des études slaves*, VI (1926), 39-41.

[2] Stanisław Słoński, "O rzekomym wplywie lacinskiej Vulgaty na staroslowianski przeklad ewangelji," *Slavia*, VI (1927-1928), 246-264.

[3] Vajs, *Byz*, I (1927), 9.

[4] Vlad. Rozov, *Slavia*, IX (1930-1931), 619-621.

[5] N. van Wijk, "Eine Vulgatalesart im slavischen Evangelium (Mat. XIII, 48) ?" *Byz*, III (1931), 89-91. In this suggestion van Wijk builds upon a study by Daniël Plooij in *Mededeelingen der koninklijke Akademie van Wetenschappen in Amsterdam*, Afd. Letterkunde, deel LXXI, serie A, no. 1, 1931.

[6] Josip Hamm, "Über den gotischen Einfluss auf die altkirchenslavische Bibelübersetzung," *Zeitschrift für vergleichende Sprachwissenschaft auf dem Gebiete der indogermanischen Sprachen*, LXVII (1942), 112-128.

Methodius in the second half of the ninth century. On the strength, therefore, of supposed parallels between the two versions, Hamm went so far as to transpose the beginnings of the Old Slavonic version to an earlier period, sometime in the sixth or seventh century. Such a theory, if it is to be proposed at all, must be supported with the strongest kind of evidence. Instead of this, however, Hamm's examples are of the most trivial sort, which, if valid, could be used to prove, *mutatis mutanda*, that the King James version is dependent upon the Old Slavonic! In a subsequent study Vajs[1] had no trouble in demolishing any semblance of validity in Hamm's position, by showing that the underlying type of text represented in the Gothic version is quite markedly different from that of the Old Slavonic version.[2]

[1] Vajs, "Je-li staroslověnský překlad evangelií a žaltáře nějak závislý na Gotském překladu Vulfilově?" (with a French résumé), *Byz*, VIII (1939-1946), 145-171. Vajs also supported his contention indirectly in another article, "Které recense byla řecká předloha staroslověnského překladu žaltáře" (with a French résumé), *ibid*., pp. 55-86, where he indicates, on the basis of an examination of 500 readings in the Old Slavonic Psalter, that 449 are pure Lucianic and the others are influenced by the Vulgate. None shows Gothic influence.

It need scarcely be mentioned that what is referred to here is something entirely different from the possibility, or even probability, of linguistic influence of the Gothic upon Proto-Slavic; see, e.g., Alfred Senn, "Verbal Aspect in Germanic, Slavic and Baltic," *Language*, XXV (1949), 402-409.

[2] Milada Paulová supports Vajs's conclusions; see *Byz*, IX (1947), 146. Josef Janko deals with the problem from the point of view of linguistics, "Měl-li Wulfilův gotský překlad Bible vliv na překlad starocírkevněslovanský?" *Časopis pro moderni filologii*, XXVIII (1942), 29-42, 121-134, 254-268.

In an article which reveals very little acquaintance with previous literature on the subject, Ferdinand Liewehr attempts to show "Wie Konstantin-Kyrill mit Wulfilas Bibelübersetzung bekannt wurde," *Beiträge zur Namenforschung*, III (1951-52), 287-290. He confines his attention to the phrase, "Russian letters," in the *Vita* of Cyril (see p. 75 above), interpreting it to mean "Gothic letters." Liewehr was answered by Dietrich Gerhardt in a richly documented article, "Goten, Slaven oder Syrer im alten Cherson?" *Beiträge zur Namenforschung*, IV (1953), 78-88. Gerhardt believes that Cyril knew Syriac (see p. 74, n. 7, above) and attempts to find support for this view in a rather inconclusive analogy, declaring that Cyril "with the textual critical interest of a missionary preacher, could have studied their version [i.e. that of the Syrian merchants of Cherson] of the Scriptures exactly as Charlemagne on the very last day of his life corrected the Gospels *cum Graecis et Siris*" (p. 85; this comment concerning Charlemagne is found in Thegan, *Vita Hludovici Imperatoris*, sect. 7 [Migne, *PL*, CVI, 409 c]). But, in view of the difficulty that Charlemagne had in learning to write ("temptabat et scribere . . . sed parum successit labor praeposterus ac sero inchoatus," Einhard, *Vita Karoli Imperatoris*, sect. 25 [= *Monumenta germaniae histo-*

In a posthumously published essay by Pechuška, edited by Kurz, attention is given to the Old Slavonic text of Acts as preserved in manuscripts of the twelfth and thirteenth century. According to the author, this text was based on a Greek original of mixed characteristics, belonging principally to the Constantinopolitan recension with pre-Syrian elements of two types, the Alexandrian and Western. Of these the Western readings predominate.[1]

Finally, attention should be drawn to several studies by Karel Horálak, professor at the Charles IV University in Prague,[2] who thinks that a progressive stylistic deterioration marks the textual transmission of the Old Slavonic texts of the Gospels. What he terms the exquisite style of the original translation has suffered from the mechanical work of the scribes who replaced many a free but happy turn with a servile imitation of the Greek model, going so far as even to adopt the Greek order of words.[3] The author also attempts to distinguish among the special characteristics of various Old Slavonic text-types. In the Balkans the Slavic translation was subsequently harmonized with the official Greek text of the Byzantine Church. The Bogomile Gospel texts have a rather pronounced archaic character; relatively well-preserved from the lexical point of view they reveal nevertheless a syntax that is strongly Hellenized. The Croatian glagolitic texts bear traces of a revision resting upon the Latin Vulgate.[4] This point of view is worked out at length in a volume which Horálek entitled, The Lectionaries and the Four Gospel Manuscripts; a Contribution to the Textual Criticism and History of the Old Slavonic Version of the Gospel.[5] The author takes

---

rica, *Scriptores*, II, p. 457, lines 2 ff.]), Thegan is probably to be understood as meaning no more than that Charlemagne asked Greeks and Syrians questions regarding the Gospels. In any case, the incident has nothing to do with the question of whether Cyril knew Syriac and used Tatian's Diatessaron.

[1] Fr. Pechuška, "Recká předloha staroslovanského textu Skutků apoštolských," *Slovanské studie; Sbírka statí, věnovaných ... J. Vajsovi k uctění jeho životního díla* (Prague, 1948), pp. 60-65.

[2] For a French summary of several of Horálek's studies, see the *bibliographie raisonnée* in *Byz*, XI (1950), 142-143.

[3] This had been pointed out earlier, e.g., by Georges Cuedet, *L'ordre des mots dans les versions gotique, arménienne et vieux slave des évangiles*; Iᵉʳᵉ partie, *Les groupes nominaux* (Paris, 1929); compare also Vaillant's article mentioned in n. 3, p. 76 above.

[4] K. Horálek, "K dějinám tekstu staroslověnského evangelia" (with a Latin summary), *Acta academiae velehradensis*, XIX (1948), 208-229.

[5] Karel Horálek, *Evangeliáře a čtveroevangelia. Příspevky k textové kritice a k dějinám staroslověnského překladu evangelia* (Stát. Pedagogické naklada-

as his starting point the generally accepted view that St. Cyril translated a Greek lectionary of the shorter variety. Subsequently the text was completed by additions taken from a tetraevangelion. During the transmission of this text two types of modifications were introduced, those which reflected variant readings in Greek manuscripts and those which were merely stylistic and due to the translator(s). Horálek shares the opinion of Vajs that the later Old Slavonic manuscripts contain a growing number of Lucianic variants, but he differs from Vajs in believing that these evolved within the Slavonic version parallel to a similar evolution within later Greek manuscripts and for the same motives (stylistic adaptation of the text, insertion of explanatory notes, and harmonizations). Horálek is pessimistic regarding the possibility of determining exactly the archetype of the Old Slavonic text, particularly since the transmission of the text discloses Slavonic readings which find no parallel in previously collated Greek manuscripts.

In an article entitled "La traduction vieux-slave de l'évangile— sa version originale et son dévélopement ultérieur,"[1] Horálek examines renderings in several Old Slavonic manuscripts, and reiterates his view that copyists made alterations in the Old Slavonic version so that little by little it lost its pure Slavonic character and more and more imitated turns of expression in the underlying Greek syntax. There is also a marked difference, he finds, between the characteristics of the Slavonic text that was translated originally from a Greek lectionary and those supplementary portions which were added later from complete Four Gospels manuscripts.

III. Analysis of the Text of Vajs's Edition of Luke

In addition to the survey above of previous contributions to the textual criticism of the Old Slavonic version, it will not be inappropriate to set forth now the results of an analysis of a collation[2]

telství, Praha, 1954). The present writer has relied on J. Jahn's French review of this volume, published in *Byz*, xviii (1957), 300-305.

[1] *Byz*, xx (1959), 267-284, being a French translation of Horálek's article, "K dějinám textu staroslověnského evangelia" (= Contributions to the History of the Old Slavic Text of the Gospels), *Acta academiae velehradensis*, xix (1948), 208-229.

[2] The present writer expresses his gratitude to Professor Giuliano Bonfante, formerly at Princeton University and now at the University of Turin, for having made the collation of Vajs's edition against the Greek text. Professor Bonfante also read over an earlier draft of this chapter and offered several valuable suggestions.

of Vajs's edition of the Gospel according to Luke made against the Greek Textus Receptus (Oxford ed. of 1873). The Old Slavonic manuscripts upon which Vajs depended for his reconstructed text are the following.[1]

Ar — evangeliarium Archangelscense, A.D. 1092, Moscow.

As — evangeliarium Assemani, saec. XI, Vatican.

De — tetraevangelium Decanense, saec. XIII, Leningrad.

Do — tetraevangelium Dobromir, saec. XII, Leningrad.

Ga — tetraevangelium Galičense, saec. XII, Leningrad.

Hv — tetraevangelium codex christiani Hval, A.D. 1404, Bononia.

Ka — evangeliarium Karpianum, saec. XIII-XIV, Moscow.

Ma — tetraevangelium Marianum, saec. XI, Moscow.

Mi — evangeliarium Miroslavi, saec. XII, Belgrade.

Ni — tetraevangelium monasterii s. Nicolai, saec. XIV, Belgrade.

Os — evangeliarium Ostromiri, A.D. 1056-1057, Leningrad.

Sa — evangeliarium Savvae, saec. XI, Moscow.

Zo — tetraevangelium Zographense, saec. XI, Moscow.

In the present investigation it was found that among these thirteen manuscripts codex Marianus[2] is decidedly closer to the Greek Textus Receptus than are any of the others. A rapid count of the variants found in the first twelve chapters of Luke shows that Marianus agrees with the Greek Textus Receptus and disagrees with some or even all the other Slavic manuscripts more than twice as often as it disagrees with the Textus Receptus against some or most of the other Slavonic manuscripts. This is in harmony with what other investigators have found regarding the characteristics of Marianus.[3]

In the presence of variants among these Old Slavonic manuscripts, how does Vajs proceed? As was mentioned above, in general

---

[1] For fuller descriptions of most of these manuscripts, with bibliographical references to philological studies on each of them, see Nicolaas van Wijk, *Geschichte der altkirchenslavischen Sprache*, I (Berlin and Leipzig, 1931), 23-37. For a discussion of criteria for judging the chronology of early Slavonic manuscripts, see Horace G. Lunt, "On Slavonic Palimpsests," *American Contriburions to the Fourth International Congress of Slavicists*, Moscow, September 1958 ('s-Gravenhage, 1958), pp. 191-209.

[2] According to F. Repp ("Zur Kritik des Codex Marianus," *Zeitschrift für slavische Philologie*, XXIV [1956], 271-276), this manuscript was written in the western area of the Balkan peninsula.

[3] E.g., A. Meillet in *Mémoires de la société de linguistique de Paris*, XI (1900), 175-177; O. Grünenthal, *Archiv für slavische Philologie*, XXXI (1910), 321.

he prefers the reading which differs from the Byzantine or late ecclesiastical type of text. The dangers inherent in slavishly following such a procedure are fully exposed by Casey and Mrs. Lake.[1] It is difficult, however, to ascertain how slavish Vajs has been in this regard. In view, therefore, of a certain amount of dubiety connected with the legitimacy of Vajs's methodology, one must rely, not upon the reconstructed Old Slavonic (still less upon the Greek text which Vajs regarded as lying inferentially behind the Slavonic),[2] but upon the evidence of the Old Slavonic manuscripts themselves as given in Vajs's apparatus. Unfortunately, however, occasionally Vajs appears to give an incomplete citation of evidence from the manuscripts which he professes to use. Thus Vajs's edition, excellent as it is in certain respects, fails in some details to satisfy the standards of impeccable scholarship.

A comprehensive study was made of the variants in chapter 8 of Luke. This chapter was chosen because it is relatively long (56 verses) and thus constitutes a significant sample, and also because there exist for this chapter relatively copious data regarding the text of the Greek lectionaries. Various *apparatus critici* (those of Tregelles, Tischendorf, von Soden, Bover, and Merk) were searched for supporting evidence. The results of this research can be summarized as follows.

A collation of Vajs's edition against the Greek Textus Receptus of Luke 8.1-56 disclosed 63 variant readings involving the reconstructed Slavonic text and/or one or more Slavonic manuscripts. (Variants which seemed to be due to the requirements of the Old Slavonic idiom were disregarded.)

The witnesses which most frequently support Old Slavonic variants are the following. One or more of the Old Latin witnesses agree with Old Slavonic variants 23 times; the Syriac Peshitta agrees 18 times; ℵ, X, and 1 agree 16 times; L, Θ, and the Latin Vulgate agree 14 times; D and 33 agree 13 times; 69, 157, 213, and 1192 agree 12 times; 1071 and the Curetonian Syriac agree 11 times; B and 124 agree 10 times; C, 13, and the Harklean Syriac agree 9 times; R, W, 22, 118, 1012, 1241, and the Coptic agree 8 times. Each of 85 other witnesses exhibits fewer than eight agreements with the Old Slavonic. Finally, it should be mentioned that fifteen variants from the Greek Textus Receptus have no support from

---

[1] *JBL*, LV (1936), 206-207.

[2] In not a few cases Vajs neglected to represent the Old Slavonic variant in the Greek text.

non-Slavonic witnesses. More than half of these variants, however, involve Slavonic renderings which might find an explanation in terms of idiomatic considerations without reflecting a different Greek original. In Luke 8.4 the Slavonic translator (as represented in the manuscripts Ga, Ma, Ni and Zo) has fallen into a gross error in rendering συνιόντος with the root *razum*, "to understand," as though the participle came from συνίημι.[1]

The significance of these statistics seems to include the following. The Old Slavonic possesses elements derived from several distinct families. The basic text is, as one would expect, the Byzantine or Koine. This, however, is not any of the later varieties, but seems to be a development of that earlier form of the Koine which also lies behind the Syriac Peshitta of the fifth century. This latter, as is well known, is a text which on the whole ranges itself with the Constantinopolitan or Koine type, yet not wholly, having a considerable intermixture of readings characteristic of the β and δ texts. The proportion of Western readings normal to this form of the Koine is, in the case of the Old Slavonic, considerably heightened by the admixture of a Western strain similar to that which appears in the Old Latin, the Vulgate, and D. One is not surprised, therefore, to find that the Old Slavonic agrees not infrequently with ℵ, X, L, and Θ, all of them being uncial manuscripts which oscillate between the β and δ texts. Among minuscule manuscripts it is 1, 33, 69, 157, 213, 1071, and 1192 with which the Old Slavonic is in agreement when differing from the Textus Receptus. In other words, the Old Slavonic shares readings with noteworthy representatives of family 1, family 13, and von Soden's "mixed" text (*I*° group).

There is another group of witnesses with which the Old Slavonic text should be compared, namely the Greek Gospel lectionaries. In view of the background of the Old Slavonic version, it is surprising that no such comparison seems to have been made before. In a study of the Lucan passages in fourteen Greek lectionary manuscripts, it was found that in Luke 8 a majority of these manuscripts differs from the Greek Textus Receptus 14 times.[2] Of these variations four are present in the Old Slavonic text. Furthermore, if one takes into account lectionary readings which sporadically appear in the

---

[1] The confusion was the easier to make, because in late Greek the participle of this verb is identical with that of σύνειμι.

[2] Cf. the present writer's monograph, *The Saturday and Sunday Lessons from Luke in the Greek Gospel Lectionary* (Chicago, 1944), pp. 94-95.

fourteen lectionary manuscripts examined, ten more parallels with the Old Slavonic are found.

Inasmuch as the Old Slavonic version of the Gospel was almost certainly made from a Greek lectionary, this number of agreements with Greek lectionaries in Luke 8 is not so high as might have been anticipated. One may account for the relatively low correlation with the Greek lectionary text in two ways. It may be that the Greek lectionary text at the time of the origin of the Old Slavonic version was somewhat different from that which is preserved today in the bulk of Greek lectionaries of later centuries. Since it is the later minuscule lectionaries which have been the object of special study, no one knows how far their text may differ from that of the earlier uncial lectionaries. In the second place, the Old Slavonic version itself was somewhat modified in the years following its original translation from a Greek lectionary. Some modification must have occurred when a Greek non-lectionary text was taken to be the base of a translation of those portions of the Gospels which are not contained in the lectionary cycle.

There is, furthermore, another circumstance which, though often overlooked, may account for the presence of certain "Western" readings in the Old Slavonic. Shortly after the arrival of Constantine and Methodius in Moravia a controversy developed regarding their introduction of the Byzantine rite, written in the language of the Slavs, into a land over which the German bishops of Passau and Salzburg claimed spiritual sovereignty. In spite of machinations against Constantine and Methodius and the temporary imprisonment of the latter in Germany,[1] eventually two Popes (Adrian II and John VIII) gave approval to the use of the Slavonic vernacular in the divine services. There was, however, one requirement that both pontifs imposed: the Scripture lessons should be read first in Latin and then in the Slavonic translation.[2] What recension of the

---

[1] Cf. P. J. Alexander, "The Papacy, the Bavarian Clergy, and the Slavonic Apostles," *Slavonic and East European Review*, xx (1941), 266-293; A. Ziegler, "Der Slawenapostel Methodius im Schwabenlande," *Dillingen und Schwaben, Festschrift zur Vierhundertjahrfeier der Universität Dillingen a. d. D.* (Dillingen a. d. D., 1949), pp. 169-189, and Franc Grivec, "Quaestiones Cyrillo-Methodianae," *Orientalia christiana periodica*, xviii (1952), 113 ff.

[2] For the order of Pope Adrian II, see his letter of 869 to Rostislav, Svatopluk, and Kocel (preserved in the *Vita Methodii*, chap. viii): "Unus vero hic servandus est mos, ut in missa primum Apostolus et Evangelium legantur lingua Romana, postea Slovenica," *Monumenta germaniae historica, Epist.*, vi (Berlin, 1925), 764; see also Ph. Jaffé, *Regesta Pontificium Romanorum* ...,

Vulgate was current in Moravia in the late ninth century may be difficult to determine with precision, but undoubtedly the way was open for a certain number of Vulgate (i.e., Western) readings to be introduced into the Old Slavonic version.

The textual analyses of the nature of the Old Slavonic version of Luke 8 appear to be supported by samplings made of other passages in that Gospel. Thus, in Luke 1.15, the Old Slavonic (except Ma and Os) agrees with Θ, 13, 157, 1071, and others,[1] reading "great before God." In 1.66 it reads the plural "their hearts" with D, L, W, Θ, and the Old Latin manuscript *e*. In 2.25 the Old Slavonic (except Ma) omits "behold" with D and the Peshitta. In 2.33 the Old Slavonic (except Ma and Os) agrees with B, ℵ, D, L, W, I, and the Latin Vulgate in reading "his father" instead of "Joseph." In Luke 10.16 it adds (except Ma) "and he who hears me hears the one who sent me" with D and several Old Latin witnesses. In 15.21 the Old Slavonic puts into the mouth of the Prodigal, "Make me as one of your hired servants," with B, ℵ, D, 33, 1241, and

ed. sec., I (Leipzig, 1885), 368 (no. 2924). The genuineness of this letter has been doubted, e.g., by Ernst Perels, *Mon. germ. hist.*, *Ep.*, VI, 763, note 1; Gerhard Ficker and Heinrich Hermelink, *Das Mittelalter*, 2te Aufl. (Tübingen, 1929), p. 54; and V. Sl. Kiselkov, "Kiril i Metodiĭ v Rim i papa Adrian II," *Istoričeski Pregled*, III (1946-1947), 98-105. On the other hand, Milko Kos, "O pismu papeža Hadriana II knezom Ratislava, Svetopluki in Koclju," *Razprave* of the Slovene Academy of Ljubljana, II, no. 12 (1944), 269-301, and F. Grivec, "Sláva na výsostech Bohu," *Slovanské studie*; *Sbírka statí, věnovaných ... J. Vajsovi k uctění jeho životního díla* (Prague, 1948), pp. 45-51, argue on the basis of certain characteristics of diplomatic style found in contemporary papal documents that the *Vita Methodii* preserves a faithful abridgment of a genuine letter of Adrian II. In any case, however, the information which it supplies regarding the use of the two languages in the reading of the Scripture must be correct; if it were not, the falsehood would be so obvious to anyone who attended the Mass in Slavic lands as to discredit the letter totally. The only uncertainty, if the letter be spurious, concerns the date at which the custom of the twofold reading was instituted.

For the order of Pope John VIII (which, in spite of the skepticism of, e.g., Leopold K. Goetz, *Geschichte der Slavenapostel Konstantinus (Kyrillus) und Methodius* [Gotha, 1897], pp. 58-71, is undoubtedly genuine; cf. V. Jagić in *The Cambridge Mediaeval History*, IV [1923], 228), see his letter of 880 to Svatopluk: "Jubemus tamen ut in omnibus ecclesiis terrae vestrae propter majorem honorificentiam, Evangelium Latine legatur, et postmodum Sclavonica lingua translatum in auribus populi Latina verba non intelligentis, annuntietur sicut in quibusdam ecclesiis fieri videtur," Migne, *PL*, CXXVI, col. 906c, and *Mon. germ. hist.*, *Ep.*, VII, 222. For further texts and bibliography, see Heinz Löwe, *Der Streit um Methodius*; *Quellen zu den nationalkirchlichen Bestrebungen in Mähren und Pannonien im 9. Jahrhundert* (Köln, 1947).

[1] Throughout this list (unlike the investigation of Luke 8), no attempt was made to do more than cite selected non-Slavic support.

the Latin Vulgate. In 23.25 the Old Slavonic (except Ma and Ni) identifies the criminal whom Pilate released in Jesus' stead as "Barabbas," with family 1 and family 13. In 24.36 the Old Slavonic adds, "It is I, be not afraid!" with W, 579, 713, 1241, the Latin Vulgate, and the Syriac Peshitta. In 24.43, after the statement that the resurrected Lord ate in the presence of the Eleven, the Old Slavonic adds that "he gave what remained to them," agreeing with A, 348, 713, 983, 1047, and the Vulgate.

On the basis, therefore, of a minute examination of a sample chapter of Luke, reinforced by additional analysis elsewhere in the Gospel, it appears that the Old Slavonic version of Luke has a quite mixed textual complexion. Basically, as one would expect, it exhibits a Constantinopolitan type of text. In this text are embedded not a few earlier readings which oscillate between the Western and Alexandrian types of text. Because many of these earlier readings are noteworthy both intrinsically and chronologically, it is little short of astonishing that no edition of the Greek New Testament published during the twentieth century includes in its *apparatus criticus* evidence from the Old Slavonic version.[1]

[1] The considered judgment of Ll. J. M. Bebb at the end of the last century has gone unheeded. He wrote in F. H. A. Scrivener, *A Plain Introduction to the Criticism of the New Testament*, 4th ed., ed. by Edward Miller, II (London, 1894), 161, that the Old Slavonic version "does not deserve to be dismissed, as summarily as has been sometimes the case, from the number of those versions which have a value for purposes of the textual criticism of the New Testament."

CHAPTER FOUR

TATIAN'S DIATESSARON AND A PERSIAN HARMONY OF THE GOSPELS

I. WITNESSES TO TATIAN'S DIATESSARON

Except for a tiny parchment fragment in Greek,[1] all the extant witnesses to the text of Tatian's famous Diatessaron are of secondary or tertiary character. These witnesses may be conveniently divided into two groups, one Eastern and the other Western.

The chief members of the Eastern group include (1) the Syriac commentary on the Diatessaron by St. Ephraem of the fourth century, preserved in its entirety in an Armenian translation which has been edited from two manuscripts,[2] and partially preserved in

---

[1] Edited by Carl H. Kraeling, *A Greek Fragment of Tatian's Diatessaron from Dura* (*Studies and Documents*, III; London, 1935). The editor dates the fragment about the year 222 (p. 7), that is, about fifty years after Tatian drew up the original Diatessaron. This is the only known witness to Tatian's work which is extant in Greek, for the leaf from a papyrus codex containing the Greek text of parts of Mt. 18 and 19, which its editor, Otto Stegmüller, believed to be a fragment of the Greek Diatessaron (see his article, "Ein Bruchstück aus dem griechischen Diatessaron (P. 16,388)," *ZNW*, XXXVII [1938], 223-229), is probably nothing more than a Greek text which contains several Tatianic readings (so Curt Peters, "Ein neues Fragment des griechischen Diatessaron?" *B*, XXI [1940], 68-77). The selections from Matthew and John which Agnes Smith Lewis published as "Fragments of a Greek Harmony of the Gospels" (in *Codex Climaci Rescriptus* [1909], pp. xxvii-xxx) were drawn up in accord with a different plan from that of Tatian's Diatessaron and the two have no connexion (so Ian A. Moir, *Codex Climaci Rescriptus Graecus* [*TS*, n.s. II; 1957]). A. Salač thought that the choice and order of the subjects of certain epigrams in the Palatine Anthology were influenced by the Greek Diatessaron (see his article "Quelques epigrammes de l'Anthologie Palatine et l'iconographie Byzantine," *Byz*, XII [1951], 1-28, especially pp. 9-12), but the resemblances are few and inconsequential.

[2] The Armenian text, *Srboyn Ephremi matenagrouthiunk'*, II, was first published in 1836 by the Mechitarist Fathers of the Monastry of San Lazzaro at Venice. This edition was made available for the use of scholars who are not expert in the Armenian language by J. B. Aucher, who prepared a Latin rendering which was edited and published by Georg Moesinger (Venice, 1876). A collection of Ephraem's citations from the Diatessaron, arranged in the order of the Arabic Diatessaron and translated into English, was supervised by J. Armitage Robinson and published as Appendix X in J. Hamlin Hill, *The Earliest Life of Christ ever Compiled from the Gospels, Being the Diatessaron of Tatian* (Edinburgh, 1894), pp. 333-377; this Appendix, accompanied by two additional essays, was reprinted with very minor alterations in J.

a fragmentary Syriac manuscript which is being edited by Leloir;[1]
(2) an Arabic Diatessaron which was translated from the Syriac
and which is extant in two forms, represented by two and four
manuscripts respectively;[2] (3) a Syriac Diatessaric lectionary for
Passiontide extant in about two dozen manuscripts;[3] (4) quotations

Hamlin Hill, *A Dissertation on the Gospel Commentary of S. Ephraem the
Syrian* (Edinburgh, 1896), pp. 75-119.

According to V. F. Büchner, of the two manuscripts of Ephraem's Com-
mentary from which the Armenian edition was prepared, it appears that
manuscript A is more reliable than manuscript B; see his note, "Some
Remarks on the Tradition of the Armenian Translation of Ephraem Syrus'
Commentary on the Diatessaron," *BBC*, v (1928), 34, and "Zu einer Stelle
der armenischen Übersetzung von Ephrem Syrus' Diatessaron-Kommentar,"
Handes Amsorya, XL (1927), cols. 685-688. This is likewise the opinion of
L. Leloir, who has published a definitive edition of the Armenian text of
manuscript A, with an apparatus of variant readings from manuscript B
(*Saint Éphrem, Commentaire de l'évangile concordant, version arménienne*
[= *CSCO*, CXXXVII; Louvain, 1953]). Leloir has also published a Latin
translation of the Armenian text (*CSCO*, CXLV; Louvain, 1954).

[1] The manuscript, which belongs to Sir Chester Beatty, contains a little
more than one half of the text of Ephraem's Commentary (see L. Leloir,
"L'original syriaque du Commentaire de S. Éphrem sur le Diatessaron,"
Studia Biblica et Orientalia; vol. II, *Novum Testamentum* [= *Analecta Biblica*,
XI; Rome, 1959], 391-402).

[2] The *editio princeps*, based on two manuscripts, A of the thirteenth or
fourteenth century, and B of a somewhat later date (so Paul E. Kahle, *The
Cairo Geniza* [London, 1947], p. 213; 2nd ed. [Oxford, 1959], pp. 297f.) was
prepared by Agostino Ciasca (later Cardinal Ciasca), *Tatiani Evangeliorum
harmoniae arabice* (Rome, 1888; anastatic reprint, 1930). Translations into
English and German, accompanied by critical introductions and notes, were
prepared by Hill (*op. cit.*), Hope W. Hogg, *The Diatessaron of Tatian* (*The
Ante-Nicene Fathers*, IX [New York, 1896], pp. 33-138), and Erwin Preuschen
with the help of August Pott, *Tatians Diatessaron aus den arabischen übersetzt* (Heidelberg, 1926). The most recent edition of the Arabic text on the
basis of three manuscripts (A and B with a much later one designated E)
is that prepared by A.-S. Marmardji, *Diatessaron de Tatien, texte arabe établi,
traduit en français* ... (Beyrouth, 1935). Unfortunately, however, it is often
impossible to determine from Marmardji's apparatus whether his printed
text is that of ms. E or is the editor's idea of what the ms. ought to read. For
further information regarding the manuscripts of the Arabic Diatessaron, see
Georg Graf, *Geschichte der christlichen arabischen Literatur* (*Studi e testi*,
CXVIII; Città del Vaticano, 1944), pp. 152-154; A. J. B. Higgins, "The
Arabic Version of Tatian's Diatessaron," *JTS*, XLV (1944), 187-199, and
"Tatian's Diatessaron" [a summary of his doctoral dissertation at the Uni-
versity of Manchester], *Journal of the Manchester University Egyptian and
Oriental Society*, XXIV (1942-1945 [published in 1947]), 28-32, and Kahle,
op. cit., pp. 211-228; 2nd. ed., pp. 297-313.

[3] See J. P. P. Martin, *Introduction à la critique textuelle du Nouveau
Testament*, Partie practique, III (Paris, 1885), 121-144, and "Le Διὰ τεσσάρων
de Tatien," *Revue des questions historiques*, XXXIII (1883), 336-378; H. H.
Spoer, "Spuren eines syrischen Diatessaron," *Zeitschrift für die deutschen*

and allusions in various Eastern Church Fathers and texts, such as Aphraates, Ephraem's *Homilies* and other works,[1] the *Liber Graduum*, Agathangelos, Eznik, and others, as well as the Armenian Breviary and Ritual, the Georgian version of the Gospels, a Jacobite marriage ritual in Old Osmanic, and certain Coptic Manichaean fragments;[2] and (5) a medieval Persian Harmony of the Gospels made from a Syriac base.

The chief witnesses of the Western group include (6) the famous codex Fuldensis, a Latin harmony of the Gospels prepared at the direction of Bishop Victor of Capua near the middle of the sixth century;[3] (7) various medieval German harmonies, the most notable of which is an Old High German (East Frankish) bilingual harmony dating from the second half of the ninth century, the Latin text of which depends upon Victor's work;[4] (8) Middle Dutch (Flemish)

morgenländischen Gesellschaft, LXI (1907), 850-859; G. A. Barton and H. H. Spoer, "Traces of the Diatessaron of Tatian in Harclean Syriac Lectionaries," *JBL*, XXIV (1905), 179-195; and the appendix in Marmardji, *op. cit.* "Évangélaire diatessarique syriaque," pp. 1*-75*. According to a note in a Syriac manuscript discovered by A. Mingana, this Passiontide Lectionary was drawn up by Rabban Daniel, of the village of Baith Bātīn near Ḥarran, and his disciple, Isaac (*Bulletin of the John Rylands Library*, XV [1931], 178).

[1] See Leloir, *L'Évangile d'Éphrem d'après les oeuvres éditées. Recueil des textes* (= *CSCO*, CLXXX; Louvain, 1958); cf. also his article, "Le Diatessaron de Tatien," *L'Orient syrien*, I (1956), 208-231 and 313-334. Here may be mentioned also the evidence (which is variously estimated) of the Greek translation of Ephraem's works; see D. Hemmerdinger-Iliadou, "Éphrem le syrien," *Dictionnaire de spiritualité*, fascicules XXVI-XXVII (Paris, 1959), cols. 788-819, and "L'authenticité de l'Éphrem grec," *Akten des XI. internationalen Byzantinisten-Kongresses, 1958* (München, 1960), pp. 232-236; cf. also idem, "Vers une nouvelle édition de l'Éphrem grec," *TU*, LXXVIII (1961), 72-80.

[2] For bibliography concerning these witnesses, see footnotes 1 to 4, p. 102 below.

[3] Edited by Ernst Ranke, *Codex Fuldensis, Novum Testamentum latine, interprete Hieronymo, ex manuscripto Victoris Capuani* (Marburg, 1868).

[4] Edited by Edward Sievers, *Tatian, lateinisch und altdeutsch mit ausführlichen Glossar*, 2te Aufl. (*Bibliothek der ältesten deutschen Litteratur-Denkmäler*, V; Paderborn, 1892). For information regarding other medieval German harmonies, see Curt Peters, *Das Diatessaron Tatians, seine Überlieferung und sein Nachwirken im Morgen- und Abendland sowie der heutige Stand seiner Erforschung* (*Orientalia christiana analecta*, CXXIII; Rome, 1939), pp. 177-188, and Cl. Van Puyvelde in *Supplément au Dictionnaire de la Bible*, VI, fasc. XXXIII (Paris, 1960), cols. 865 f.

G. Quispel's recent attempt to revive the view that the Heliand, an Old Saxon epic poem on the Saviour, is a reliable source for the reconstruction of Tatian's Diatessaron (*NTS*, V [1959], 276-290), has been severely criticized from the standpoint of Germanic philology by Willy Krogmann ("Heliand, Tatian und Thomasevangelium," *ZNW*, LI [1960], 255-268).

harmonies preserved in nine manuscripts of the thirteenth to fifteenth centuries,[1] the best known of which are the manuscript at Liège[2] and the one at Stuttgart;[3] (9) two Old Italian harmonies of the thirteenth and fourteenth centuries, one in the Tuscan dialect preserved in twenty-four manuscripts, the other in the Venetian dialect preserved in one manuscript;[4] (10) a Middle English harmony (which once belonged to Samuel Pepys) dating from about the year 1400 and based upon an Old French harmony;[5] and (11) the harmonized Gospel text on which Zacharias Chrysopolitanus

[1] For a list of these see Peters, *Das Diatessaron Tatians*, pp. 140-142.

[2] Edited first by G. J. Meijer, *Het Leven van Jezus, een nederlandsch Handschrift uit de dertiende Eeuw* (Groningen, 1835), the significance of which for New Testament scholarship was discovered sixty years later by J. A. Robinson, *Academy*, XLV (24 March 1894), 249-250. The manuscript was re-edited with evidence from other Middle Dutch harmonies by J. Bergsma, *De Levens van Jezus in het Middelnederlandsch* (*Bibliotheek van middelnederlandsche Letterkunde*, LIV, LV, LXI; Groningen, 1895-98). The lack of an index in Bergsma's volume is supplied by C. A. Phillips, *Index to the Liège Diatessaron* (*Edition of Dr. J. Bergsma*), privately printed for the members of the Bezan Club. It is to be hoped that the magnificent edition which has been in the course of publication under the auspices of the Royal Academy at Amsterdam will be brought to a conclusion, namely, *The Liège Diatessaron*, edited with a Textual Apparatus by Daniël Plooij, C. A. Phillips, and A. H. A. Bakker, Parts I-V (*Verhandelingen der koninklijke nederlandsche Akademie van Wetenschappen*, Afd. Letterkunde, Nieuwe Reeks, Deel XXXI; Amsterdam, 1929-1938). For a general discussion of this and other Middle Dutch harmonies, see C. C. De Bruin, *Middelnederlandse Vertalingen van het Nieuwe Testament* (Groningen, 1935), pp. 32-68, and for a stemma showing the relationship of several Dutch Harmonies, see the incisive critique of Plooij's preliminary work on the Liège Diatessaron, *A Primitive Text of the Diatessaron* (Leyden, 1923), by the Germanist, Th. Frings, in *Literaturblatt für germanische und romanische Philologie*, XLVII (1926), cols. 150-155.

[3] The text is printed by Bergsma, *op. cit.*

[4] These have been edited by Venanzio Todesco, Alberto Vaccari, and Marco Vattasso, *Il Diatessaron in volgare italiano, testi inediti dei secoli XIII-XIV* (*Studi e testi*, LXXXI; Città del Vaticano, 1938). For an investigation of the type of text in the Italian Harmonies see Curt Peters, "Die Bedeutung der altitalienischen Evangelienharmonien im venezianischen und toskanischen Dialekt," *Romanische Forschungen*, LXI (1942), 181-192. Contrary to Vaccari, who thought that the Tuscan text goes back to the Codex Fuldensis (*op. cit.*, p. iii), Peters argues that the most that can be said is that the Tuscan Harmony may belong to the orbit of that branch of the Western transmission of the Diatessaron to which the Codex Fuldensis also belongs (*op. cit.*, p. 182). The Venetian Harmony, according to both Vaccari (*ibid.*) and Peters (p. 187), contains more remnants of an older text form than does the Tuscan Harmony, and Peters finds that it even agrees occasionally with Aphraates in singular readings (pp. 191-192).

[5] Edited by Margery Goates, *The Pepysian Gospel Harmony* (*Early English Text Society*, Original Series, CLVII; London, 1927).

ܙ ܘܩܝܒ

(Zachary of Besançon)[1] wrote a commentary during the first half of the twelfth century.[2]

The testimony of these witnesses to Tatian is of two kinds. Some of them, such as the Codex Fuldensis and the Arabic Diatessaron, represent more or less closely, it is thought, the framework of Tatian's Diatessaron, but possess essentially a non-Tatianic form of text. In the case of the Codex Fuldensis, Victor accommodated almost perfectly the Old Latin form of text of the original to the current Vulgate. As regards the Arabic Diatessaron, the Syriac base on which it rests is largely the Peshitta which has in most places supplanted the Old Syriac text of Tatian's harmony.[3] The chief evidence, therefore, which these two witnesses provide is not textual but structural; the frequent agreements of the sequence of sections may be presumed to reflect accurately the framework of the original Diatessaron. On the other hand, other witnesses, which are constructed according to utterly divergent sequences of Gospel material having no connection with the framework of Tatian's work, preserve

---

[1] The text of Zachary's *In unum ex quatuor, sive de concordia evangelistarum libri quatuor* is published in Migne, *Patrologia Latina*, CLXXXVI, cols. 11-620. On the nature of the Biblical text, see J. P. P. Martin, "Le Διὰ τεσσάρων de Tatien," *Revue des questions historiques*, XLIV (1888), 36-40; Otto Schmid, "Zacharias Chrysopolitanus und sein Kommentar zur Evangelienharmonie," *Theologische Quartalschrift*, LXVIII (1886), 531-547; LXIX (1887), 231-275; J. Rendel Harris, "Some Notes on the Gospel-Harmony of Zacharias Chrysopolitanus," *JBL*, XLIII (1924), 32-45; D. Plooij, "De Commentaar van Zacharias Chrysopolitanus op het Diatessaron," *Mededeelingen der koninklijke Akademie van Wetenschappen*, Afd. Letterkunde, Deel LIX, Serie A., No. 5 (Amsterdam, 1925); and C. A. Phillips, "The Winchester Codex of Zachary of Besançon," *Bulletin of the Bezan Club*, II (1926), 3-8 (this last presents selected readings from a text of Zachary which is earlier than the text printed in Migne).

[2] It may be profitable to seek for further traces of the Diatessaron in the West by examining Latin manuscripts of works attributed to Ephraem, of which there are many in European libraries; for a list see Albert Siegmund, *Die Überlieferung der griechischen christlichen Literatur in der lateinischen Kirche bis zum zwölften Jahrhundert* (= *Abhandlungen der bayerischen Benediktines-Akademie*, Band V; München, 1949), pp. 67-71. Cf. also Gustav Grau, *Quellen und Verwandtschaften der älteren germanischen Darstellungen des jüngsten Gerichtes* (Halle a.S., 1908), pp. 8 ff. August C. Mahr's monograph on *Relations of Passion Plays to St. Ephraem the Syrian* (Columbus, Ohio, 1942), though interesting and ingenious, does not touch upon the Diatessaron.

[3] Higgins (*JTS*, XLV [1944], 187-199) shows that the form of the Arabic Diatessaron which is preserved in mss. BEO has been less thoroughly accommodated to the Peshitta than has ms. A (which latter Ciasca printed as representing the text of Tatian). Burkitt's judgment that "there is no doubt that the Arabic is intrinsically a *better* Gospel Harmony than that in Codex Fuldensis; but this rather suggests that the Arabic may be a later, improved

Lincoln Christian College

Tatianic readings transmitted to these witnesses via the Old Syriac or Old Latin forms of text. This kind of Tatianic testimony is on a par with the type of text represented in Gospel quotations in, for example, Aphraates,[1] the Syriac *Liber graduum*,[2] the Armenian version and Liturgy,[3] and certain Manichaean literature[4]—all of which appear to embody in varying degrees Diatessaric readings. In fact, it is likely that the policy of approving as genuinely Tatianic only those readings in the Arabic Diatessaron which differ from the Peshitta has been unwarrantably rigorous, for even where the Arabic Diatessaron agrees with the Peshitta, if the Old Syriac also agrees, such readings are proved to be more ancient than the Peshitta and may therefore be Tatianic. Such a possibility becomes a probability with overwhelming compulsion when Ephraem and other witnesses unrelated to the Peshitta add their support.[5]

form" (*JTS*, xxv [1923-24], 116) is reiterated by A. Vaccari in his examination of "Le sezioni evangeliche di Eusebio e il *Diatessaron* di Taziano nella letteratura siriaca," *Scritti in onore di Giuseppe Furlani*, 1 (= *Rivista degli studi orientali*, xxxii [1957]), 433-452.

[1] The *Demonstrations* of Aphraates have been edited by J. Parisot, *Patrologia syriaca*, 1, i (Paris, 1892), ii (Paris, 1907). For Aphraates' Gospel text, see F. C. Burkitt, *Evangelion da-Mepharreshe*, ii (Cambridge, 1904), 109-111, 180-186.

[2] The Syriac *Liber graduum*, which dates from c. A.D. 320, has been edited by M. Kmosko, *Patrologia syriaca*, I, iii (Paris, 1926). For the type of text in this work see A. Rücker, "Die Zitate aus dem Matthäusevangelium in syrischen 'Buche der Stufen,' " *Biblische Zeitschrift*, xx (1932), 342-354.

[3] F. C. Conybeare, "An Armenian Diatessaron ?" *JTS*, xxv (1924), 232-245; P. Essabalian, *Le Diatessaron de Tatien et la première traduction des évangiles arméniens* (*Bibliothèque nationale*, cxlii; Vienna, 1937) [in Armenian with a French résumé]; and S. Lyonnet, "Vestiges d'un Diatessaron arménien," *B*, xix (1938), 121-150; "La première version arménienne des évangiles," *RB*, xlvii (1938), 355-382; "Notes philologiques sur la première version arménienne des évangiles," *Revue des études indo-européennes*, 1 (1938), 263-270 and *Les origines de la version arménienne et la Diatessaron* (Rome, 1950); and L. Leloir in *Supplément au Dictionnaire de la Bible*, vi, fasc. xxxiii (Paris, 1960), cols. 810-818. Cf. also p. 49, n. 1, above.

Other witnesses derived from the Armenian which appear to preserve harmonistic readings include the Old Georgian version of the Gospels (see A. Baumstark, "Zum georgischen Evangelientext," *OC*, 3. Ser., iii-iv [1928-29], 117-124) and the text of Matt. 19 in a Jacobite marriage ritual preserved in Old Osmanic (see W. Heffening-C. Peters, "Spuren des Diatessarons in liturgischer Überlieferung. Ein türkischer und ein karschuni-Text," *OC*, 3. Ser., x [1935], 225-238).

[4] Anton Baumstark, "Ein 'Evangelium'-Zitat der manichäischen Kephalaia," *Oriens christianus*, 3. Ser., xii (1937), 169-191, and Peters, *Das Diatessaron Tatians*, pp. 125-132.

[5] For a sane and balanced statement of the correct methodology of Tatianic-*Forschung*, which is drawn up with lapidary succinctness, see August Merk, *Novum Testamentum graece et latine*, ed. sexta (Rome, 1948), pp. 17*-18*.

II. A Persian Harmony of the Gospels

Among the more extensive witnesses to the Tatianic text of the Gospels is a Persian Harmony of the Gospels. Though the manuscript had been described by Assemani[1] so long ago as 1742, and again by Italo Pizzi[2] in 1886, it was not until the twentieth century that the nature and importance of this document was fully appreciated. In 1943 Giuseppe Messina published a general description[3] of the manuscript and its Harmony, and eight years later made the text available, with an Italian translation and an extensive Introduction.[4] The manuscript, which is number XVII (81) in the Laurentian Library of Florence, was copied in the year 1547 by a Jacobite priest, Ibrahīm ben Shammas 'Abdullāh, in the city of Ḥiṣn Kaif on the Tigris River, from a parent manuscript dating probably from the thirteenth century. This earlier Persian Diatessaron appears to have been translated (not always quite accurately) from a Syriac base by a Jacobite layman of Tabrīz who calls himself Īwānnīs 'Izz al-Dīn, that is, "John, Glory of the Religion." Although Īwānnīs undoubtedly wished the reader to believe that he had himself composed the Harmony de novo, Messina finds reasons to believe that in preparing the Persian work he utilized two slightly divergent Harmonies already existing in Syriac.[5]

The Persian Harmony is divided into four main divisions, containing respectively 71, 61, 60, and 58 paragraphs. The compiler has

---

[1] *Bibliotheca Mediceae Laurentianae et Palatinae codicum MSS. orientalium catalogus* (Florentiae, 1742), p. 59.

[2] *Cataloghi dei codici orientali di alcune biblioteche d'Italia*, III (Firenze, 1886), p. 301.

[3] *Notizia su un Diatessaron Persiano tradotto dal siriaco* (Roma, 1943).

[4] *Diatessaron Persiano*. I, *Introduzione*; II. *Testo e traduzione* (*Biblica et orientalia*, N. 14; Roma, 1951). This edition, excellent though it is, does not render obsolete Messina's earlier *Notizia*. Indeed for a fuller discussion of certain stylistic features (e.g., conflate readings) and evidence bearing on the history of the Persian manuscript and its translator, including the complete text and translation of one of the chief colophons, one must refer to the earlier volume. It is a cause for regret also that, although Messina indicates the location and length of sporadic comments interspersed in the Harmony (some of which extend to a column or more in length), yet in the interests of saving space he neither transcribes nor translates any of them. One cannot but wonder whether these comments might reveal or corroborate some characteristic of the Harmonist. To learn even a modicum as to his methods of exegesis would contribute directly to a fuller understanding of his background and mental processes.

[5] Pp. xxi sq.

indicated the derivation of the various passages from the four
Gospels by using the appropriate letters, M, S (the final letter of
Markōs), L, and Y (Yuḥannā).[1] When the sequence of the sections
is compared with Tatian's work, represented in codex Fuldensis
and the Arabic Diatessaron, only a relatively few sections are found
to be in the same order, and these can be explained on the basis
of natural coincidence. Indeed, the underlying plan as well as the
execution seems to differ from Tatian's very carefully wrought
Diatessaron. Thus, the compiler of this Harmony occasionally
presents parallel Synoptic passages at different places in his work
(e.g. "the salt which has lost its saltiness" Mt. 5.13 appears in I, 34,
while the parallel in Lk. 14.34 is given in IV, 11). At other times but
one of two slightly divergent passages is utilized, the peculiarities
of the other being omitted entirely in a way quite unlike Tatian's
meticulous care in embodying practically everything distinctive
in the four Gospels (as III, 8, where Mt. 10.26b-28 is cited without
the Lucan details of Lk. 12.2-4). The Persian Harmony begins with
Mk. 1.1 and not with Jn. 1.1, as Tatian, on the explicit testimony of
Dionysius bar Ṣalibi,[2] began his Diatessaron. Furthermore the
Persian Harmony contains the Matthean and Lucan genealogies of
Jesus, both of which, according to Theodoret, Bishop of Cyrrhos,[3]
were omitted by Tatian. So far, therefore, as the external framework is concerned, the Persian Harmony manifests no relationship
with Tatian.

[1] In one form of the Arabic Diatessaron these *sigla* are: M for Mt, R for
Mk, Ḳ for Lk, Ḥ for Jn; in the other form two letters are used for each Gospel:
Mt, Mr, Lk, Yu. Zachary explains that he uses M for Mt, R for Mk, L for Lk,
and A for Jn (here Zachary chooses the first letter of *Aquila* to show that
John is the eagle in the tetrad of living creatures in Ezekiel; Migne, *PL*,
CLXXXVI, col. 40 A-C).

[2] Joseph S. Assemani, *Bibliotheca orientalis*, II (Rome, 1721), 159-160.
Bar Ṣalibi's statement is confirmed by evidence from Ephraem's commentary
but is apparently contradicted by the Arabic text (which begins with Mark)
and by the Codex Fuldensis (which begins with Luke). If the introductory
notices in the Arabic manuscripts are carefully studied, however, it appears
that the original Arabic text began with Jn. 1.1. Similarly, it is almost
certain that the first four verses of Luke were not in the original text of the
manuscript which Victor found, for they are not mentioned in the (old) table
of contents, which begins with John.

[3] Theodoret, *Treatise on Heresies*, I, 20 (Migne, *PG*, LXXXIII, cols. 369-372).
The two forms of the Arabic text of the Diatessaron are distinguished also
(see footnote no. 1 above) by the way in which they dispose of the genealogies; in one form the genealogies are included in the midst of the text, in the
other they appear at the end as a kind of appendix.

In several other particulars besides sequence of material this Harmony differs from what is generally understood to be Tatian's Diatessaron. Which of these features are actually Tatianic, for which there had previously been no explicit evidence, and which were introduced into an ancestor of the Persian Harmony at a later date than Tatian, will be variously estimated. One of the most remarkable of these characteristics is the presence of nearly a score of passages which betray knowledge of the Protoevangelium of James. Thus, to cite only one example, the Persian text at I, 3 presents Lk. 1.44 with a remarkable addition. Elizabeth addresses Mary as follows (in Messina's translation): "Divenne molto esultante questo bambino, che è nel mio seno, *e adorò quel bambino, che è nel tuo seno.*" The italicized matter is paralleled in the Protoevangelium in its Syriac and Ethiopic versions.

Furthermore, numerous stylistic peculiarities and tendential modifications seem to indicate that the hand which formed this Harmony was characteristically Hebraic.[1] Several of the more salient features include numerous examples of additions of words and phrases to the text of the Gospels, producing thereby typical Hebraic parallelism; the presence of many Semitisms which reflect Hebrew syntax (such as the use of a noun indicating action which is identical or analogous to the action expressed in the verb; the co-ordination of final, concessive, explicative, adversative, and circumstantial clauses by "and"); the altering of quotations from the Old Testament so as to conform them more exactly to the Hebrew text; and a certain rabbinical familiarity with targumic traditions. In addition to these there also occur several of the traits which have been generally recognized to be Tatianic, such as an encratitic lack of sympathy for matrimony and normal family life, and an antipathy against wine. Other minor modifications of text display a tendency to eliminate phrases which refer to "king" or "kingdom," particularly where these represent Jesus as the heir to the throne of David. (In this respect one can perhaps detect the influence of Marcion.)

From this evidence Messina concludes that in addition to the four canonical Gospels the author of the Syriac Harmony underlying the Persian translation utilized the Protoevangelium of James and

---

[1] *Op. cit.*, pp. lii-lxxxiv. For a discussion of the stylistic characteristics of the Arabic Diatessaron, see A. A. Hobson, *The Diatessaron of Tatian and the Synoptic Problem* (Chicago, 1904), pp. 46-74.

another Gospel written in Hebrew.[1] He is inclined to identify the latter with the *Hebraicum evangelicum* to which Eusebius and Jerome refer. This source, however, is not to be confused with the *Evanglium iuxta Hebraeos*, which Phillips,[2] Baumstark,[3] and Peters[4] thought was a fifth source of the Diatessaron, thus accounting for the otherwise puzzling statement made by Victor of Capua concerning Tatian's "diapente."[5]

Another complicating factor is involved in the circumstance that the Persian Harmony exhibits numerous readings which are also present in the Bodleian manuscript used by Brian Walton for the Persian text of the Gospels in his Polyglot Bible. Some of these are the result of interpretative effort, as Lk. 1.36, ἡ συγγενίς σου] *tua zia materna*; some of them involve amplification, as Lk. 4.26, Σάρεπτα τῆς Σιδωνίας] *città di Tiro e Sidone*; and some are the result of simple inattention, as Jn. 1.1, καὶ θεὸς ἦν ὁ λόγος] *e Dio è il Verbo*. Since Messina was unable to find any Greek or Syriac evidence for most of these readings, he concludes that the Harmony and the

---

[1] *Op. cit.*, pp. li and lxxxiv. Recently G. Quispel has attempted to show that the Coptic Gospel according to Thomas depends upon a Semitic source which Tatian also utilized in making his Diatessaron ("L'Evangile selon Thomas et le Diatessaron," *Vigiliae christianae*, XIII [1959], 87-117). A similar view is expressed by A. F. J. Klijn ("De stand van het onderzoek naar de geschiedenis van de tekst van het Nieuwe Testament," *Nederlands theologisch tijdschrift*, XV [1961], 161-168), who observes that the parallels between Thomas and the Diatessaron may point to their common indebtedness to a very old Gospel text in which the influence of the primitive oral tradition had produced these variants. But one cannot rule out, Klijn thinks, the possibility that the Gospel to the Hebrews or some other apocryphal work was the origin of these readings (see also Klijn, "Het evangelie van Petrus en de Westerse tekst," *ibid.*, XV [1961], 264-269). A different relationship is suggested by Tjitze Baarda, who thinks that the Coptic Thomas goes back to a Syriac exemplar which was influenced by the original Syriac Diatessaron (in R. Schippers, *Het evangelie van Thomas* [Kampen, 1960], p. 155); cf. also Baarda in *Vox theologica*, XXXII (1961-62), 107-119.

[2] C. A. Phillips, *BBC*, IX (1932), 6-8.

[3] Anton Baumstark, *B*, XVI (1935), 288, and *OC*, 3 Ser., XIV (1939), 19-27.

[4] Curt Peters, *Acta orientalia*, XVI (1938), 258-294.

[5] Victor says that "Tatianus ... unum ex quattuor conpaginaverit evangelium cui titulum diapente composuit" (Ranke, *op. cit.*, p. 1, lines 16-18). Isaac Casaubon commented on this statement as follows: "Videtur scribendum *Dia panton*, quod consentit cum Eusebio. Alioquin scimus et *Dia pente* concentus nomen esse apud Musicos, ut *Dia tessaron* et *Dia pason*: quas appellationes et Latini retinuerunt, ut Vitruvius," *De rebus sacris et ecclesiasticis exercitationes XVI ad cardinalii Baronii Prolegomena in Annales ...* (London, 1614), p. 236. Casaubon's tentative suggestion is worked out convincingly by Franco Bolgiani in his monograph, *Vittore di Capua e il "Diatessaron"* (Torino, 1962).

Bodleian manuscript go back to a common origin. Yet because of still more numerous differences between the two, it is impossible to postulate direct dependence of one upon the other.

As to the date of the composition of the underlying Syriac Harmony, Messina argues repeatedly for a relatively early date. First, the numerous agreements with the Old Syriac text and the frequent divergencies from the Peshitta text leave no doubt in his mind that the Harmony "was composed at a time in which the translation of the Peshitta either did not yet exist or at any rate was not completely dominent."[1] Second, the presence of non-canonical material "proves that the work was composed when the canon of the New Testament had not yet been universally recognized."[2] Third, Messina inclines, in fact, to attribute to Tatian himself the composition of this Harmony, "We know," he writes, "various sides of Tatian's mentality, and we have found in the Persian Diatessaron readings undoubtedly conformed to this thought. But we do not have even the slightest hint that Tatian had had a rabbinical mentality; on the contrary, all that is known of him excludes this. Consequently, the Hebraizing and rabbinical coloring present in our document did not come from Tatian himself, but was derived from a source which he used, other than the four Gospels."[3]

To the present writer these arguments for an early date of the underlying Syriac Harmony are inconclusive. If the Harmony is to be proved to be ancient, the proof must rest on grounds other than those which Messina has adduced. Against the first mentioned argument, evidence is now coming to light that (contrary to Burkitt's *obiter dicta*, accepted by almost all subsequent scholars) the Peshitta version did not immediately supplant all Old Syriac readings. Vööbus, for example, has unearthed a large amount of evidence which shows that non-Peshitta (Vööbus would say, Old Syriac) readings appear relatively frequently down to the thirteenth century.[4] Even within the general orbit of Persian Christianity, Peters found evidence in a Sogdian Gospel Lectionary of the tenth century of significant variations from the current Peshitta text.[5]

---

[1] *Op. cit.*, p. xxviii.

[2] *Ibid.*, p. lxxxi.

[3] *Ibid.*, pp. lxxxii ff.

[4] Arthur Vööbus, *Studies in the History of the Gospel Text in Syriac* (*CSCO*, vol. cxxviii; Louvain, 1951).

[5] Curt Peters, "Der Text der soghdischen Evangelienbruchstücke und das Problem der Pešitta," *OC*, 3te Serie, xi (1936), 153-162.

Thus, Messina's first argument for an early date loses much of its cogency.

Messina's second argument for an early date, based on the degree of freedom which the Harmonist allowed himself in using non-canonical material, takes on a quite different appearance in the light of the ample evidence from the Middle Ages that authors of a somewhat similar type of literature, namely devotional lives of Christ, did not feel themselves at all inhibited by "a universally recognized canon of the New Testament" from introducing into their works many incidents not contained in the New Testament.[1] Furthermore, an added difficulty standing in the way of dating the composition of the Harmony as early as Messina desiderates is the lack of proof and, indeed, the unlikelihood that all of the readings in the Syriac and Ethiopic versions of the Protoevangelium (but not in Greek) which were adopted by the Harmonist were current as early as Messina's theory necessitates.

Finally, two considerations weigh heavily in the present writer's mind against Messina's proposal that Tatian himself is to be regarded as the author of the Harmony. In the first place, not only is the order of material in the other Harmonies which have been generally attributed to Tatian quite different from the framework of the Persian Harmony, but also one must suppose that all or almost all of the non-canonical material had been expurgated from the other extant forms of Tatian's Diatessaron. In the second place, Tatian's dislike of the Jewish antecedents of Christianity would almost certainly have prevented him from choosing as one of his sources a document so Hebraistic and rabbinic as must be postulated in the ancestry of this Harmony.

Thus, the conclusion appears to be that the structure of the Persian Harmony has no discernible connection with Tatian's Diatessaron. At the same time, it is legitimate to regard this Harmony, resting upon a Syriac original of uncertain age, as a valuable Tatianic witness of the second variety mentioned above; it contains many readings which are of undoubted Tatianic ancestry. In order to exhibit this feature of the Persian Harmony[2] the following list

---

[1] See, e.g., Sister Mary Immaculate Bodenstedt, *The Vita Christi of Ludolphus the Carthusian* (Washington, 1944), pp. 47-49.

[2] For a comparison of the Persian Harmony with the Arabic Gospel Harmonies see A. J. B. Higgins in *Studia Evangelica*, ed. by K. Aland *et al.* (= *TU*, LXXIII; Berlin, 1959), pp. 793-810; cf. also his article, "The Persian Gospel Harmony as a Witness to Tatian's Diatessaron," *JTS*, n.s. III (1952), 83-87.

of about one hundred variants was compiled by comparing the text
of the first main section of the Persian Harmony (in Messina's
Italian translation) with other Eastern and Western witnesses to
Tatian mentioned at the beginning of this chapter. For purposes of
comparison evidence from the Syriac versions is also cited. (It
must not be supposed that the autograph of Tatian's Diatessaron
contained each of the following variants, for in some cases the
testimony of the Tatianic witnesses is divided.)

Sigla used in the Apparatus

Ar	Arabic Diatessaron	Sy[s]	Sinaitic Syriac
Aph	Aphraates	Sy[c]	Curetonian Syriac
E	Ephraem	Sy[p]	Peshitta
L	Liège ms.	Sy[pal]	Palestinian Syriac
LG	Syriac *Liber graduum*	Sy[har]	Harclean Syriac
Pep	Pepsian Harmony	Tus	Tuscan form of Italian Harmony
Per	Persian Harmony	Ven	Venetian form of Italian Harmony
St	Stuttgart ms.	Z	Zachary of Besançon

Direct quotations from editions of Tatianic witnesses are cited
in italics; translations of words and sentences into English are
enclosed in quotation marks.

MATTHEW

1.19 Ιωσηφ δε ο ανηρ αυτης, δικαιος ων] Ιωσηφ δε ανηρ δικαιος Per
E Ven: *unde Iosep veçando çò, cum ello iusto et bono* Tus:
uomo giusto L Sy[c]

2.5 — αυτω Per A | — γαρ Per A

2.6 ουδαμως] μη Per A L St Z [(Winchester codex)]

2.9 οι δε ακουσαντες του βασιλεως] cum audivissent (hoc) a rege
Per: *la parole del re* A Ven Sy[s, c]

2.14 δε] + Ιωσηφ Per A Ven Tus L St Sy[s, c, p]

2.23 δια των προφητων] δια του προφητου Per: *per la lingua del
profeta* Ar L St Tus Ven: *cossì fo conpiude le profeçie*
Sy[s, c, p, pal]

3.6 — ποταμω Per Tus L St

4.6 επι χειρων] brachiis Per: *sulle loro braccia* E[(com)] A
Sy[s, c, p] [2 mss.]

5.13   — ετι Per A Sy^{s, c, p}

5.14   κειμενη] aedificata Per: *fondamento sia* A Sy^{s, c, p}

5.18   ιωτα ... κεραια] Per: *una parole* Ven: *una letera* L and St: *ene lettre* Aph, LG, and Sy^s (cf. Lk. 16.17): "one yôd letter"

5.27   ερρεθη] + τοις αρχαιοις Per Ven Tus St Z Sy^{c, pal, har*}

5.28   — ηδη Per E Sy^{s, c}

5.32   γαμηση] λαβη Per: *prende* A Ven Tus L Sy^s: ܢܣܒ Sy^{c, p}: ܠܗ ¹

6.5   — εστωτες Per Tus L: *gaen staen* LG^{vid} Sy^{c, p (s hiat)}

6.19   θησαυριζετε] ponite Per: *riponete* A Ven Tus L Aph Sy ^{c (s hiat)}

6.24   ανθεξεται] honorabit Per: *onorerà* A Sy^p

7.24   — ουν] Per A Ven Tus Sy^{c (s hiat)}

7.26   ομοιωθησεται] ομοιος εστιν Per Ven L St Z

7.29   αυτων] + και οι Φαρισαιοι Per: *i loro grandi (farisei)* A Tus L Z Sy^{c, p, har (s hiat)}

8.4   τω ιερει] τοις ιερευσι Per A Ven Tus L E Sy^{s, c, p, pal}

8.8   — μονον Per E

8.17   νοσους] +ημων Per A Ven Tus L Sy^{s, c, p}

11.17 ηυλησαμεν] cantavimus Per: *cantammo (sarwad guftīm)* A Ven Tus L Sy^{s, c, p}

12.12 ουν] + μαλλον Per A Sy^{s, c}

MARK

2.27   εγενετο] εκτισθη Per A L Pep Sy^{s, p (c hiat)}

LUKE

1.13   σου (1)] + ενωπιον θεου Per E Aph Pep Sy^{s (c hiat)}: "for lo, God has heard the voice of thy prayer" | γεννησει] Per: *concepirà e ti partorirà* Pep: *conceyuen & beren*

1.25   οτι] τουτο Per A L Sy^{(s, c hiant) p}: ܗܕܐ

1.28   αυτην] + ο αγγελος Per A L St Pep Sy^{(s, c hiant) p, pal} | σου] + ευλογημενη συ εν γυναιξιν Per A Ven Tus L St Pep E Aph Sy^{(s, c hiant) p, har}

1.29   διελογιζετο] + εν εαυτη Per: *nel suo cuore rifletteva (mīandēšīd)* L: *wart si geturbeert in hare seluen* (Sy^{s, c hiant})

1.35   γεννωμενον + εκ σου Per A Ven Tus L E Pep Sy ^{(s, c hiant) p, pal} [ms. C] | αγιον] + εστι και Per A Ven St Sy^{p (s, c hiant)}

---

¹ See Daniël Plooij, "Traces of Syriac Origin of the Old-Latin Diatessaron," *Mededeelingen der koninklijke Akademie van Wetenschappen*, Afd. Letterkunde, Deel LXIII, Ser. A, No. 4 (Amsterdam, 1927), pp. 20 (120) ff.

1.56 — ως Per Ven St

1.61 εκ της συγγενειας] εν τη συηγενεια Per A Tus L St Sy^s (c hiat), p, har

1.64 incipit και παραχρημα Per A Ven Tus L Sy^s (c hiat), p

1.66 — γαρ Per A Ven Sy^s (c hiat), p, har*

1.71 σωτηριαν] ut liberaret nos Per: *che ci libererebbe* A Sy^p; ut liberavit nos Ven: *salvati n'à da li nimici* Tus: *àcci salvati da' nimici nostri* Sy^s (c hiat): "he has snatched us away unto life from the hand of our enemies"

2.5 απογραψασθαι ... ουση εγκυω] εγκυω α. εχει Per A Sy ^s, p (c hiat

2.8 τη αυτη] ταυτη Per A Ven Tus Sy^pal

2.14 εν (2)] και Per: *e lieto annuzio di buona speranza agli uomini* A Sy^s (c hiat) p, har ; E omits εν (2)

2.15 ὁ] ως Per A Sy^s, p (c hiat)

2.17 — τουτου Per A L St Sy^s, p (videntur: c hiat)

2.21 αυτον (1)] το παιδιον Per A L St Pep Sy^s (c hiat), p, pal

2.25 — ιδου Per A Tus L Sy^s, p, pal [mss. A,C] (c hiat)

2.26 πριν η] εως αν Per A Sy^s, p, pal (c hiat)

2.33 ο πατηρ αυτου και η μητηρ] η μητηρ αυτου και Ιωσηφ Per A: "Joseph and his mother" Tus: *Gioseppo e Maria* (Ven hiat) L: *Ioseph ende Maria* St: *Joseph ende Maria Jhesus moeder* Pep: *Joseph & Marie* Sy^s, p (c hiat)

2.35 ρομφαια] Per: *lancia di dubbio* E^(com) Ishô'dâd of Merv (*Horae Sem.*, V, 159)

2.36 — ζησασα Per: *era rimasta* E: "seven days she had been with a husband" (ed. Lamy, III, 813) Sy^s: "seven days only with a husband she was" (Sy^c hiat) | απο της παρθενιας] Per: *vergine* (*bikr*) St: *in haren magedomme* (= "in her virginity")

2.38 και (1)] + αὑτη Per A L St Sy^s, p (c hiat)

2.41 οι γονεις αυτου] Per: *la gente di Gesù* A L: *Joseph ende Maria* Pep: *Joseph and Marie* Tus: *Gioseppo e Marie* Sy^s (c hiat) p: "and his kinsfolk"

2.43 οι γονεις αυτου] η μητηρ αυτου και Ιωσηφ Per A: "Joseph and his mother" Sy^p: "Joseph and his mother"

2.48 ο πατηρ σου καγω] εγω και ο πατηρ σου Per A E | οδυνωμενοι] + και λυπουμενοι Per: *afflitti con ansietà* E Pep: *wiþ mychel sorou3* Sy^c: "in trouble and in much perturbation"

2.49 ηδειτε] οιδατε Per A Ven L St

2.52 σοφια και ηλικια] ηλικια και σοφια Per A L: *in ijaren ende in wijsheiden* Z Sy^s, p, pal

3.19 γυναικος] + Φιλιππου Per A Pep Sy^p, har

3.23   — αρχομενος Per A Ven Aph Sy^{s, p (c hiat)}

5.3   εμβας δε εις εν των πλοιων ο ην Σιμωνος. ηρωτησεν αυτον απο
της γης επαναγαγειν ολιγον καθισας] και το εν αυτων ην του
Σιμωνος και ενεβη ο Ιησους εκαθισεν Per: *una nave era di
Simone Ṣafā. Gesù . . . sedette in quella nave, e commandò che
andassero un pochino lontano dalla terra* A Sy^{s, p (c hiat)} |
ολιγον] + in aquam Per A Sy^{s, p (c hiat)}

5.8   γονασιν] ποσιν Per A Ven Tus Sy^{s, p (c hiat)}

5.25   εφ ο κατεκειτο] την κλινην Per A Tus L Pep Sy^p

5.29   αυτων] αυτου Per A Sy^{har mg}

5.33   σοι] + μαθηται Per A Tus L St

6.10   αυτου] + ως η αλλη Per Tus L St Sy^{p, pal, har}

6.37   και ου (1)] ινα Per A Sy^s

7.11   — εγενετο Per A Ven L Pep Sy^{s (c hiat)}

7.18   — τινας Per A Ven Tus Sy^{s, p (c hiat)}

7.24   αγγελων] μαθητων Per A Sy^{s, p, har* (c hiat)}

11.2   λεγετε] + ουτως Per A Ven Sy^p

11.6   — προς με Per A St

11.7   ηδη] γαρ Per A Ven Tus Sy^{s, c}

11.8   φιλον αυτου] φιλιαν Per A Ven L^{mg} St Sy ^{s, c, p}

11.12   και] + εαν Per A Ven Tus Sy^{s, c, p}

12.15   — ορατε και Per A Sy^{s, c, p}

12.18   μειζονας οικοδομησω] οικοδομησω και ποιησω αυτας μειζονας
Per A L and St: *sal* (St: *salse*) *meerre maken* Pep: *he wolde
breke his berne and make it more* Sy^{s, c, p}

12.38   εισιν] + οι δουλοι Per A Ven Tus L Sy^{s, p}

JOHN

1.4   ην (2)] εστιν Per A Sy^{c, p (s hiat)}

1.16   — και (2) Per A L St

1.18   εξηγησατο] + ημιν Per E L Tus Sy^{c, pal (s hiat)}

1.27   incipit αυτος εστιν ο οπισω Per A (L hiat) Sy ^{p, har} | ερχομενος]
+ ην γεγονεν Per A Ven (L hiat)

1.29   βλεπει] + ο Ιωαννης Per A Pep Sy^p (L hiat)

1.31   βαπτιζων] βαπτιζειν Per: *affinchè battezzi* A Pep Sy^{s, c, p}

1.35   — παλιν Per A Ven Tus L Pep Z ^(Winchester codex) Sy^{s, c, p}

1.43   ηθελησεν] + ο Ιησους Per A Tus L Pep Sy^p

1.46   — και (1) Per A Sy^{s, p} | ειναι] εξελειν Per E Sy^s

2.6   — κειμεναι Per Tus Pep

2.10 τοτε] affert Per: *allora presenta* A Ven: *dali* [ms.: *dati*] Tus:
è dato L: *gheft* St: *geift* Pep: *setten forþ*

2.11 αρχην] primum Per: *primo* A Ven: *in prima* L Pep Sy^P

3.27 λαμβανειν] + αφ εαυτου Per A Sy^{P, pal, har}

3.32 ο] και ο Per A Tus L St Sy^{s, p, har}

Several of these readings are worthy of more extended comments.
The following remarks will serve to indicate the significance of the
Persian Harmony in relation to certain Tatianic variants preserved
in other witnesses.

Five of the readings in the list above reflect the embarrassment
that Tatian, with his encratite leanings,[1] felt regarding certain
expressions in the Gospels which refer to the relationship of Joseph
to Mary and of both of them to Jesus. Thus, for example, in Mt.
1.19 instead of representing the generally accepted Greek text,
'Ιωσὴφ δὲ ὁ ἀνὴρ αὐτῆς, δίκαιος ὤν, the Persian Harmony reads *e
Giuseppe era un uomo giusto* and thus avoids referring to Joseph as
Mary's husband by omitting the Greek definite article and possessive
pronoun and by taking ἀνήρ in a general and not a marital sense.
Ephraem quotes the same reading in his Commentary on the
Diatessaron, "Joseph, because he was a just man." Among the
other medieval harmonies, the Venetian Diatessaron reads *unde
Iosep veçando çò, cum ello fosse iusto et bono.* It may be added that
the Curetonian Syriac likewise avoids offending the ascetically
minded and reads, "Joseph, because he was a just man."

In Lk. 2 there are four references to Joseph and Mary which, in
the ordinary Greek text, doubtless appeared to certain in the early
church to require rephrasing in order to safeguard the virgin birth
of Jesus. In Lk. 2.33 ὁ πατὴρ αὐτοῦ καὶ ἡ μήτηρ is adjusted in the
Persian Harmony to read *la madre di lui e Giuseppe*, and in several
other Tatianic witnesses the proper name "Joseph" is used in
order to avoid referring to him as ὁ πατὴρ αὐτοῦ [*sc.* 'Ιησοῦ]. Thus,
the Arabic Diatessaron reads "Joseph and his mother," and the
Dutch Harmonies read *Ioseph ende Maria* (Liège ms.) and *Joseph
ende Maria Jhesus moeder* (Stuttgart ms.). The Pepysian Harmony
and the Tuscan form of the Italian Diatessaron (the Venetian form
omits this verse) agree with the Liège ms. in reading the two proper
names.

[1] See Daniël Plooij, "Ein enkratitische Glosse im Diatessaron; ein Beitrag
zur Geschichte der Askese in der alten Kirche," *ZNW*, XXII (1923), 1-16
(deals with an addition to Mt. 19.5-6).

In Lk. 2.41 and 43 the phrase οἱ γονεῖς αὐτοῦ is used in the Greek text in referring to Jesus' parents. In the former passage, however, the Persian Diatessaron prefers the more general term "people" in the phrase *la gente di Gesù*, as does also the Arabic Diatessaron (وابله).[1] The Sinaitic Syriac (Curetonian hiat) and Peshitta likewise use a word meaning "his kinsfolk" (ܐܝܢܣܚ). The Tuscan, Liège, and Pepysian Harmonies avoid the word for "parents" by using the proper names, "Joseph and Mary." In the latter passage the Persian Harmony also refuses to speak of Jesus' father and refers to *la madre di lui e Giuseppe*. The Arabic Diatessaron and the Peshitta similarly abstain from calling Joseph his father (but these two witnesses reverse the order, "Joseph and his mother").

In Lk. 2.48 the Greek text is less violently altered by the Persian Harmony. Here the words ἰδοὺ ὁ πατήρ σου κἀγώ have resisted substitution by synonyms; only the order of words has been altered, thereby putting, significantly enough, Mary in a position of prominence (as is also the case, it will have been observed, in each of the other three passages of Lk. 2 in the Persian Harmony). Both Ephraem and the Arabic Diatessaron agree with this inversion of order.[2]

The Persian Harmony partially supports the famous Tatianic variant of ascetical import regarding Anna, the prophetess (Lk. 2.36). The text, according to, א BGLXΞ 13 33 69 131, is ζήσασα μετὰ ἀνδρὸς ἔτη ἑπτα ἀπὸ τῆς παρθενίας αὐτῆς. Tatian, in accord with his encratite tendencies, had very probably read this verse, "seven days she had been with a husband,"[3] for so Ephraem refers to the passage in one of his Hymns[4] and so the Sinaitic transmits the passage (indeed, here the statement is even more emphatic by the presence of ܪܐܘܠܒ, "seven days *only* she ..."; Curetonian hiat). Though the Persian text does not reduce the conjugal life enjoyed by Anna to such a short time, it fails to render ζήσασα, a word which suggests a normal married life, and transforms the married estate into a celibate life: "She remained seven years a virgin with her

---

[1] Marmardji translates, with unjustifiable laxity, "ses parents."

[2] For a full discussion of these four passages see H. J. Vogels, "Die 'Eltern' Jesu (Textkritisches zu Lk. 2, 33 ff)," *Biblische Zeitschrift*, XI (1913), 33-34.

[3] Adelbert Merx argued that this reading is to be regarded as the original; *Die vier kanonischen Evangelien nach ihrem ältesten bekannten Texte*; II, ii, *Die Evangelien des Markus und Lukas nach der syrischen im Sinaikloster gefundenen Palimpsesthandschrift* (Berlin, 1905), pp. 207-208.

[4] Edited by T. J. Lamy, *Sancti Ephraem Syri hymni et sermones*, III (Mechliniae, 1889), col. 813, verse 17.

husband" (*era rimasta sette anni vergine* [كذا] *con suo marito*).
With this one may compare the Stuttgart Harmony which, instead
of reading ἀπὸ τῆς παρθενίας, has *in haren magedomme* ("in her
virginity").[1]

There were, it goes without saying, other reasons besides an
ascetical tendency which prompted Tatian to make adjustments
in the text of the Gospels. He was doubtless moved, for example,
by literalistic considerations. When he read in Mt. 2.23 that Jesus
"dwelt in a city called Nazareth that what had been spoken through
the prophets (διὰ τῶν προφητῶν) might be fulfilled, 'He shall be called
a Nazarene,' " he would have been uncertain and perplexed—as
others have been since his day—in attempting to discover the
precise Old Testament references to which the Evanglist alludes.
So far from there being a plurality of prophets who had spoken of
this matter, it is difficult enough to find in but one prophet an
allusion which could have suggested to the author of the First
Gospel such a prediction.[2] Tatian, it appears, sought to avoid the
multiplication of difficulties and read the singular number (διὰ τοῦ
προφήτου). This variant was perpetuated in the Tatianic tradition
of the following centuries. The Arabic Diatessaron (النبي), the
Dutch Harmonies (Liège: *die prophetie*; Stuttgart: *den prophete*),
both forms of the Italian Harmonies (Tuscan: *per lo profeta*; Venetian: *cossì fo conpiude le profeçie*), as well as the Persian Diatessaron
(*per la lingua del profeta*)—all preserve the singular number either as
"prophet" or "prophecy." The Sinaitic, Curetonian, Peshitta, and
Palestinian Syriac agree in reading ܟܬܒܐ.

Another attempt to conform a quotation to the Old Testament
(in the Syriac version) appears in Mt. 4.6. Here the promise that
angels will bear one up on their hands (ἐπὶ χειρῶν) was brought into
closer harmony with the Syriac Psalter (91.12), which reads ܥܠ
ܕܪ̈ܥܝܗܘܢ, "on their arms (or shoulders)"—contrary to the Hebrew,
עַל־כַּפַּיִם, and the Septuagint, ἐπὶ χειρῶν.[3] The reading of the

---

[1] For a discussion of the evidence as far as it was known in 1913, see H. J.
Vogels, "Lk. 2, 36 im Diatessaron" *BZ*, XI (1913), 168-171. Cf. also the
brief remarks by Messina, *Notizia*, 57-59.

[2] Doubtless it was the Hebrew נֵצֶר of Is. 11.1 which supplied the Evangelist
with the germinal idea developed in Mt. 2.23; there is no evidence, however,
that Tatian could read Hebrew. For a discussion of the problems involved in
Mt. 2.23, see any critical commentary, especially those by Strack and
Billerbeck and by Lagrange.

[3] The meaning of χείρ, "hand and arm, arm," is confined almost entirely
to poetry and medical authors (see, *inter alios*, Stephanus, *Thesaurus graecae
linguae, s.v., init.*).

Persian Harmony, *sulle loro braccia*, is in conformity with the Arabic Diatessaron, على ازرعهم, "upon their arms." Furthermore, even though Ephraem does not quote the entire promise (simply "they shall keep thee, lest at any time thy foot be dashed against a stone"), in his subsequent comments he discloses that he is aware of the tradition regarding the arms or shoulders of the angels.[1] This variant, it may be remarked, has left no trace among the Western witnesses to Tatian, being confined to the Eastern orbit, including also the Sinaitic and Curetonian Syriac and two manuscripts of the Peshitta.[2]

In addition to variants which are the result of ascetic or harmonistic tendencies, there are many others of a miscellaneous character which appear in both the Persian Harmony and in one or more of the Eastern and Western witnesses to Tatian. A Diatessaric reading which Peters detected in the West-Saxon version[3] seems to have left a trace in the Persian Harmony also. The statement in Mt. 2.9 regarding the Magi: οἱ δὲ ἀκούσαντες τοῦ βασιλέως ἐπορεύθησαν, appears in slightly divergent forms in the following Tatianic witnesses. The reading of the Venetian Harmony, *e li magi aldito çò, partironssi dal re*, suggests an underlying Old Latin text running something like *magi cum audivissent (hoc) a rege abierunt*, which reappears in the West-Saxon version *ðā hī þaet gebod gehȳrdon, þā fērdon hī* ("When they had heard the command, then they went").[4] Similarly in the East the Arabic Diatessaron by its reading, وهم لما سمعوا من الملك انط لقوا ("and they, when they had heard [this] from the king, went on their way"), presupposes a form of the

---

[1] Ephraem's comment uses the Armenian word *Թիկանց* , which usually means "shoulders, middle of the back" (Moesinger translates: *in medio dorso suo*; Leloir translates: *in dorso suo*), but it also may mean "arms" (see the Armenian lexica by Ciakciak and by Miskgian).

[2] They are manuscripts 2 and 40 in Pusey and Gwilliam's *Tetraevangelium*, of the sixth century and A.D. 548 respectively. The Peshitta text of the parallel in Lk. 4.11 reads "on their arms."

[3] Curt Peters, "Der Diatessarontext von Mt. 2, 9 und die westsächsische Evangeliumversion," *B*, XXIII (1942), 323-332.

[4] Peters could have strengthened his case by mentioning the fact that two similar readings appear in (1) the Old Mercian version, printed by Skeat in his edition of the Anglo-Saxon Gospels: *þa hie þa geherdon ðæs kyninges word eodun þonan*, and (2) in an Old German rendering of Gospel pericopes (Rheinau ms. 158b, Zürich): *do si des koniges rede gehorten* ... (see Hans Vollmer, *Verdeutschung der Evangelien und sonstiger Teile des Neuen Testaments von den ersten Anfängen bis Luther* [*Bibel und deutsche Kultur*, V; Potsdam, 1935], p. 97).

Syriac like that which is preserved in the Curetonian, ܗܘ ܕܝ
ܟܕ ܫܡܥܘ ܡܠܟܐ ܡܢ ܡܠܟܐ ܐܙܠܘ ("now they, when they received the command from the king, went"); the Sinaitic reads
ܡܠܟܐ.1 instead of ܡܢ ܡܠܟܐ.1 Likewise in the Persian Harmony,
quando sentirono la parola del re obviously represents a form of the
Matthean text which, instead of construing the genitive τοῦ βασιλέως
as the object of ἀκούσαντες, inserted a noun or pronoun as the object
of the Greek participle, as is preserved today in the various circum-
locutions set forth above.

In Mt. 11.17 (and the parallel in Lk. 7.32) the complaint, "We
have piped (ηὐλήσαμεν) to you, and you did not dance; we have
wailed, and you did not mourn," was undoubtedly read by Tatian
with a verb of singing instead of playing. Both Eastern and Western
branches of Tatianic tradition agree in this variant. Thus, the
Arabic (غنّينا) and the Persian Harmony (*cantammo [sarwad
guftīm]*) join with the Venetian (*noi avemo chantato*), the Tuscan
(*noi cantamo*), and the Dutch Harmonies (*wi habben u g(h)esongen*).

Several variants are the result of a certain fullness of expression.
For example, instead of representing exactly the Greek text of Lk.
1.13, μὴ φοβοῦ, Ζαχαρία, διότι εἰσηκούσθη ἡ δέησίς σου, καὶ ἡ γυνή σου
Ἐλισάβετ γεννήσει [*var. lect.* γενέσει] υἱόν σοι,, the Persian Harmony
reads, *non temere, o Zaccaria, perchè la tua preghiera fu udita presso
Dio; e Elisabetta, tua moglie, concepirà e ti partorirà un figliolo.*
The phrase represented by *presso Dio* in the Persian is quoted
thrice by Ephraem from Tatian's Diatessaron ("thy prayer is heard
before God") and once by Aphraates (ܐܠܗܐ ܩܕܡ). The Pepysian
Harmony contains both of the expansions which are designated
above by spaced type in the Persian: *And þe aungel reconforted hym
and seide þat þe bisechyng þat he had beden for þe folk was herd
tofore God, and that his wife schulde conceyuen & beren a son.*

Another example of a certain redundance of expression is in
Lk. 12.18 where, in the usual Greek text, the Rich Fool says to
himself: "I will pull down my barns and build larger ones (μείζονας
οἰκοδομήσω)." This is represented in the Persian Harmony by *dist-
meggerò i magazzini, e edificherò e farò altri più amplii.* The Arabic
Diatessaron reads, "... I will build again and will make greater
ones," and the Syriac tradition (both Old Syriac and Peshitta)
agrees, "I will build and enlarge (ܐܘܪܒ) them."

---

1 This variant escaped Burkitt's attention in his *Evangelion da-Mepharreshe.*

On the other hand, a few Tatianic readings, such as the following example, are somewhat abbreviated. In Mt. 5.18 the saying about ἰῶτα ἓν ἢ κεραία οὐ μὴ παρέλθῃ probably appeared in the Diatessaron in the form, "the iota [or, yôd] letter will not pass away," as is disclosed by the following evidence. The verse occurs twice in Aphraates and both times he quotes it, ܪܝܘ ܐܬܘܬܐ ܚܕܐ ("one yôd letter"). This is also the reading of the Sinaitic Syriac. In the Syriac *Liber graduum* the saying is quoted in the same form, and the comment is added to the effect that this means the entire ten commandments, for the letter yôd is equivalent to the numeral ten.[1] In medieval times the Venetian Diatessaron read the saying in the form, *una letera non se perderà*. The Liège and Stuttgart manuscripts of the Dutch Harmonies read, *sal ene lettre van der wet nie(e)t achter bliven*.[2] In the Persian Harmony the saying appears in the form, *una parola . . . non svanirà*.

In Lk. 11.8 Tatian introduced a slight variant which unaccountably escaped von Soden's keen eye while combing the Arabic Diatessaron for evidence of Tatian's all-pervading influence. Instead of reading "though he will not get up and give him anything because he is his friend" (. . . διὰ τὸ εἶναι φίλον αὐτοῦ, with B אCLX33 124 157 etc.), Tatian substituted φιλίαν for φίλον αὐτοῦ. Eastern representatives, such as the Arabic Diatessaron (الصداقة) and the Persian Harmony (*a causa dell'amicizia*), agree with the testimony of Western witnesses to the Diatessaron, such as the Venetian (*per l'amistade*), the Liège (*om de vrinschap*), and the Stuttgart (*dor die vrienscap*), in the support of φιλίαν. The Syriac tradition (Old Syriac and Peshitta) likewise preserves the word which undoubtedly appeared in Tatian's Diatessaron, ܪܚܡܘܬܐ.

Finally it may be mentioned that the Persian Harmony contains a reading which may have stood in two different Harmonies of the second Christian century. In addition to Tatian's Diatessaron it appears that Theophilus of Antioch had also drawn up a Harmony of the four Gospels which, according to the testimony of Jerome, was a monument of his genius.[3] Though many scholars have be-

---

[1] *Liber graduum*, XXII, 21; col. 684, ed. Kmosko.

[2] Cf. Daniël Plooij, *A Primitive Text of the Diatessaron* (Leyden, 1923). p. 38.

[3] Jerome, *Ep.* CXXI, 6, 15 (ed. Hilberg, III, 24-25): Theophilus, Antiochenae ecclesiae septimus post Petrum apostolum episcopus, qui quattuor evangelistarum in unum opus dicta conpingens ingenii sui nobis monumenta demisit . . . .

lieved that Jerome confused Theophilus with Tatian, recently attention has been drawn to what may well be a citation from Theophilus's Harmony. It is found in the celebrated *Liber sancti Iacobi*, or the Codex Calixtinus.[1] In the course of one of the spurious sermons attributed to Pope Calixtus II (died A.D. 1124), reference is made as follows to the incident recorded in Luke 9.54, "Cum vidissent autem discipuli eius Iacobus et Iohannes, dixerunt: Domine, vis dicimus ut ignis descendat de celo et consummat illos, sicut Elias fecit? Istud verbum 'sicut Elias fecit' non multis codicibus habetur, sed in quibus scribitur melius est ut in illis sit quam absit, quia beatus Lucas in evangelio suo et inde Theophilus Antiocenus episcopus qui prius quatuor evangelia in uno volumine rescripsit."[2] This passage not only seems to confirm what Jerome wrote regarding Theophilus's Harmony, but more significantly quotes a reading from it, "sicut Elias fecit." Other Harmonies which also contain this variant are the Persian, the Stuttgart manuscripts, and the Arabic (here, however, the Arabic Diatessaron may rest upon the Peshitta text, which, unlike Sy[s] and Sy[c], also has the addition).

The history of the investigation of Tatian's Diatessaron leads one into many byways. Though the Mechitarists' edition of the Armenian text of Ephraem's commentary on the Diatessaron was published in 1836, it was not until nearly half a century later (1876) that Aucher's Latin rendering made it available to a wider public.[3] Even then, in some unaccountable way, several years elapsed

---

[1] See B. de Gaiffier, "Une citation de l'harmonie évangélique de Théophile d'Antioche dans le 'Liber sancti Iacobi,'" *Mélanges en l'honneur de Monseigneur Michel Andrieu* (Strasbourg, 1956), pp. 173-179.

[2] Edited by Walter M. Whitehill, *Liber sancti Iacobi. Codex Calixtinus* (Saint-Jacques de Compoatelle, 1944), p. 121. In the quotation, as de Gaiffier points out (*op. cit.*, p. 176), after the word "Lucas" it is necessary to understand some formula such as "ita habet."

[3] Curiously enough, during those very years it was debated whether Tatian had in fact composed a Diatessaron at all! In an erudite but wrong-headed anonymous work entitled *Supernatural Religion: an Inquiry into the Reality of Divine Revelation* (London, 1874; revised edition 1879), the author (said to have been Walter Richard Cassels) soberly set forth arguments for disbelieving Eusebius, Theodoret, and other Fathers when they speak of the Diatessaron. Even J. B. Lightfoot, in his elaborate reply to Cassels in *The Contemporary Review* (1877), could not point to any irrefutable proof of the existence of the Diatessaron—though ironically enough he had in his own library a copy of the Mechitarists' edition of Ephraem's Commentary on the Diatessaron! Twelve years later in a note appended to his *Essays on the Work Entitled Supernatural Religion reprinted from the Contemporary Review*

before New Testament scholars began to be aware of its importance.[1] Since then, however, unrelenting efforts have been expended
in the attempt to reconstruct the original text of the Diatessaron.[2]
The preceding analysis will have suggested something of the significance of the Persian Harmony for Diatessaron-*Forschung*. Although
this medieval Harmony has no relationship with Tatian's Diatessaron so far as its external framework is concerned, it is by no
means worthless as a witness to the original Diatessaron. Its value
for the textual criticism of the Gospels lies in the presence of many
undoubted Tatianic readings which are embedded within its text.
These Tatianisms show a remarkable affinity with similar readings
preserved in other Eastern and Western witnesses to the Diatessaron.

(London, 1889), Lightfoot confesses: "I had for some years possessed a copy
of this work in four volumes, and the thought had more than once crossed my
mind that possibly it might throw light on Ephraem's mode of dealing with
the Gospels, as I knew that it contained notes on St. Paul's Epistles or some
portions of them. I did not, however, then possess sufficient knowledge of
Armenian to sift its contents, but I hoped to investigate the matter when I
had mastered enough of the language" (pp. 287 f.).

[1] Apparently the first notice taken of Aucher's Latin translation was by
Ezra Abbot in his book, *The Authorship of the Fourth Gospels; External
Evidence* (Boston, 1880), p. 55. In the following year Theodor Zahn published
his reconstruction of Tatian's Diatessaron from Ephraem's Commentary
(*Tatians Diatessaron*, being vol. 1 of his *Forschungen zur Geschichte des neu-
testamentlichen Kanons* [Erlangen, 1881]).

[2] Among peripheral studies J. Rendel Harris's investigation of "The
Gospel Harmony of Clement of Llanthony" (*JBL*, XLIII [1924], 349-362) is
valuable chiefly in showing how Tatian must have gone about the task of
constructing his harmony.

CHAPTER FIVE

RECENT SPANISH CONTRIBUTIONS TO THE TEXTUAL CRITICISM OF THE NEW TESTAMENT

It has been the fate of more than one significant contribution to theological and Biblical knowledge to remain unnoticed, sometimes for many years, by the scholarly world in general because the authors of these studies happened to have written in languages other than German, French, Latin, or English. One thinks, for example, of Kierkegaard's carefully polished treatises in Danish, or of Andrej N. Popov's publication in Russian (in 1866) of parts of the Slavonic version of Josephus's *History of the Jewish War*, the significance of which was not appreciated until many decades later.

The present chapter reports the gist of about fifty contributions to the textual criticism of the New Testament made by Spanish scholars from the year 1925 onwards. Although certain of these publications are of great significance, they have been ignored by most German, British, and American textual critics. The date 1925 has not been chosen arbitrarily; it is a quite appropriate *terminus a quo* inasmuch as, with the exception of three or four earlier publications,[1] the bulk of serious textual work by Hispanic scholars began in that year. Within this period the principal authors who have contributed in various ways to the advance of the textual criticism of the New Testament are Mateo del Álamo (1878-1947), Teófilo Ayuso Marazuela,[2] and José M. Bover, S. J. (1877-1954).[3]

---

[1] They include Z. García Villada, *Catálogo de los códices y documentos de la catedral de León* (Madrid, 1919), and Marino Revilla, "El códice Ovetense de los Evangelios y la Biblia de Valvanera," *CD*, cxvii (1919), 393-399; cxviii (1919), 23-28; cxx (1920), 48-55, 190-210. This was published separately as *Fragmenta Biblica Scurialensia*; *la Biblia de Valvanera y el códice Ovetense de los Evangelios* (El Escorial, 1920), 46 pp. Z. García Villada, "Nota a un artículo de Lowe sobre la fecha del códice Toledano de la Vulgata," *EE*, iii (1924), 324-325, called attention to Dionisio Fernández Zapico, "Sobre la antigüedad del códice Toledano de la Vulgata," *RF*, xxxix (1914), 362-371, who argued on the basis of philological data that this manuscript should be dated, not in the eighth century (as E. A. Lowe dates it), but in the ninth or tenth century.

[2] While these pages were passing through the press, word was received of the death of Mons. Ayuso on September 18, 1962.

[3] Bover died October 22, 1954; see "In memoriam Bover," *Revista*

The first mentioned was a Benedictine at Silos in Burgos; Ayuso was formerly at the Roman Catholic Seminary in Segovia and latterly Canónigo Lectoral at Zaragoza; and the last mentioned was Professor of the Holy Scriptures in the Colegio Máximo de S. Ignacio at Barcelona (Serriá) and Adviser to the Papal Biblical Commission. For convenience of listing, the following survey will (1) report general articles and textual analyses of Greek manuscripts of the New Testament; (2) report textual analyses of Latin manuscripts, concluding with an account of work done by Spanish scholars on the Latin Vulgate; (3) summarize critical studies on certain individual variants; and (4) describe and evaluate the plan and execution of Bover's edition of the Greek and Latin New Testament.

I. TEXTUAL ANALYSES OF GREEK MANUSCRIPTS

In 1925 Bover began his textual publications with a survey of the chief developments in the textual criticism of the New Testament from about 1900 onwards.[1] In his discussion of the merits and demerits of the Western text there appeared a significant statement which revealed Bover's dissatisfaction with various one-sided emphases and which was prophetic of the direction his own work was to take in the future: "If there does not exist a text truly neutral as Westcott and Hort pretended, to which the Western must yield first place, and if the contaminating influence of Tatian upon all the codices and versions of the New Testament, as von Soden imagined, is pure fancy, the value of the Western text remains, which, though one may not admit it *in toto*, neither can he discredit it *in toto*."[2]

Española de teología, XV (1955), 107-126; "In memoriam el P. José M. Bover y Olivar," EE, XXIX (1955), 5-12; and "El Padre José María Bover, S. J." EB, segunda época, XIII (1954), 333-368.

[1] "Boletín Bíblico del Nuevo Testamento; la crítica textual," EE, IV (1925), 306-318, 416-434.

[2] *Ibid.*, p. 424. This position was amplified and elaborated in Bover's inaugural lecture, *Critica textualis Novi Testamenti in crisim revocata, principia tenenda atque applicanda*, oratio habita in Collegio Maximo Sarrianensi S. Ignatii Societatis Iesu (Madrid, 1930), pp. 10 f. and 21, note 19. A few sentences of this note are worthy of quotation: "At incorruptus ille textus hodie ubi servatur? In documentis occidentalibus? An in recensionibus alexandrina ac caesariensi? Indubia facta prorsus evincunt purum textum neque in solis occidentalibus, neque in solis recensionibus integrum conservari. Occidentalia enim documenta a pristina puritate saepe desciverunt; recensiones vero, dum eam restituere contendunt, ad eam saepe nequaquam redierunt. Igitur partim in his partim in illis genuinus textus servatur." Bover's inaugural lecture was also published in EB, I (1930) 329-354; compare his "Crítica de los críticos," *ibid.*, 301-312.

During the same year Bover published a study of "Un fragmento de San Lucas (22, 44-63) en un papiro recientemente descubierto."[1] In this he analyzes the text of the parchment (not papyrus, as the title wrongly indicates) fragment[2] designated 0171, dating from the fourth century, and shows it to be "indisputably Western."

In 1930 while analyzing "Dos papiros egipcios del N.T. reciente-mente publicados,"[3] Bover defended certain textual theories of central importance to an editor of the Greek Testament. The two fragments are P^{47}, containing Matt. 26.15-52 and edited first by H. A. Sanders,[4] and 0162, a leaf of vellum containing John 2.11-22 and first published by Grenfell and Hunt as P. Oxy. 847.[5] Refining Sanders's methods of textual analysis of P^{37}, by which the Michigan scholar maintained that the papyrus was Western in textual complexion, Bover showed that it belongs to family θ. Contrary to Lagrange, who regarded[6] the θ type of text as a mixture of the β and δ types, Bover argued that the three are independent and equally primitive.[7] The other fragment, 0162, is unmistakably Alexandrian and discloses the closest affinity with codex B.[8] In discussing the value of the β type of text Bover questioned the validity of the almost universal high regard for this type of text and for the canon of textual criticism, "lectio brevior, potior."[9]

A year later in his discussion of the "Textus codicis Claromontani (D) in epistula ad Galatas,"[10] Bover concluded that, contrary to the opinion held by some scholars that there is no Western text in the Pauline Epistles,[11] in Galatians codex Claromontanus preserves a second century text which corresponds in complexion to that

[1] *EE*, IV (1925), 293-305.
[2] It was first edited in *Pubblicazioni della Società Italiana per la ricerca dei papiri greci e latini in Egitto; Papiri greci e latini*, I, no. 2, and II, no. 124, and then by Carl Wessely in *PO*, XVIII, 452.
[3] *EE*, IX (1930), 289-320.
[4] *HTR*, XIX (1926), 215-226.
[5] *The Oxyrhynchus Papyri*, VI (London, 1908), 4-5.
[6] "Un nouveau papyrus évangelique," *RB*, XXXVIII (1929), 161-177. Lagrange disputed Sanders's evaluation of the papyrus and termed it Alexandrian.
[7] *EE*, IX (1930), 305.
[8] *Ibid.*, p. 306.
[9] *Ibid.*, pp. 311-315. See p. 140 below.
[10] *B*, XII (1931), 199-218.
[11] E.g. Lagrange in his commentaries on Romans and Galatians. He subse-quently changed his opinion, *Critique textuelle; II, La critique rationnelle* (Paris, 1935), pp. 481-485.

exhibited by codex Bezae in the Gospels. In discussing the critical value of this type of text, he warned against an uncritical acceptance of an Alexandrian reading simply because it is Alexandrian.[1]

A similar note is struck in Bover's article, "Un notable códice bíblico (2005 = α 1435) de la Biblioteca Escurialense."[2] From an analysis of the variants in Galatians, Philippians, and Colossians in this fourteenth century minuscule manuscript, he concluded[3] that its text preserves many primitive and archaic elements whose affinities lie with the Western text, namely, with D F G and Sy[h]. Bover again insisted that "though B and Θ are the better manuscripts, they are not the only good ones,"[4] and that it has not been proved that "they contain such a monopoly of the good readings that not one can be found which is not represented in them."[5]

Of equal if not greater significance than these articles by Bover are two studies by Ayuso. Shortly after the publication of the Chester Beatty papyrus of the Gospels (P[45]), Ayuso set himself to the task of examining its text in comparison with the so-called Caesarean text.[6] He first pointed out that the critical apparatus prepared by Kenyon, the editor of the papyrus, occasionally is erroneous and more frequently is incomplete, because Kenyon neglected to utilize the evidence of manuscript 28 and of the Sinaitic Syriac, Armenian, and Georgian versions. On the basis of independent research in the Caesarean witnesses, Ayuso collected 55 variant readings in which P[45] in Mark agrees with other Caesarean witnesses but disagrees with B, D, and the Textus Receptus. In comparing his statistics with the less elaborate tables drawn up by Kenyon, Ayuso showed that P[45] in Mark is much more closely related to the

[1] Bover certainly is correct when he says: "Fatendum quidem est, alexandrinos testes, ubi sive occidentales sive alios secum sentientes habent, genuinam fere praebere lectionem. At vero ubi, a ceteris omnibus discrepantes soli incedunt, eorum testimonium concordi ceterorum suffragio praeponere nimis arbitrarium videtur. Nisi enim alexandrinos ab omni prorsus errore immunes censeas,—quo autem iure, nescio,—facilius credo explicueris variantem alexandrinam a recensore esse creatam, quam ceteros testes universos, tam inter se dispares, in errorem convenisse. Universalem testium corruptionem facilius asseras quam probes," B, XII (1931), 214.

[2] EB, IV (1934), 249-267.

[3] Ibid., p. 267.

[4] Ibid., p. 263.

[5] Ibid., p. 264.

[6] "El texto cesariense del papiro de Chester Beatty en el Evangelio de San Marcos," EB, IV (1934), 268-281.

Caesarean group (W, fam. 13, 565, 28, Θ, 700, and fam. 1, in this sequence) than had heretofore been supposed.[1]

In the second of Ayuso's important investigations of P[45], entitled "¿ Texto cesariense o precesariense?"[2] he subjects its text in four chapters of Mark (chs. 7, 8, 9, 11) to a painstaking and methodical examination, comparing it in almost every possible way with the witnesses of the so-called Caesarean text, and comes to the following conclusions.[3]

1. There exists a homogeneous family of Greek codices and versions which represent a type of text different from those of von Soden and Westcott-Hort; a type which is not represented in B, in D, or in the Textus Receptus.

2. To this family has been given the name Caesarean, because it was believed that it had its origin in Caesarea. In reality, it is anterior to the transfer of Origen to that city. Therefore, it is not Caesarean but pre-Caesarean. One must seek its origin in Egypt, and, as it seems, not in Alexandria but in the central region (Fayyum-Gizeh).

3. This family exhibits manifest cohesion and homogeneity. But within that unity there is in the family a double modality or tendency, represented by P[45], W, 28, λ, and φ, on the one hand, and by Θ, 565, 700, Origen, Eusebius, the Georgian, the Armenian, and perhaps the Sinaitic Syriac, on the other.

4. This diversity has a reasonable explanation. There exists a primitive element and a recensional element. The primitive element is represented by the first of these two sub-groups; the recensional is due to Origen in Caesarea and is represented by the second.

5. There is a marvellous correlation between the critical element and the topographical situation. In fact, if a dividing line were drawn at Suez, the witnesses which represent the primitive element and which have more affinity among themselves belong to the West, and the others to the East.

6. For the reconstruction of the archetype, one must pay more attention to the first sub-group than to the second, because it is more ancient and represents better the primitive state of the text.

7. It is evident that this family will provoke a most severe repercussion in textual criticism. We find ourselves with a most ancient and perfectly defined text, which is carried back by the documents themselves to the beginning of the third century,

---

[1] *Ibid.*, p. 280.

[2] *B*, XVI (1935), 369-415; the subtitle is "su realidad y su trascendencia en la crítica textual del Nuevo Testamento."

[3] *Ibid.*, pp. 414-415. Except for certain minor condensations, the language of this summary is Ayuso's.

and in its origin toward the end of the second century; therefore, apart from internal considerations of its value, its antiquity demands the primacy.[1]

Of considerably less scientific value is the popularly written article, "El gran problema de la crítica textual y los Evangelios,"[2] in which Ayuso surveys the state of textual criticism before and after the most recent discoveries of New Testament papyri.

In a wide-ranging historical survey and critique of the methods of editing the text of the Greek Testament,[3] Ayuso first traces the chief stadia of criticism ("the hegemony of the *Textus Receptus*; the hegemony of the critical text; the return to the second century"), and then treats of the multiplicity of theories which have been set forth by way of attempting to isolate and evaluate the several types of New Testament texts. After the "arrecensional" method of editing the New Testament had been discovered to be false and inconvenient, as regards both the text and the apparatus, editors began to group the evidence into families and to attempt to go behind the major recensions of the third and fourth centuries to the "prerecensional" text of the second and third centuries. This latter has been transmitted independently, Ayuso argues, through the Western and the pre-Caesarean texts. He concludes, "If each of these families or groups has primal value in isolation, the sum of the two conjointly can have decisive value."[4]

A contribution to our knowledge of the Greek text of the Apocalypse, and, indeed, to the advance of methodology in analyzing the relationship and critical value of codices, was made by Bover in an article entitled, " ¿ El códice 1841 (= 127) es el mejor representante del Apocalipsis?"[5] Here he attempted to refine the usual methods of ascertaining the affinities of a newly discovered manuscript. Kenyon had counted, for example, the number of agreements and disagreements of P^{47} with ℵ, A, C, P, B, and the Textus Receptus. From his table of these figures, however, it is exceedingly

[1] For another summary of Ayuso's elaborate analyses, giving a somewhat different selection of data, see pp. 63 ff. above.

[2] *Arbor*, I (1944), 165-183.

[3] " ¿Texto arrecensional, recensional o prerecensional? Contribución al estudio de la crítica textual de los Evangelios " *EB*, segunda época, VI (1947), 35-90.

[4] *Ibid.*, p. 90.

[5] *EE*, XVIII (1944), 165-185. In this article Bover follows Hoskier's numbers of manuscripts of the Apocalypse; I have substituted the more usual Gregory equivalents.

difficult to form more than a rather vague judgment of the degree
of relationship of P⁴⁷ with any or all of the manuscripts. Bover, by
a simple additional step, expressed the exact proportion of affinity
(or lack of affinity) between the papyrus and each manuscript.
Since in every instance in Kenyon's table the number of discrepan-
cies exceeds the number of agreements with P⁴⁷, Bover subtracted
the latter from the former and found that the difference in the case
of א is 14; of C, 14; of P, 24; of A, 42; of B, 86; of the Textus
Receptus, 120. Thus it is possible to measure the degree of dimin-
ishing affinity with P⁴⁷, with automatic adjustment in the case of
manuscripts (such as C) which have serious lacunae.

Bover also utilized other methods of discovering relationship
among manuscripts. He confirmed the results of the process just
described by evaluating P⁴⁷ on the basis of readings in which this
papyrus agrees with only one or two other manuscripts, finding
that in such readings it agrees with א far more often than with any
other manuscript. Next he counted the number of times that P⁴⁷
agrees or disagrees with 67 variant readings approved as primitive
by himself and other critics. The figures are as follows: with codex
1841, 45 agreements; with א, 45; with C, 35; with P, 32; with B,
32; with A, 24. An analysis of the affinities of the papyrus with
minuscule codices reveals that it agrees most often with 1841, 1006,
2053, 1611, 2321, 1778 (and others) in descending order.

In summing up the critical value of P⁴⁷ Bover's judgment is that
"the papyrus is a mediocre copy [copia mediana] of an excellent
type of text."[1]

In Bover's stemma of the probable reconstruction of the families
of some of the more important manuscripts of the Apocalypse,[2] he
distinguishes three series of manuscripts: the pre-recensional, the
archetypes or bases of the recensions, and the representatives of
the different recensions or families. Among the manuscripts with
a pre-recensional type of text, P⁴⁷ and 1841 excel, after which
follow 1778, 1611, 2053, 2329, and others, more or less contami-
nated by the recensions. In the second series are the unknown
archetypes of the three principal recensions: the Caesarean (X),
the Alexandrian (Y), and the Antiochian (Z), with affinities between the first two and P⁴⁷ and 1841 respectively. The rest of the
diagram, which involves the usual *sigla* of manuscripts and of von

[1] *Ibid.*, p. 174.
[2] *Ibid.*, p. 183.

Soden's three main types of texts (which are enclosed within parentheses), is self-explanatory.

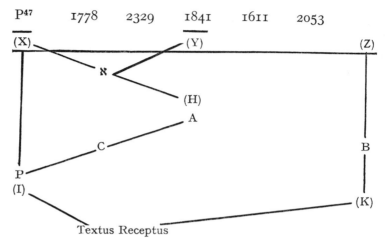

II. Textual Analyses of Latin Manuscripts

Both Bover and Ayuso have also given some attention to the text of the Old Latin version and Jerome's Vulgate. In 1925 the former briefly described and analyzed three Vulgate manuscripts of about the thirteenth century, each with a text generally similar to that in Irish manuscripts of the Vulgate.[1] In an article published two years later and entitled, "Un fragmento de la vetus latina (Act. I, 15-26) en un epistolario del siglo XIII,"[2] Bover provided a collation of a pericope from a medieval lectionary in the Archaeological Museum of Barcelona. Its text, he found, is in closest agreement with Gigas (twenty-one agreements) and with Perpinianus (eighteen agreements). The remainder of the lectionary presents the common Vulgate text.

In his "Boletín de Sagrada Escritura; la nueva edición de la Vulgata," Bover examined and rejected Dom Quentin's *règle de fer*.[3] The same author, in his "La Vulgata en España,"[4] set the

---

[1] "Tres códices Tarraconenses de la Vulgata," *EE*, iv (1925), 382-391.
[2] *EE*, vi (1927), 331-334.
[3] *EE*, vi (1927), 79-95, 186-207, 415-428.
[4] *EB*, segunda época, I (1941-42), 13-40, 167-185. A summary of this article, which Bover delivered as an address entitled, "La Vulgata en España; lo poco que se sabe y lo mucho que queda por investigar," appeared in the official report, *La primera semana Bíblica española*, prepared by Ayuso and published by Asociación para el fomento de los estudios Bíblicos espa-

history of the Latin Bible in Spain in a wider European framework of three periods: "The first epoch, which extends from the fifth to the eighth century, is the epoch of local texts and of autonomous transcriptions. During it two great families predominated: the Spanish and the Italian, or, better, the Italo-Anglican: besides these, two other families of less importance appear: the Irish and the French."[1] The two primitive Spanish editions by Peregrinus[2] and St. Isidore belong in this period. "The second epoch is characterized by two great recensions made about the year 800: that of Alcuin, based on the Italian or Italo-Anglican text, and that of Theodulf, of Visigothic origin, based on the Spanish or Hispanicized text .... The third epoch is that of an artificial, uniform text, produced by the Sorbonne of Paris."[3] In tracing the fortunes of the Vulgate in Spain, the author indicates the relationship between various codices of the Vulgate and their position in his chronological outline.

Of more significance are Ayuso's dozen or more publications in the series, "Contribución al estudio de la Vulgata en España." With the exception of a general article, "El texto de la Vulgata,"[4] these are chiefly palaeographical descriptions of various Spanish manuscripts of the Vulgate, with collations of selected chapters in the Old and New Testaments, and critical analyses of the nature of the variants.[5] The most elaborate of these studies is his edition of *La Biblia de Oña*,[6] which, in addition to the customary information,

ñoles (Zaragoza, [1941]), pp. 87-90. Bover had dealt earlier with the same subject, "Para la historia de la Vulgata en España, un proyecto y un llamamiento," *EB*, I (1930), 89-93.

[1] *EB*, segunda época, I (1941-42), 13.

[2] In " ¿Bachiarius Peregrinus?" *EE*, VII (1928), 361-366, Bover argued that a good case can be made for the identification of Peregrinus with the famous monk Bachiarius.

[3] *EB*, segunda época, I (1941-42), 13-14.

[4] *EB*, segunda época, II (1943), 23-74.

[5] Those which include material pertaining to the New Testament are: "La Biblia de Calahorra," *EB*, segunda época, I (1941-42), 241-271; "La Biblia de Calatayud," *U*, XVIII (1941), 529-550; "La segunda Biblia de Calatayud," *U*, XX (1943), 201-231; "La Biblia de Lérida," *U*, XXI (1944), 25-65; "La Biblia de Huesca," *U*, XXIII (1946), 161-210; "Las Biblias de Escorial; el códice latino B-II-17, interesante y poco conocido," *CD*, CLVIII (1946), 127-177, and *Las Biblias de Zaragoza* (Zaragoza, 1947), In addition to these Ayuso has published certain other articles in *EB*, segunda época, which pertain entirely to the Vulgate text of the Old Testament.

[6] This is further defined in the subtitle, *Notable fragmento casi desconocido de un códice Visigótico homogéneo de la Biblia de San Isidoro de León* (Zaragoza, 1945).

includes a complete photographic reproduction, a collation, and an essay on the classification of Spanish Biblical manuscripts.

These several studies were climaxed in 1953 by the publication of the first of eight projected volumes dealing with the Old Latin Bible in Spain, its origin, relationships, value, and influence.[1] The preliminary volume, which is handsomely printed in folio format, contains a comprehensive bibliography embracing some 5500 items, a general introduction relating to the Old Latin version, and a study of the problems of isolating the Spanish form of the Old Latin version. Ayuso finds that the Spanish Old Latin is distinct from the Italian and African forms of the Old Latin, and that it was not a single version but existed in several forms. These have been preserved in four types of sources: the Biblical manuscripts, the marginal notes, the Mozarabic liturgy, and Spanish church fathers.

Ayuso furnishes a most useful catalogue of manuscripts containing some form of Old Latin text. These manuscripts are listed according to the Biblical (including apocryphal) books involved— the Psalms being represented by the greatest number of manuscripts, namely 287. Equally valuable is the list of nearly one thousand ecclesiastical writers of the first seven centuries who quote the Latin scriptures. Under each writer is given a list of his extant works and available editions, with a selected bibliography relating to his latinity, the type of text he quotes, and the like. Ayuso also classifies the materials which have some connection with Spain. He catalogues 255 Biblical manuscripts dating from the fifth to the fifteenth century, each with a brief palaeographical description and a full bibliography, and 374 Spanish ecclesiastical writers, each treated with even greater fullness than those listed earlier among the general writers of the church. An astounding amount of bibliographic information is included in these several catalogues.[2]

---

[1] Teófilo Ayuso Marazuela, *La Vetus Latina Hispana*, I, *Prolegómenos, introducción general, estudio y análisis de las fuentes*, Madrid: Consejo Superior de Investigaciones Científicas, 1953. For a review-article on this work see R. Creado and A. Segovia, *EE*, xxx (1956), 67-79.

[2] One thinks at once of comparing this volume, which was submitted to the publishers in 1949, with the somewhat similar German project, the *Vetus Latina; die Reste der altlateinischen Bibel*, begun in about 1914 by a pastor, Josef Denk, and continued during the last decades by the late Father Dold and Father Fischer at the Monastry of Beuron. Although there is much duplication, there are also certain differences. Fischer's first volume, the *Verzeichnis der Sigel*, published in 1949 and containing 104 pages, was purposely restricted to bare lists of manuscripts and fathers, with no discussion of text

III. Critical Studies of Individual Passages

The following are summaries of articles in which Spanish scholars discuss variant readings in individual passages.

In his first article of this nature, entitled "Justificata est sapientia a filiis suis (Mt. 11, 19): *a filiis* an *ab operibus*?"[1] Bover decides against ἔργων, which is supported (to quote from his own edition) by B* ℵ bo. W 124 788 2145. sy^pesh har*, and argues in favor of τέκνων, which is the text of the parallel passage, Lk. 7.35. The chief part of his argument against accepting ἔργων is that this reading would introduce a discrepancy between Matthew and Luke.

Bover's article was vigorously opposed by Père M.-J. Lagrange,[2] who, appreciating the force of the textual evidence, sought to convince Bover that, although ἔργων were admitted to be the true text of Matthew, a proper exegesis of the two passages would prevent their coming into conflict. Bover, in rebuttal, was unmoved by the force of Lagrange's plea and still maintained that τέκνων should be accepted on both critical and dogmatic grounds, because "by this reading even the shadow of a discrepancy in the Gospels vanishes."[3]

A few years later Bover considered the *hapax legomenon*, δευτερο-πρώτῳ, in Lk 6.1, a word which has bewildered scholars of every age from the time of Gregory of Nazianzus and Jerome to the present. On the basis of textual and exegetical considerations Bover approved of the text which includes this word, concluding that to suppose that the word had been added in the majority of codices would involve a circumstance more strange than the word itself! But in so doing, he went against the evidence (quoting again from his edition) of P⁴ B ℵ L W 33 579 2141 sa bo. *b c f^c l q r¹ fi* 69*.157. sy.^pesh. pal. har. mg. Ta, which testify to the omission of the word.[4]

history and theory, such as Ayuso provides in his volume of *Prolegómenos*. The Spanish work contains certain information (pertaining to marginal notes and the identification of several fathers who are quoted by other authors) which Fischer does not cite. Furthermore, the isolation of the Spanish *bloc* of witnesses, with a discussion of their significance, is peculiar to Ayuso's volume. It must be said, on the other hand, that the proofreading of the German work is superior to that of the Spanish.

[1] *B*, VI (1925), 323-325.

[2] "Iterum Mt. 11, 19: *a filiis* an *ab operibus*?" *B*, VI (1925), 461-463.

[3] *Ibid.*, pp. 463-465. Interestingly enough, in his critical edition of the Greek New Testament, published in 1943, Bover prints ἔργων in the text and relegates τέκνων to the apparatus, marking it, however, as possessing equal or even superior worth to the reading in the text.

[4] "In sabbato 'secundo-primo,' Lc. 6,l," *EE*, VII (1928), 97-103.

Still another passage which, from the days of Origen, has perplexed textual critics is the name of the sheep pool in Jn. 5.2. Bover decided in favor of Βηθεσδά, found in A, C, I, Γ, Δ, Λ, Π sy[cu. pesh. har.], and against all the other forms, "Bethsaida," "Bethzatha," "Bezatha," and "Belzetha."[1]

The next textual problem which engaged Bover's attention was the variant transmission of Matt. 1.16. Bover argued in favor of the generally accepted reading and against von Soden's text[2] (which translated into Greek the testimony of Syr[s]).

In 1943 Fr. Mateo del Álamo reviewed the history of "El 'Comma Joaneo.' "[3] After considering the doctrinal interpretation of the text in the Vulgate of I Jn. 5.7-8, he traced its varying forms from the fourth to the thirteenth century. Because Spanish Bibles exhibit two main forms of the passage, del Álamo believed that the reading had a double origin, one form originating in Africa from a marginal annotation in the Old Latin text of I John, and the other originating in Spain in the writings of the heretic Priscilianus. Neither form, he admitted, can be authentic, and the Clementine Vulgate text here is deutero-canonical.

In the same year Bover contributed a short note in which he argued against the view that harmonization has played a prominent role in the transmission of the text of the New Testament. He pointed out that in Mt. 22.32, Mk. 12.27, and Lk. 20.38, where conditions are most favorable for the operation of harmonistic adjustments, there is actually no evidence (reported in Tischendorf, von Soden, or Wordsworth and White), with the exception of one manuscript, that scribes succumbed to the temptation to harmonize these parallel passages. Bover concluded that, although there may be some harmonization in the New Testament, the influence of Tatian and other harmonizers upon the canonical text has been more imagined than real.[4]

What is the reason for the multiplicity of endings to the Second

---

[1] "El nombre de la Piscina," *EB*, II (1931), 192-198.

[2] " ¿ Cuál es la lección auténtica de Mt. I, 16 ?" *EE*, XIII (1934), 338-354. In this article Bover points out not a few errors in von Soden's critical apparatus on Matt. 1.16.

[3] *EB*, segunda época, II (1943), 75-105. This article was later condensed and published under the title, "Los 'Tres Testificantes' de la primera Epístola de San Juan, V. 7," in *Cultura Bíblica*, IV, nr. 32 (Enero, 1947), 11-14.

[4] "Harmonizaciones e interpolaciones en el texto del Nuevo Testamento," *EB*, segunda época, II (1943), 121-122.

Gospel? Bover answered this question on the basis of logic and syllogism.[1] His first proposition is, ' The Second Gospel is the close reproduction of the evangelical catechesis of St. Peter." The second is, "The recounting of the resurrection of the Lord and his appearances to his Apostles, who were to be his witnesses, did not pertain to the evangelical catechesis, directed to those who believed, but to the previous apologetic proof, directed to those who had not yet embraced the faith. The narration of the appearances, being known by the previous proof, did not need to be repeated in the evangelical catechesis." Accepting these two propositions as true, Bover offered two hypotheses either of which, he thought, would account for the textual phenomena.

According to one hypothesis, when Mark published his Gospel, he added to the Petrine catechesis his own account of the appearances of Jesus (Mk. 16.9-20). This explains, Bover believed, the difference of style between the body of the Gospel and the canonical conclusion. This difference of style was detected by certain persons in the early church, who were led thereby to suspect the authenticity of the last twelve verses. As a result of their suspicions and doubts, these verses were omitted by several subsequent copyists, a circumstance which accounts for their absence in codices B, ℵ, etc. But the Second Gospel, in this shortened form, seemed to others in the early church to lack a proper conclusion. These undertook to supply various endings, two of which are extant today, one brief (in codex L, etc.) and one longer (in W).

According to the second hypothesis, Mark published two editions of his Gospel, the former which ended with the close of the Petrine catechesis (16.8), and the latter which was supplied with Mark's own ending (vss. 9-20). Consequently some codices, copies of the former edition, giving the impression of being incomplete or mutilated, provoked various attempts to add apocryphal endings.

Another reading which Bover investigated[2] involves the variant τὸ ναὶ καὶ τὸ οὔ in II Cor 1.17, found, according to Tischendorf, in only a very few witnesses, namely the Vulgate, the margin of 424, and a citation by Pelagius. So slight did this evidence seem that neither von Soden nor Vogels nor Merk thought it worth while to

---

[1] "El final de San Marcos (16, 9-20)," *EB*, segunda época, III (1944), 561-562.
[2] "El 'SI' y el 'NO'; un caso interesante de crítica textual," *EB*, segunda época, V (1946), 95-99.

indicate the presence of a variant at all. Bover, on the contrary, argued strongly in favor of this variant, partly upon the basis of his exegetical understanding of the context, but chiefly upon the circumstance that P[46] must now be added to the witnesses for the shorter text. These four witnesses, in Bover's opinion, represent several widely divergent local texts. "Papyrus 46 seems to represent a pre-Caesarean type; the margin of 424 belongs very likely to the Alexandrian recension; the Greek codices represented in the Vulgate are of a type not sufficiently characterized; Pelagius perhaps represents the Old Latin and consequently the Western type of text." On the basis of these observations, Bover concluded that this variant ought to be regarded as the original words which the apostle Paul penned.[1]

In a series of textual studies in the Gospels, Bover dealt with several Antiochian readings in Matthew (in 11.23; 12.31-32; 15.6, 8; 26.60; 27.43),[2] the Western variant ὀργισθείς in Mark 1.41,[3] the nest of variant readings in Luke 9.54-56,[4] and the variants in John 5.3b-4.[5] In all of these passages Bover came to the conclusion that the true reading has been preserved in the traditional text. On the other hand, in a study of Heb. 9.11 he argued for the originality of γενομένων, found in P[46] B* 1739 D* etc.,[6] thus going against the text which he had printed in both the first and the second editions of his Greek New Testament.

When one surveys all of these studies of individual passages, one gains the impression that sometimes Bover permitted dogmatic considerations to sway his judgment even in cases where the textual

---

[1] Bover had not yet come to this opinion when he published the first edition of his Greek Testament, where he prints the usual geminated form of the reading *in loco*. The text is altered in the second edition (1950).

[2] "Variantes semíticas del texto antioqueno en san Mateo," *Miscellanea biblica B. Ubach*, curante Romualdo M.ª Días (*Scripta et documenta*, I; Montisserrati, 1953), pp. 323-321; compare Bover's remarks on Gergesenos in "Dos casos de toponimia y de crítica textual," *S*, XII (1952), 271-282, especially pp. 279 f.

[3] "¿ Ὀργισθείς ο σπλαγχνισθείς? crítica textual de Mc. 1, 41," *EE*, XXIII (1949), 355-357.

[4] "Autenticidad de Lc. 9,54-56," *EE*, XXVII (1953), 347-349.

[5] "Autenticidad de Jn. 5.3b-4," *EB*, segunda época, XI (1952), 69-72.

[6] "Las variantes μελλόντων y γενομένων en Hebr. 9, 11," *B*, XXXII (1951), 232-236. For another instance when Bover changed his mind regarding the text he had printed in both his editions, see his "Notas de crítica textual neotestamentaria," in *Emerita*, XVIII (1950), 381-385, in which he argues for the superiority of the reading οἴκῳ in Acts 7.46.

evidence seems to argue quite strongly for the reading which he rejected. It is significant that almost all the variants which he considered to be original agree with the Textus Receptus. It may be that scholars since Westcott and Hort have been too chary of accepting readings of this type, but nevertheless it will doubtless appear to most critics that Bover went too far in the opposite direction.[1]

This section dealing with discussions by Spanish scholars of the textual criticism of individual passages may be brought to a close by noticing Ayuso's comprehensive study of I John 5.7-8, entitled, "Nuevo estudio sobre el 'Comma Ioanneum,' acompañado de la edición crítica del Cap. V de la primera Epístola de San Juan."[2] Ayuso first disposes of any question regarding ecclesiastical restriction which might inhibit free investigation of the problem by observing that, when the principle of universality is applied to the history of the *Comma Johanneum*, one is warranted in drawing the conclusion: "We believe that we stand on *terra firma* in denying the authenticity of the verse."[3] On the basis of about seventy manuscripts of the Vulgate, the author edits the text of I John 5 and traces the history of the origin and the evolution of the diverse forms of the *comma*.[4]

IV. BOVER'S EDITION OF THE GREEK AND LATIN NEW TESTAMENT

In 1943 Bover garnered the fruits of his textual studies and published an edition of the Greek and Latin New Testament with a critical apparatus.[5] The idea of editing the text was conceived,

---

[1] For an evaluation of Bover as a textual critic, see John R. Janeway, *An Investigation of the Textual Criticism of the New Testament done by Spanish Scholars, with Special Relation to the Theories and Text of Westcott and Hort* (unpublished dissertation, University of Southern California, 1958), especially pp. 386-429. For a summary of Janeway's dissertation, see *EE*, XXXII (1958), 472-473. It may be added here that the article by Antonio Gil Ulecia, "Actualidad de crítica textual griega neotestamentaria" (*EB*, segunda época, IX [1950], 235-243) is general and elementary. The survey by Manuel F. Galiano, "Veinte años de crítica textual de la Biblia griega," (*Estudios clásicos*, I [1950-51], 3-10, 57-72) deals chiefly with recently discovered papyri of both the Septuagint and the New Testament.

[2] *B*, XXVIII (1947), 83-112, 216-235; XXIX (1948), 52-76.

[3] *Ibid.*, p. 96.

[4] Significantly, Bover not only does not print the spurious words in the Greek text of his edition of the New Testament, but he does not even honor them by mentioning them in his Greek apparatus.

[5] *Novi Testamenti biblia graeca et latina, critico apparatu aucta*, Consejo

so he informs the reader in his Preface, in 1913—in which year, one will recall, von Soden's critical edition first saw light. Bover began his work in 1921 and had almost completed it by 1931. Inasmuch as it was not published until twelve years later, one may surmise that during the interval the editor was busy taking into account the new material furnished by the discovery of the Chester Beatty Biblical papyri, the first announcement of which was made by Kenyon in 1931.[1]

The volume is of convenient size, its dimensions being 4⅛ by 6⅜ by 1¾ inches. Happily the beautiful font of type used in the publications of the Guillaume Budé Society of France was chosen for this edition, and as a result the appearance of the printed page is exceptionally pleasing. Other than supralinear numerals for the verses, no symbol appears within the Greek text. Poetical passages, such as the prologue to the Fourth Gospel, parts of the Apocalypse, and certain quotations from the Old Testament, are printed in stichs. The right-hand pages contain the text of the Clementine Vulgate, with some slight modifications as to punctuation in the Pauline Epistles. This text is broken into pericopes with appropriate captions and (in the Gospels) references to parallel passages. The apparatus to the Vulgate is in two parts, one of which supplies information regarding the identity of quotations from the Old Testament, and the other of which contains some of the more notable variants from the Wordsworth and White text and an occasional variant from the Sixtine Vulgate (1590).[2]

In eighty introductory pages of elegant and pellucid Latin, Bover sets forth the necessary information regarding the arrangement of his text and apparatus, his understanding of the history of the critical text, and the criteria of textual criticism which he followed.

Bover's text is, as he states, resultant or even eclectic; yet it is

Superior de Investigaciones Científicas (Madrid, 1943), lxxx + 771 pp. In the second edition (1950), besides correcting a good number of misprints, Bover more than once altered his preference for text and apparatus. Spanish reviews of the first edition were prepared by Ayuso in *S*, IV (1944), 199-204 and in *Arbor*, I (1944), 267-270, and by Romualdo Galdós in *Cultura Bíblica* (1944), 164 f. (the last is known to me through *Bibliotheca Hispana*, III [1945]).

[1] In *The* (London) *Times*, November 19, pp. 13-14.

[2] In the second edition (1950) the apparatus of Latin variants has been eliminated, and the number of cross-reference to parallel passages has been greatly augmented.

not an eclecticism which lacks a foundation in basic principles.[1]
He collated the critical editions of Tischendorf, Westcott and Hort,
Bernhard,Weiss, von Soden, Vogels, and Lagrange (in the Gospels,
Romans and Galatians), and added information derived from
Merk's edition and the work of Jacquier (in Acts), A. C. Clark (in
Acts), and Allo (in I Corinthians and Revelation). From the criti-
cal texts of these scholars Bover chose those readings which, in his
opinion, "are approved by the testimony of the most ancient and
best codices, versions, and ecclesiastical authors."[2]

Bover's text differs not infrequently from Nestle's. The Stuttgart
edition, it will be recalled, was formed mechanically by printing
the text which two of three previous editors had printed (Tischendorf, Westcott-Hort, and B. Weiss). The Madrid text, on the other
hand, being formed subjectively, possesses what the other does not,
the personal stamp of a single scholar's critical evaluation. When
the text on a sample page[3] of Bover's edition was collated with
Nestle's text, eight differences were noted.[4] It is certainly not
without significance that in all of these, Bover's text agrees with
the Textus Receptus.

As regards the choice and disposition of evidence in the critical
apparatus the following may be noted. Bover is more interested
than is Nestle in modern editions and orthographic details, while
Nestle thinks it more important than does Bover to supply information regarding variants involving the order of words. Of greater
significance is the relative proportion of the amount of evidence
cited. When Bover mentions a variant he usually provides consider-

---

[1] *Novi Testamenti biblia graeca et latina*, p. xiii.

[2] From the publisher's prospectus of Bover's edition, p. [4].

[3] Page 7, containing Matt. 3.16-4.4, was selected for collation against the
17th edition of Nestle, which was published two years earlier (1941).

[4] The following are the eight readings of the Madrid text as compared
with the Stuttgart text (readings involving merely differences of punctuation
and the use of upper case initial letters have not been taken into account).
Information has also been added involving a comparison between Bover's
edition and two other critical editions prepared by Roman Catholic scholars;
the symbols V and M are to be interpreted that Vogels's edition (1928) and
Merk's edition (1933) agree with Bover against Nestle. Title ΚΑΤΑ ΜΑΤ-
ΘΑΙΟΝ, VM; 3.14 ὁ δὲ Ἰωάννης, VM; 3.15 πρὸς αὐτόν, V; 3.16 ἀνεῴχθησαν,
V / + αὐτῷ VM / τὸ Πνεῦμα τοῦ Θεοῦ, V / καὶ (3), VM; 4.2 νύκτας τεσσεράκοντα,
V. Thus, in all eight readings Vogels agrees with Bover against Nestle, and
Merk agrees with Bover against Nestle four times. For other statistical com-
parisons of these editions, see K. Aland, "The Present Position of New Testa-
ment Textual Criticism," *Studia Evangelica*, ed. by Aland *et al.* (= *TU*,
LXXIII [1959]), 719-721.

ably more data from minuscules, versions, and lectionaries than does Nestle. Thus, in Matt. 3.12, where Nestle cites only B *pc* for the variant ἀποθήκην] + αὐτοῦ, Bover cites B. W *b.* 372 828 1391 1279 443. 157.[1] Again, to give another example from the same sample page, the Stuttgart edition quotes B ℵ *al* in support of the sequence of εὐθὺς ἀνέβη in 3.16, but the Madrid edition adds to these two witnesses 33 lect.1043 co. W D lat syᶜ. 600 *f*1. On the other hand, Nestle supplies evidence of certain variants not mentioned by Bover, as, for example, the Old Latin addition at the end of 3.15 regarding the light on the Jordan at the Baptism of Jesus, and in 3.17 he cites two Western variants which Bover passes over. Bover has a total of 28 variants on this sample page; Nestle [17] has a total of 25.

Where did Bover derive his information about variants? He states[2] that he utilized von Soden's repository of variants, correcting his citation of evidence by collating it with Tischendorf and supplementing both by much additional information derived from personal collations and from the work of Legg, Merk, Huck, and Hoskier. Bover cites the witnesses in a sequence which resembles that used by von Soden.

From the information supplied thus far, certain of Bover's critical presuppositions may have been gleaned. It will be useful, however, to set forth on the basis of information contained in his Preface a summary of his views regarding the history of the text of the New Testament and his criteria for choosing among variant readings.

Bover divides the manuscripts and versions into four families, the Alexandrian, the Western, the Caesarean, and the Antiochian. The chief witnesses to these,[3] at any rate as far as the Gospels are concerned, are:

Alexandrian type, B, ℵ, 0162, 33, etc.

Western type, D, (W), 0171, sa, syrˢᶜ, vet. Lat.

Caesarean type, P³⁷, P⁴⁵, Θ, (W), 565, 700, 28, *f*1, *f*13, arm.

Antiochian type, A, K, Π, V, Ω, Ξ, E, F, G, H.

---

[1] In accordance with Bover's practice, the occurrences of the full stop following certain *sigla* signify that only these witnesses in their respective families support the reading.

[2] *Novi Testamenti biblia graeca et latina*, p. xxii.

[3] *Ibid.*, pp. xx-xxi.

After indicating the special characteristics of each of these families Bover reconstructs the early history of the text. This history falls into two well defined divisions, the pre-recensional period and the period of the great recensions. What is called the Western text was dominant in the former period; the Alexandrian and Caesarean recensions were prepared in the third century, and the Antiochian in the fourth.

The Western text of the second century was not, as a whole, the result of any deliberate or formal editorial effort. The stages through which the primitive text passed and which were productive of variant reading were the following.[1]

1. In the earliest times a living oral tradition, particularly of Gospel material, was added to the written tradition both by private possessors of codices and by scribes and booksellers.

2. During the same period, because greater weight was accorded to deeds than to written words, it would happen that scribes, who knew the Gospels by heart, would not pay strict enough attention to their work in producing new codices. These new manuscripts, discrepant among themselves, became archetypes of many other manuscripts, which, in turn, formed many small families.

3. The work of correctors, who were eager to guard against heresies, modified the text by seeking to avoid those expressions which were susceptible of perverse interpretations.

4. Various standards of fidelity in the transcription of manuscripts prevailed, especially among private individuals. Some would favor the shorter reading; others, the longer; others would alter the more rude form of expression into the more polished. In these ways many new types of text arose.

5. Local manuscripts of single churches migrated to other churches. This produced the greatest amount of inter-mixture of texts and created still other new types.

Thus during the second century the types of text were many and varied. Yet not all manuscripts, if Irenaeus can be believed,[2] were corrupted, but some were preserved immune from contamination.

The recensions of the third and fourth centuries, being based on the pre-recensional (commonly called Western) type of text of the second century, contain a mixture of good and bad readings, in proportion to the success of the early editors in choosing from among the welter of variants current in the second century.

---

[1] *Ibid.*, pp. xxix-xxxi. I have slightly abbreviated Bover's statements, while retaining so far as possible his phraseology.

[2] Bover refers to Irenaeus, *contra Haeresis*, V, xxx, 1, ἐν πᾶσι τοῖς σπουδαίοις καὶ ἀρχαίοις ἀντιγράφοις (ed. Harvey, II, 406).

What principles should the modern editor follow in choosing the best readings? Bover discusses the two kinds of criticism, the external and the internal (which he calls "documentalia criteria" and "rationalia criteria"). Evidence which is evaluated in terms of the former will lead the editor back to the second century; evidence judged in terms of the latter will enable him to decide which of several readings, all current in the second century, is likely to be the original. Among the "rationalia criteria," Bover accepts as valid those which he formulates as follows: the "originalis lectio" (i.e. that reading which explains the origin of another is to be preferred), the "lectio non harmonizans" (although Bover would be quite parsimonious in applying this rule; see p. 132 above), the "lectio impolitor," and the reading which is in accord with the "scriptoris stilus."[1] It will be noted that Bover does not admit as valid the generally accepted canon, "brevior lectio, verior."[2]

Although these canons have long been in general use among textual critics, it is, of course, in their application that individual differences among editors emerge. In assessing the general result of Bover's critical procedure, one observes that his text recedes from the Alexandrian type and approaches somewhat to the Western and Byzantine types. That is to say, in many respects it deserts the text preferred by Tischendorf, Westcott and Hort, or Bernard Weiss, and agrees with that which, in varying degrees, was approved by von Soden, Vogels, and Merk.

In addition to discussing the textual criticism of the New Testament in general and of the Gospels in particular, Bover deals with the special problems peculiar to the Pauline Epistles, the Catholic Epistles, and the Apocalypse.[3] The results of his analyses are that manuscripts B and 1739 approve themselves as the best witnesses to the Pauline Epistles (along with codex 1852 in Romans).[4] The text represented by D G F has often been accused of showing traces of Latinization; Bover thinks, however, that the extent of such

[1] *Novi Testamenti biblia graeca et latina*, pp. xxxvii-xl.

[2] *Ibid.*, pp. xviii and xl; see also p. 123 above. It may be mentioned that recent editors of the Iliad and the Mahābhārata, contrary to Bover's reluctance to accept the shorter reading, deliberately prefer the shorter to the longer variant; see pp. 152 ff. below.

[3] In his discussion of the text of the Apocalypse (*ibid.*, pp. lvi-lxv), Bover presents practically the same material which he published in expanded form in *EE* and which has been summarized above on pp. 126ff.

[4] *Novi Testamenti biblia graeca et latina*, pp. xlvii.

Latinization has been considerably overestimated, and that what does exist may be easily detected by the critic.[1] In the Catholic Epistles, codices 1739 and 1852 approve themselves as the best among ten cursive manuscripts which Bover analyzed.

In his discussion of the textual complexion of P^{46} Bover refines Kenyon's and Sanders's work on this papyrus. He conjectures that as P^{45} represents a pre-Caesarean type of text in the Gospels, so P^{46} represents the same type of text in the Pauline Epistles.[2] In an analysis of fifty variant readings in the first four chapters of Galatians, in which only a few codices agree with P^{46}, Bover found that the text of the papyrus shows the greatest affinity with 1739, whose archetype seems to have been written at Caesarea.[3] Bover believed that the Caesarean type of text in Paul is to be sought in von Soden's sub-group I^{a3} (containing 467, f.1319, 436, 255, 69, 462, and 330), and supported his view with a wealth of detail which must be read to be appreciated.[4]

[1] *Ibid.*, p. xlviii. The matter is not, however, quite so simple as Bover would have one believe; see the careful study of Karl Th. Schäfer, "Der griechisch-lateinische Text des Galaterbriefes in der Handschriftengruppe D E F G " *Scientia Sacra; theologische Festgabe zugeeignet seiner Eminenz dem hochwürdigsten Herrn Karl Joseph Kardinal Schulte, Erzbischof von Köln ...* (Köln und Düsseldorf, [1935]), pp. 41-70, the chief merit of which is to let the reader see how exceedingly complicated the problem really is.

[2] *Novi Testamenti biblia graeca et latina,* p. liii.

[3] M.-J. Lagrange, *Critique textuelle*; II, *Critique rationnelle* (Paris, 1935), p. 471.

[4] *Novi Testamenti biblia graeca et latina,* p. liv. It may be mentioned here that, according to preliminary announcement, Bover's edition of the Greek text will be the basis of the New Testament section in the forthcoming Spanish Polyglot Bible (see the *Prooemium* volume of the *Biblia Polyglotta Matritensia* [Matriti, 1957]). Necessary additions in the citation of evidence will be made by José O'Callaghan Martínez, S.J.

CHAPTER SIX

RECENT TRENDS IN THE TEXTUAL CRITICISM OF THE ILIAD AND THE MAHĀBHĀRATA

An ever present danger besets the specialist in any field; it is the temptation to neglect taking into account trends of research in other fields. Confining one's attention to a limited area of investigation may result in the impoverishment rather than the enrichment of scholarship. On the other hand, the history of research in the broad expanse of the humanities includes many examples of the cross-fertilization of ideas and methods, thereby providing sometimes a stimulus and sometimes a corrective to research in a related discipline.

From the time of the Renaissance onward the study of the classics has more than once furnished the Biblical scholar with new methods and tools of criticism, as the following two instances illustrate. At the end of the eighteenth century, F. A. Wolf's theory of the composite authorship of the Homeric poems[1] indirectly stimulated the inquiry into the composition of the Pentateuch, and subsequently New Testament scholars began a similar systematic analysis of the sources of the Synoptic Gospels. Again, it was the great German classicist of the past generation, Eduard Norden, who first applied to Graeco-Roman literature the discipline of *Gattungsgeschichte*, the study of the categories of literary genre and style.[2] Shortly thereafter Hermann Gunkel, who had been thinking along somewhat similar lines, made use of the same principles in his study of the sagas of Genesis.[3] About a score of years later Martin

---

[1] *Prolegomena ad Homerum* (Halis Saxonum, 1795), chapters xii-xxxv.

[2] *Die antike Kunstprosa vom VI. Jahrhundert v. Chr. bis in die Zeit der Renaissance*, 2 vols. (Leipzig and Berlin, 1898; reprinted with supplements, 1909). Prior to Norden the method had found a limited use by Germanists investigating fairy tales in German folklore.

[3] *Genesis* in Nowack's *Handkommentar zum Alten Testament* (Göttingen, 1901; 3rd ed., 1910). The introductory material setting forth Gunkel's theory was translated by W. H. Carruth and published serially in *The Open Court*, xv (1901), 261-283, 385-398, 450-463, 526-539, 582-595, and 650-673, as well as in a separate volume entitled *The Legends of Genesis* (Chicago, 1901).

Dibelius[1] and Rudolf Bultmann[2] applied Norden's (and Gunkel's) methods to the study of the transmission of the Gospel materials. Thus the application of *Formgeschichte* to the Gospels as well as the earlier efforts directed toward the purely literary solution of the Synoptic Problem were stimulated by influences from classical and Semitic scholarship.

In the sphere of textual criticism New Testament scholars have profited more than once from the research of editors of classical texts. Westcott and Hort adopted and refined the genealogical method of classifying manuscripts—a method which, ever since the classicists Immanuel Bekker[3] and Karl Lachmann[4] first developed it in a systematic way, has been taken for granted by almost[5]

---

[1] *Die Formgeschichte des Evangeliums* (Tübingen, 1919); the 2nd ed., 1933, was translated into English by B. L. Woolf under the title *From Tradition to Gospel* (New York, 1935).

[2] *Die Geschichte der synoptischen Tradition* (Göttingen, 1921; 3te Aufl., 1957).

[3] Bekker (1785-1871) was the editor of sixty volumes of Greek texts and the collator of some four hundred manuscripts, many made available by their transfer to public libraries as a result of the upheaval following the French Revolution. Discovering that many received texts rested on an unsound foundation and that a mass of earlier material existed, he analyzed available manuscripts of an author and grouped them into families where one derived from another. He made the mistake, however, of thinking that the oldest manuscript was necessarily the best.

[4] In textual criticism Lachmann (1793-1851) went further than Bekker. He sho wed how, by comparison of manuscripts, it is possible to draw inferences as to their lost ancestors or archetypes, their condition and pagination. Besides his famous edition of Lucretius, Lachmann distinguished himself by critical editions of Propertius, Catullus, Tibullus, Gaius, the Niebelungenlied, Walther von der Vogelweide, and Wolfram von Eschenbach. As is well known, the beginning of the downfall of the supremacy of the *textus receptus* of the Greek New Testament dates from the work of the same scholar: his object was to restore the text to the form in which it had been read in the ancient Church about the year 380 (see his article, "Rechenschaft über seine Ausgabe des Neuen Testaments," in *Theologische Studien und Kritiken*, 1830, pp. 817-845, and the preface to his larger edition of the Greek New Testament [2 vols., Berlin, 1842-1850]). For a glowing appreciation of Lachmann's erudition, see Sir J. E. Sandys, *A History of Classical Scholarship*, III (Cambridge, 1908), pp. 127-131, who writes, *inter alia*, "Lachmann was the true founder of a strict and methodical system of textual criticism" (p. 130).

[5] The qualification is made because the views of, e.g., Joseph Bédier, who, in his edition of *Le Lai de l'Ombre par Jean Renart* (Paris, 1913), denounces the genealogical method of textual criticism as a snare and delusion for the reason that in many instances one can argue persuasively for several methods of classification. His own method was to choose what seemed to him to be the best manuscript, making the choice on the basis of grammar,

all editors of works whose autographs have perished. More recently, still another classicist and humanist has advanced the science and art of textual criticism. The New Testament scholar may read with pleasure and profit A. E. Housman's pungent and piquant, not to say caustic, paragraphs exposing the absurdities involved in following mechanically and bindly certain stereotyped canons of textual criticism.[1] A small but none the less important advance in the study of manuscripts was Housman's recognition that not only were homoeoteleuton and homoeoarchon predisposing factors in the production of errors in transcription, but that homoeomeson must also be taken into account as liable to occasion parablepsis.[2]

It is the purpose of this chapter to inquire whether recent textual investigation in two great epics of ancient Greece and India, the Iliad and the Mahābhārata, may offer the textual critic of the New Testament helpful suggestions as to methodology.

I

Of all the literary compositions by the Greek people, the Homeric poems are the best suited for comparison with the Bible. In antiquity men memorized Homer as later they were to memorize the Scriptures. Each was held in the highest esteem and quoted in defence of arguments pertaining to heaven, earth, and Hades. Homer and the Bible served as primers from which different generations of school boys were taught to read. Around both there grew up a mass of scholia and commentaries; they were provided with

coherent sense, simple and regular orthography, and then to use the other manuscripts eclectically. His opinions are set forth more fully in an article entitled, "La tradition manuscrite du Lai de l'Ombre: réflections sur l'art d'éditer les anciens textes" (*Romania*, LIV [1928], 161-181, 321-356). Bédier's scepticism of the validity of the "orthodox" methods of textual criticism has influenced several New Testament critics. Leo Vaganay, e.g., asserts that "applied to New Testament text this system [Lachmann's genealogical method] is useless" (*Initiation à la critique textuelle néotestamentaire* [*Bibliothèque catholique des sciences religieuses*, LX] Paris, 1934, p. 60; Eng. tr., *An Introduction to the Textual Criticism of the New Testament* [London, 1937], p. 71). For a refutation of Bédier's skepticism, see Paul Collomp's *La critique des textes* (Paris, 1931), pp. 65-72, and, from a different point of view, Jean Irigoin, "Stemmas bifides et états des manuscrits," *Revue de philologie*, IIIe sér. XXVIII (1954), 211-217.

[1] A. E. Housman, *D. Iunii Iuvenalis saturae* (2nd ed., Cambridge, 1931), xi-xvi; see also the preface in his edition of Lucan (Oxford, 1926) and the preface in his edition of Manilius (new ed., Oxford, 1937) for many wise and witty observations concerning the art and science of textual criticism.

[2] *M. Annaei Lucani belli civilis libri decem*, pp. xix f.

glossaries. Both fell into the hands of allegorists. Both were imitated and supplemented—one with the Homeric Hymns and writings such as the Batrachomyomachia, the other with apocryphal books. Homer was made available in prose analyses; the Gospel of John was turned into epic hexameters by Nonnus of Panopolis. The manuscripts of both Homer and the Bible were illustrated. Homeric scenes appeared in Pompeian murals; Christian basilicas were decorated with mosaics and frescoes of Biblical episodes.[1] Moreover, the textual transmission of Homer and the New Testament exhibit many similarities, some of which are the following.

In the entire range of ancient Greek and Latin literature, the Iliad ranks next to the New Testament in possessing the greatest amount of manuscript testimony. The most recent figures (1962) for the Greek New Testament are: 76 papyri, 297 uncial manuscripts, 2647 minuscule manuscripts, and 1997 lectionaries.[2] In 1955 Hans Joachim Mette listed 453 papyri of the Iliad.[3] Besides these the Iliad is contained in two uncial and 188 minuscule manuscripts.[4] In both the Iliad and the New Testament several passages are without fixed location in the manuscripts. For instance, as the *pericope de adultera* appears at various places in different manuscripts of the Fourth Gospel and after Luke 21.38 in the Ferrar group of manuscripts, so the section concerning the Trojan scout, Dolon, probably did not always appear in the tenth book of the Iliad, as it does in printed editions.

In order that the most recent trends in the textual criticism of the Iliad may be understood in a wider context, a brief résumé will be given first regarding the present state of the text of Homer as the result of ancient and modern criticism.[5]

---

[1] For other comparisons, see Ernst von Dobschütz, "Homer und die Bibel, eine überlieferungsgeschichtliche Vergleichung," *Neue Jahrbücher für Wissenschaft und Jugendbildung,* 1 (1925), 331 ff.

[2] This information was kindly supplied by Prof. Kurt Aland of Münster in a letter to the author, dated 11 July 1962.

[3] "Neue Homer-Papyri," *Revue de philologie,* IIIᵉ sér. XXIX (1955), 193-199, 202-204. For statistics regarding the number of papyrus fragments of Homer in roll-format and in codex-format, see J. A. Davison, "The Study of Homer in Graeco-Roman Egypt," *Akten des VIII internationale Kongresses für Papyrologie* (= *Mitteilungen aus der Papyrussammlung der österreichischen Nationalbibliothek,* N.S., V. Folge; Wien, 1956), pp. 51-58.

[4] T. W. Allen, *Homeri Ilias;* 1, *Prolegomena* (Oxford, 1931), p. 55.

[5] It need scarcely be mentioned that theories regarding the origin of the Homeric poems—whether they are the work of one poet or many—do not come into the orbit of the present survey.

The earliest critics of Homer were certain members of the famous Alexandrian School,[1] and included Zenodotus of Ephesus (*fl. c.* 285 B.C.), his pupil, Aristophanes of Byzantium (*fl. c.* 195 B. C.), and the latter's pupil, Aristarchus of Samothrace (*fl. c.* 150 B.C.), all of them librarians of the great Library at Alexandria. Zenodotus produced the first critical edition of the Iliad and the Odyssey, and all three scholars invented and used certain explanatory symbols in the margins of manuscripts to denote various conditions of the text thus marked.[2]

In modern times the printed text of the Iliad which has come to be regarded as the vulgate or Textus Receptus is that which was drawn by Wolf from the mediaeval manuscripts known to him, with the addition of a few lines preserved only in quotations. Within the last fifty or sixty years it has been discovered that this Wolfian text, which contains 15,693 lines, is substantially the same as that found in all papyri from about 150 B.C. onward.[3] So far as can be determined on the basis of evidence contained in Homeric scholia,[4] the text which Aristarchus annotated and that of the papyri subsequent to about 150 B.C. were identical and contained about 15,600 lines. Thus, only about 100 lines have been added by interpolation into the accepted text of the Iliad during the course of the last two thousand years.

Regarding the state of the text prior to about 150 B.C. Homeric scholarship has been sharply divided. The difference of opinion arises from the varying weight accorded the evidence derived from certain Ptolemaic papyri and from quotations made by pre-Aristarchian authors. Grenfell and Hunt discovered that the Homeric papyri before about 150 B.C. possess an "eccentric" text which differs from that which is found in later papyri and mediaeval

---

[1] For a good account of this School reference may be made to Sandys, *op. cit.*, I (2nd ed., 1906), 105 ff., esp. 119 ff.

[2] For an account of these symbols see, e.g., Arthur Ludwich, *Aristarchs Homerische Textkritik nach den Fragmenten des Didymos*, I (Leipzig, 1884), 19-22 and 94; R. C. Jebb, *Homer, an Introduction to the Iliad and the Odyssey* (Boston, 1887), p. 94, note 2; and Robert Devreesse, *Introduction a l'étude des manuscrits grecs* (Paris, 1954), pp. 73 f.

[3] The amount of the Iliad preserved in the papyri is considerable; Collart ("Les papyrus de l'Iliade," *Revue de philologie*, IIIᵉ sér., vi [1932], 317) reports that 13,207 lines of the Iliad are represented in papyri.

[4] Concerning these T. W. Allen admits, "The age and origin of the collections of scholia which we possess upon the *Iliad* is still a mystery," *The Homeric Scholia* (= *Proceedings of the British Academy*, XVII; London, 1931), p. 3.

manuscripts. The divergence is particularly marked in the insertion of new lines.[1] Some scholars immediately concluded that these Ptolemaic papyri represent a prolix pre-Alexandrian text before it was shortened and fixed in the current text by the criticism of Zenodotus, Aristophanes, and Aristarchus. But this conclusion is opposed by the evidence of the scholia which record the readings preferred by the Alexandrian critics and show that the opinions of this School had next to no effect upon the traditional text.[2] Furthermore, as Grenfell and Hunt observed, "the new lines are in many cases no doubt interpolated from other portions of the poems," and in the remaining cases "are often due to the unconscious influence of parallel passages."[3]

On the other hand, an attempt was made to prove from the quotations in pre-Alexandrian authors that their text of Homer was substantially the same as the vulgate. In an elaborate discussion of the subject, Arthur Ludwich offered statistics which show that out of 480 verses quoted by various authors before 300 B.C., not more than nine to eleven are absent from the vulgate.[4] From this he concluded that, so far from its being true that the Alexandrian grammarians fabricated a unified Homeric text from a chaotic condition, actually most of the pre-Alexandrian writers (24 or 25 out of 29) used the vulgate and not the "eccentric" ("erweiterte oder wilde") text.

But, as several scholars were quick to point out, Ludwich's conclusion is greatly weakened by the circumstance that most of the quotations are so short as to afford very slender evidence for or against the vulgate text, and of the remainder a sizeable proportion disagrees with the vulgate.[5]

Present-day Homeric scholarship seeks to avoid both extreme

[1] B. P. Grenfell and A. S. Hunt, *The Hibeh Papyri*, I (London, 1906), 67-75. The "eccentric" texts contain about 70 new lines in 547 lines, i.e. approximately one in eight.

[2] "The influence of [the Alexandrian] critics on the vulgate was *nil* in antiquity and sporadic in the middle ages" (Allen, *Homeri Ilias*, p. 204).

[3] *Op. cit.*, p. 75.

[4] *Die Homervulgata als voralexandrinisch erwiesen* (Leipzig, 1898), pp. 67 ff., esp. p. 140.

[5] Only 26 of the total number of quotations contain more than three consecutive lines; see Grenfell and Hunt, *op. cit.*, pp. 72 f., and Gilbert Murray, *The Rise of the Greek Epic* (3rd ed., Oxford, 1924), pp. 290 ff. Cf. Günther Jachmann, *Vom frühalexandrinischen Homertext* (= *Nachrichten der Gesellschaft der Wissenschaften zu Göttingen*, phil.-hist. Kl., 1949, 7), pp. 167-224.

positions. Although clear evidence for the widespread use of the vulgate can be traced back only to the time of Aristarchus, this textual critic can scarcely have been its creator. Nor on the other hand, did it reign supreme prior to the Alexandrian School. Though Plato[1] and Aristotle[2] quote a text of Homer that in the main agrees with the vulgate text, each occasionally either attributes to Homer lines which are "eccentric" or omits lines from a context which they otherwise quote exactly.

One of the most significant of recent contributions to Homeric criticism is George M. Bolling's monograph entitled *The Athetized Lines of the Iliad*.[3] Believing that the whole tradition of the Iliad goes back to a single Athenian text not earlier than the sixth century, Bolling attempts to bridge the gulf between this text and the emergence of the vulgate in about 150 B.C. by studying the lines said in the scholia to have been athetized by any one of the Alexandrians. He finds that 764 lines were athetized, or about one verse in twenty.[4]

Why did the Alexandrians mark about five per cent of their text

---

[1] Cf. Jules Labarbe, *L'Homère de Platon* (Liège, 1949), pp. 385-425.

[2] Cf. W. S. Hinman, *Literary Quotation and Allusion in the Rhetoric, Poetics and Nicomachean Ethics of Aristotle* (Diss. Columbia University, 1935), pp. 39-46, 106-117, and 142-146.

[3] Baltimore, 1944. Bolling had long been a student of Homer. Beginning in 1898 he published at short intervals in books, transactions, and journals his numerous and varied Homeric studies. Those which bear upon the textual criticism of Homer include the following: "The Archetype of our *Iliad* and the Papyri" (*American Journal of Philology*, XXXV [1914], 125-148); "The Latest Expansions of the *Iliad*" (*ibid.*, XXXVII [1916], 1-30); "The Latest Expansions of the *Odyssey*" (*ibid.*, pp. 452-458); "Vulgate Homeric Papyri" (*ibid.*, XLII [1921], 253-259); "On the Interpolation of Certain Homeric Formulas" (*Classical Philology*, XVII [1922], 213-221); *The External Evidence for Interpolation in Homer* (Oxford, 1925); "The New Ptolemaic Papyrus Containing Parts of *Iliad*, XII, 128-263," (*Journal of Egyptian Archaeology*, XIV [1928], 78-81); "Zur homerischen Textüberlieferung" (*Philologische Wochenschrift*, XLVIII [1928], 1014-1021); "παραιτεῖσθαι = ἀθετεῖν?" (*Classical Quarterly*, XXII [1928], 101-106); "The Quotations from Homer in Polyainos 1. Proem. 4-12," (*Classical Philology*, XXIV [1924], 330-334). Several of Bolling's students have likewise published material bearing on the textual criticism of Homer; e.g. Barbara P. MacCarthy, "Line Omissions in Homeric Papyri since 1925" (*Classical Philology*, XXVII [1932], 151-155), and Stanley T. Vandersall, "Line Omissions in Homeric Papyri since 1932 " (*ibid.*, XXXVII [1942], 299-306).

[4] The athetizing of these lines, however, did not have the effect of removing them from the text. In this one observes a parallel to the work of the Masoretes, who expressed their disapproval of certain words in their Hebrew text by applying dots to them, but the words remained in the text.

of the Iliad with an obelus? In answering this question Bolling postulates that "neither Zenodotus, nor Aristophanes, nor Aristarchus would athetize a line unless its attestation seemed to him seriously defective."[1] If this proposition is accepted, it follows that "whenever a passage is presented to us both in a longer and a shorter version, the latter is to be preferred in a reconstruction" of the sixth century text of the Iliad.[2] Instead of arguing for the probability of the postulate, Bolling, in true Socratic manner, examines its consequences (τὰ συμβαίνοντα). As he quite correctly points out, "If these are untenable, the postulate falls; if not, the postulate works, and we must, at least tentatively, accept it, and seek for it an explanation."[3] The bulk of Bolling's volume is devoted to just this kind of testing.

It is quite impossible to quote here the wealth of material which Bolling takes into account in his analysis of the athetized lines;[4] it will be sufficient to indicate three of the reasons for which the postulate suggested itself to him: (1) the way in which the text of the Iliad was transmitted from about 150 B.C. onward, namely, with additions but without excisions; (2) "the fact that the Ptolemaic papyri contain many additions but no excisions";[5] and (3) the "recognition that the text which Zenodotus is supposed to have produced by 'hacking' is often in Wecklein's phrase 'ursprünglich und offenbar auf handschriftlicher Überlieferung beruhend.' "[6] In

---

[1] *Athetized Lines*, p. 30. Earlier Bolling formulated his understanding of ἀθέτησις in similar language: "ἀθητεῖν is to put a mark (ὀβελός) before a line of the text to indicate that it was believed by the editor to be unhomeric" (*The External Evidence for the Interpolation of Homer*, p. 46).

[2] *Athetized Lines*, p. 6.

[3] *Ibid.*, p. 26.

[4] The validity of his conclusions has impressed more than one reviewer who have a right to an opinion; e.g., John A. Scott, in *Classical Weekly*, XXXVIII (December 18, 1944), 74 f., and C. Bradford Welles, in *Language*, XX (1944), 255-257. On the other hand M. H. A. L. H. van der Valk, who had previously argued for the unity of Homer and the reliability of the vulgate text of the Odyssey (*Textual Criticism of the Odyssey* [Leiden, 1949]), remains unconvinced (*Mnemosyne*, 4th Series, V [1952], 245-246).

[5] This is not quite correct; the Ptolemaic papyri omit a very few lines; see G. A. Gerhard, *Griechische literarische Papyri*; I, *Ptolemäische Homerfragmente* (Heidelberg, 1911), p. 5. Bolling doubtless means that, in his opinion, such lines were not excised from these papyri but have been inserted elsewhere.

[6] *Athetized Lines*, p. 6. The reference to Wecklein (not supplied by Bolling) is his *Über Zusätze und Auslassung von Versen im Homerische Texte* (= *Sitzungsberichte der königlich bayerischen Akademie der Wissenschaften*, phil.-hist. Klasse, 1917, 7. Abh.), p. 59.

other words, whenever we can test it, the text of the epic has had a tendency to grow.[1]

II

During the past third of a century a group of scholars has been working on the first critical edition of the Mahābhārata, one of the two national epics of India. Before the methodology employed by this team of scholars is described, however, a brief account concerning the nature of the Mahābhārata may not be out of place.

The title comes from two Sanskrit words, mahā-, "great," and Bhārata, "a descendant of a king or a member of a tribe named Bharata," and is susceptible of being resolved into either the "Great Battle of the Descendants of Bharata,"[2] or "The Great Narrative of the Battle of the Bharatas."[3] The kernel of this work involves the history of a contest for supremacy between two great regal families of northern India, the Pāṇḍavas and the Kurus or Kauravas, ending in the victory of the former and the establishment of their rule. In reality this narrative occupies but a fourth of the poem, the other three-fourths being a vast number of old legends about gods, kings, and sages; accounts of cosmogony and theogony; disquisitions on philosophy, law, and religion, and the duties of the military caste. Entire works are sometimes inserted to illustrate a particular statement. For example, while the two armies are drawn up prepared for battle, a whole philosophical poem in eighteen cantos, the lofty Bhagavad gītā, is recited to one of the generals. The Mahābhārata thus became a kind of encyclopedia designed for the religious instruction of those classes who by their position were debarred from studying the Vedas and the Vedānta.[4]

The magnitude of labor involved in preparing a critical edition of the Mahābhārata far exceeds any of the tasks with which classicists are confronted, both because of the length of the text (it is

---

[1] Bolling's edition of the Iliad sets forth the text as it presumably existed in Athens at the time of Peisistratos, i.e. with some one thousand lines less than in the vulgate text; see his *Iliad Atheniensium; the Athenian Iliad of the Sixth Century B.C.* (Lancaster, Pa.; and Oxford, 1950).

[2] Arthur A. Macdonell, *A History of Sanskrit Literature* (London, 1900), p. 283.

[3] M. Winternitz, *A History of Indian Literature*, I (Calcutta, 1927), p. 317.

[4] For an outline of the contents of the Mahābhārata reference may be made to Macdonell, *op. cit.*, pp. 291-298, and Winternitz, *op. cit.*, pp. 327-442. The latter discusses its date, *ibid.*, pp. 454-475.

by far the longest poem known to literary history, being about eight times as long as the Iliad and Odyssey together), and because of the complexity of the tradition. The text exists in nearly a dozen more or less independent versions, whose extreme types, the Northern and the Southern recensions, differ in extent by about 13,000 stanzas or 26,000 lines. Under the devoted leadership of Vishnu S. Sukthankar (died 1943) and his associate, S. K. Belvalkar, and with the assistance of a corps of other scholars, the enormous task of preparing the first critical edition of the Mahābhārata has made exceptionally good progress.

The critical procedure followed by Sukthankar and his collaborators is indicated in the prolegomena of the first volume. Sukthankar writes, "The main principle underlying all speculation as to authenticity is the postulated originality of agreement between what may be proved to be (more or less) independent versions."[1] Critical analysis makes it probable that "our manuscripts contain all that was there originally to hand down, and more."[2] In the Introduction to his edition of the Sabhāparvan, which is the second book of the Mahābhārata, Franklin Edgerton states, "I have come to believe that any passage, long or short, which is missing in *any* recension or important group of manuscripts *as a whole*, must be very seriously suspected of being a secondary insertion. For the Mbh., I should now hesitate long before including any such case in the edited text. This was not a preconceived notion. Indeed I started with a quite different attitude.... But I should now go so far as to assert that probably not one of the some fifty MSS. I have studied for Book 2, nor any of their genealogical ancestors, ever *deliberately or intentionally* omitted a single line of the text.... It appears that no scribe, no redactor, ever knowingly sacrificed a single line which he found in his original."[3]

More might be written concerning the ramifications and difficulties met with in applying this principle,[4] but sufficient has been

[1] *The Mahābhārata*, for the first time critically edited by Vishnu S. Sukthankar ... and other scholars, vol. i, *The Ādiparvan* (Poona, 1933), pp. lxxxvi f. After Sukthankar's death and upon becoming the General Editor of the project Belvalkar indicated that he found no "reason to depart from the rules and procedure for text-constitution as adopted in the volumes of the Critical Edition already published" (*The Bhishmaparvan* [Poona, 1947], p. cxxv).

[2] *Ibid.* p. xcv.

[3] *The Mahābhārata* ..., vol. ii, *The Sabhāparvan* (Poona, 1944), p. xxxiv.

[4] Some of these are pointed out by Walter Ruben in his article, "Schwierig-

indicated for the present purpose. Sukthankar's edition, it may be mentioned, has met with wide and hearty approval and commendation on the part of reviewers. Moreover, his canon of criticism has received independent corroboration by Ferdinando Belloni-Filippi, who analyzed a small section of the epic on the basis of intrinsic probability and came to the same conclusions as Sukthankar regarding the superiority of the shorter form of the text.[1]

III

The New Testament scholar is struck at once by certain parallels between the textual history of these two great national epics and that of the Gospels. In the case of all three, the material circulated for a longer or shorter time in an oral form. Most of those who retold the material, whether in oral or written form, were interested in preserving all that had been handed down to them. In some instances additional material, more or less similar to the original, was incorporated into the textual transmission. As a result certain "wild" or "eccentric" texts were formed. In the case of the Mahābhārata this process proceeded quite unchecked and produced at least two diverse forms of the text with many sub-varieties, each much mixed with the others. In the case of the Iliad learned recensions were made by Alexandrian critics who athetized lines which seemed to them to be supported by less than adequate testimony. Their work was apparently successful in preventing further heterogeneous accretions of a major sort, but, so far as it is known, their texts were never reproduced without including the lines which they had athetized. That is, the vulgate text, with roots that antedated the Alexandrians, emerged as a compromise between the prolix "eccentric" texts and the purified text not marked with obeli.

In the case of the New Testament, the earliest textual efforts of which we have knowledge were those of Marcion (c. 144), Tatian (c. 170), and certain Monarchian heretics, the disciples of Theodotus,

keiten der Textkritik des Mahābhārata," *Acta Orientalia*, VIII (1930), 240-256. Cf. Sukthankar's rejoinder in the *Annals of the Bhandarkar Oriental Research Institute*, XI (Poona, 1929-1930), 259-283 (reprinted in the *V. S. Sukthankar Memorial Edition*, ed. P. K. Gode, I [Poona, 1944] 226-245), and H. Weller, "Zur Textkritik des Mahābhārata," in Moriz Winternitz's *Festschrift*, pp. 37-40.

[1] "L'episodio di Kadrū e di Vinatā nell' edizione critica del Mahābhārata " in *Silloge linguistica dedicata alla memoria di Graziadio Isaia Ascoli* ... (Torino, 1929), pp. 174-180.

a leather merchant from Byzantium.[1] During the second and third centuries different types of text gained currency in various localities. By about the end of the fourth century a compromise text embodying certain features of the earlier texts gained the ascendancy and became the ecclesiastical text approved throughout the Middle Ages and down to the nineteenth century. It has become customary among textual scholars to associate the names of specific editors with several of these types of text—such as Hesychius with the Alexandrian, Pamphilus with the Palestinian, and Lucian with the Koine or Byzantine type of text.[2] The text current at Alexandria betrays the editorial care for which scholars in that city were famous. The other main types of text, current before the Koine type gained the supremacy, exhibit many differences among themselves, but they are frequently opposed, individually or collectively, to the Alexandrian in preferring a fuller, more expanded form of text. The problem confronting the New Testament textual critic is how to evaluate these two main types of text.

New Testament scholars have been well acquainted for more than two centuries with the canon of criticism, *brevior lectio praeferenda est*.[3] It goes without saying that responsible textual critics have never applied this canon in a mechanical way. The merits and demerits of the Alexandrian, Western, and Koine texts of the New Testament must be evaluated by weighing the evidence for each variant reading and forming from these separate judgments an opinion regarding the text as a whole. At the same time, one's confidence in the general validity of this canon[4] is strengthened by

[1] See Hermann Schöne, "Ein Einbruch der antiken Logik und Textkritik in die altchristliche Theologie; Eusebios' KG 5.28, 13-19 in neuer Übertragung erläutert," in *Pisciculi, Studien zur Religion und Kultur des Altertums* [Franz Joseph Dolger's *Festschrift*], edd. Theodor Klauser und Adolf Rücker (Münster in W., 1939), pp. 252-265.

[2] This last has more probability than the others; see pp. 3 ff. above.

[3] J. J. Wettstein appears to be the first editor of the Greek Testament to formulate this canon fully. In his *Prolegomena ad Novi Testamenti Graeci editionem accuratissimam* (Amsterdam, 1730), p. lx, and again in his celebrated *Novum Testamentum Graecum*, II (Amsterdam, 1752), 862, he laid down the rule that, "Inter duas variantes lectiones non protinus amplior atque prolixior breviori est praeferenda, sed contra potius," etc.

[4] The validity of this canon has been challenged, however by A. C. Clark in his volumes on *The Primitive Text of the Gospels and Acts* (Oxford, 1914); *The Descent of Manuscripts* (Oxford, 1918); and *The Acts of the Apostles; a Critical Edition with Introduction and Notes on Selected Passages* (Oxford, 1933), and by Bover (see pp. 123 and 140 above). Robert Eisler, who was not primarily a textual critic, went so far as to suppose that a deliberate

the knowledge that scribes and redactors of the Iliad and the Mahābhārata were reluctant to omit anything from the text of these
epics which had been transmitted to them.

and drastic shortening of all four Gospels took place so early as to leave
little or no trace in any extent manuscripts, even of the Western variety
(*BBC*, XII [1937], 5-6). Still further from sober scholarship was the view of
E. S. Buchanan, who thought that most New Testament manuscripts have
been altered in the interests of Arianism to remove references to the deity
of Christ and the deity of the Holy Spirit ("More Light on the Western Text,"
Bibliotheca Sacra, LXXIII [1916], 422-444; cf. other publications by Buchanan
listed in my *Annotated Bibliography of the Textual Criticism of the New
Testament, 1914-1939* [*SD*, XVI; Copenhagen, 1955]).

APPENDIX

WILLIAM BOWYER'S CONTRIBUTION TO
NEW TESTAMENT TEXTUAL CRITICISM[1]

According to Allibone's famous and useful *Dictionary*, William Bowyer the younger (1699-1777) will "long be remembered as the most learned English printer of whom we have any account."[2] The third generation in a line of printers, Bowyer attended Cambridge but does not appear to have taken a degree. In 1722 he entered the printing business with his father. From this time until his death he was engaged in superintending his press and contributing to various scholarly works by supplying corrections, prefaces, annotations, and the like. Indeed, the learned men of the day found it a great advantage to have in the person of their printer a scholar whose erudition and classical taste could rectify their errors and improve their publications.[3] Among his own scholarly productions in the field of the classics it will be sufficient to mention two. In 1774 he published a new edition of Cornelius Schrevelius's *Greek Lexicon*, to which he added words (distinguished by an asterisk) which he had himself collected in the course of his own studies. At the close of his life he produced a new edition of Bentley's famous *Dissertation on the Epistles of Phalaris*, inserting various learned remarks and critical comments. It is indicative of the general reputation for trustworthiness and accuracy in printing which the Bowyer press enjoyed that for nearly fifty years this house printed the votes of the House of Commons and in 1776 was appointed to print the *Journal of the House of Lords* and the rolls of Parliament.

After publishing several editions of the Textus Receptus of the

---

[1] Most of the material in this Appendix was published originally in an article in the *Journal of Religion* (October, 1952), copyright by the University of Chicago Press, under the title, "Three Learned Printers and their Unsung Contribution to Biblical Scholarship." The two other printers dealt with in the article are Isaiah Thomas, Jr. (1749-1831) and Robert Young (1822-1888).

[2] S. Austin Allibone, *A Critical Dictionary of English Literature*, 1 (Philadelphia, 1871), 229.

[3] A full account of Bowyer's editorial labors is found in John Nichols's *Literary Anecdotes of the Eighteenth Century* (9 vols., 1812-15); continued as *Illustrations of Literary History* (7 vols., 1817-48).

Greek New Testament, Bowyer decided to produce a critical edition worthy of the reputation of his printing house. The time-honored ecclesiastical text of the New Testament, which goes back to the edition that Erasmus prepared "at breakneck speed" (as he himself confessed) from a small handful of late Greek manuscripts, had secured an almost unbroken monopoly. Only a few hardy souls had been brave enough to question the validity of such a universally accepted text.[1] It is to the credit of Bowyer that he not only questioned the validity of the Textus Receptus but published a critical edition[2] which in many passages anticipated the general critical opinion which was to prevail after the time of Westcott and Hort. By a system of square brackets Bowyer marked in his text not a few familiar passages which lacked good manuscript support. Thus he bracketed the doxology of the Lord's Prayer (Matt. 6.13), the *pericope de adultera* (John 7.53-8.11), the *comma Johanneum* (I John 5.7-8), and single verses (such as Acts 8.37 and 15.34) and words throughout the New Testament.[3]

In addition to marking some readings with square brackets, Bowyer departed in many other passages from the Textus Receptus by introducing into his printed text the reading which the better

---

[1] One of the earliest of these appears to have been a Presbyerian minister named Daniel Mace. In 1729 he published at London a New Testament in Greek and idiomatic English in two volumes, "containing the original text corrected from the authority of the most authentic manuscripts" (see H. McLachlan, "An Almost Forgotten Pioneer in New Testament Criticism," *Hibbert Journal*, XXXVII [1938-39], 617-25).

[2] Novum / Testamentum / Graecum, / ad fidem / Graecorum solûm codicum mss., nunc primùm expressum, / adstipulante Joanne Jacobo Wetstenio: / juxta sectiones Jo. Alberti Bengelii / divisum; / Et novâ interpunctione saepius illustratum. / Accessere / in altero volumine / emendationes conjecturales / virorum doctorum undecunque collectae. / Londini, / cura, typis, et sumptibus *G. B.* [i.e. Guilelmi Bowyer], MDCCLXIII. / Pp. iv, 278. The second volume contains the following title page: Novi / Testamenti / volumen alterum: / complectens / epistolas / apostolicas, / cum / apocalypsi / S. Joannis. / Accessere / emendationes conjecturales. /Vol. II. / Pp. *279, *280, 280-488. Both volumes are duodecimo. A synoptic table of readings differing from Mill's text is on pp. 464-75. On page 476 ("ne vacet pagina," as Bowyer quaintly introduces it) is given a table of dates of the Passover starting from A.D. 26. This page concludes with a bold "FINIS." On pages 477-88, however, Bowyer adds a "P.S." showing where Old Testament quotations in the New Testament differ from either the Septuagint, or from both the Hebrew and the Septuagint. In 1783 a second edition of the Greek text appeared in handsome quarto format (vii+460 pp.).

[3] In the Book of Revelation (for which Erasmus used only a single manuscript) Bowyer is most liberal with square brackets.

manuscripts support. Here also he was a precursor of much of present-day scholarship. To select only a few examples, one may note αὐτῷ for αὐτοῖς in Matt. 8.15, the reversed sequence of James and John in Luke 8.51, υἱός for ὄνος in Luke 14.5, Βηθανίᾳ for Βηθαβαρᾷ in John 1.28, καρδίας for διανοίας in Eph. 1.18, ναί for καί in Phil. 4.3, ὅ for θεός in I Tim. 3.16, and ἀσελγείαις for ἀπωλείαις in II Pet. 2.2. He omitted the doxology found at the end of Romans in the Textus Receptus (Rom. 16.25-27) and printed it as verses 24-26 at the close cf chapter 14.

Most remarkable of all, Bowyer introduced a conjecture into his text at Eph. 1.1, namely, Λαοδικείᾳ instead of Ἐφέσῳ (although he did not change the title of the Epistle!).

In many of these alterations of the Textus Receptus, Bowyer depended upon the critical judgment of Johann Jakob Wettstein, who had published his magnificent folio edition of the Greek New Testament at Amsterdam in 1751 and 1752. Whereas, however, Wettstein continued to print the Textus Receptus at the top of the page and relegated his judgments about the better readings to his footnotes, Bowyer must be credited with the courage of introducing many of the earlier and better attested readings into the text itself.

The second volume of his critical edition contains a sizeable collection of conjectural emendations which Bowyer and other scholars suggested for the text and punctuation of the New Testament. Although some readers, as would be expected, boggled at what they considered the unwarranted license of several of these conjectures, the work received the highest commendation from many scholars.[1] In 1767 the president and fellows of Harvard College wrote a letter to thank Bowyer for several benefactions of his

---

[1] See quotations from favorable reviews cited by Allibone, *op. cit.*, p. 230, especially the full text of the (anonymous) review in the *Monthly Review; or Literary Journal*, xxx (London, 1764), 300. For a modern appraisal see Caspar René Gregory, *The Canon and Text of the New Testament* (New York 1907), p. 449. On the other hand, the contemporary Bishop Warburton took offense at certain parts of the work; see John Nichols, *Biographical and Literary Anecdotes of William Bowyer, Printer, F.S.A.* (London, 1782), pp. 432-39. So recently as the close of the nineteenth century, Scrivener (or his editor, Miller) refers in connection with Bowyer to "the utter fruitlessness of the attempt to illustrate Scripture by ingenious exercise of the imagination" (F. H. A. Scrivener, *A Plain Introduction to the Criticism of the New Testament*, ed. Edward Miller, II [4th ed.; London, 1894], 245, n. 1).

to that college, in which they refer to his critical edition as follows:

"It is a particular pleasure to us to mention your very curious edition of the Greek Testament, in two volumes, with critical notes, and many happy conjectures, especially as to the punctuation, an affair of the utmost importance as to ascertaining the sense. This work, though small in bulk, we esteem as a rich treasure of sacred learning, and of more intrinsic value than many large volumes of the commentators."[1]

An edition of the Conjectures, with extensive additions, was published separately at London in 1772 under the following title, *Critical Conjectures and Observations on the New Testament, Collected from Various Authors, as well in regard to Words as Pointing: With the Reasons on which both are founded.* It is noteworthy that this enlarged edition was translated into German by Joh. Chr. F. Schulz, professor of theology and oriental languages at Giessen.[2] Two other editions, enlarged still further, were published posthumously at London, one in 1782 and the last in 1812 from the annotated, interleaved copy of Dr. Henry Owen.

Several typical examples of Bowyer's comments on the text of the New Testament will reveal his acuteness better than many eulogies. In more than one of these proposals Bowyer antedated similar suggestions made by modern scholars. An example is the conjecture that the name "Enoch" originally stood in the text of I Pet. 3.19, "Enoch went and preached to the spirits in prison." Although both Moffatt and Goodspeed, in adopting this conjecture for their translations of the New Testament, attribute it to Rendel Harris,[3] it has a far older pedigree than was supposed. As a matter of fact, it was suggested by M. R. James (in 1901),[4] by J. Cramer (in 1891),[5] van Manen (in 1880),[6] Stier and Theile (in 1855),[7]

---

[1] The full text of the letter is given by Nichols, *op. cit.*, pp. 405 f.

[2] Johann Christoph Friedrich Schulz, *Konjekturen über das Neue Testament, zuerst gesammelt von Wilhelm Bowyer. Aus dem Englischen der zwoten Ausgabe übersetzt und durchaus mit Zusätzen und Berichtigungen bereichert*, Vol. I (Leipzig, 1774) and Vol. II (paged continuously with the first) (Leipzig, 1775).

[3] Harris had published several articles on the subject in *Expositor*, Ser. 6, IV (1901), 346-49; V (1902) 317-20; and VI (1902), 378-90. Compare George Farmer's comment in *Expositor*, Ser. 6, VI (1902), 377-78.

[4] See *Expositor*, Ser. 6, V (1902), 318.

[5] J. Cramer, "Exegetica et Critica," *Nieuwe bijdragen op het gebied van godgeleerdheid en wijsbegeerte* VII (1891), 130.

[6] W. C. van Manen, *Conjecturaal-Kritiek, toegepast op den tekst van de schriften des Nieuwen Testaments (Verhandelingen ... Teylers godgeleerd genootschap*, n.s. IX, I [Haarlem, 1880]), p. 339.

[7] R. Stier and K. C. W. Theile, *Polyglottenbibel*, IV (Bielefeld, 1854), 490.

J. J. Griesbach (in 1806),[1] and G. C. Knapp (in 1797).[2] The fountainhead of this long stream of tradition appears to be the second edition[3] of Bowyer's *Critical Conjectures* (1772).[4]

In Acts 15.20 and 28 Bowyer proposed that the words καὶ τοῦ πνικτοῦ and καὶ πνικτῶν be regarded as later intrusions into the transmission of the text of the Apostolic Decree, and was inclined to leave them out. This is also the conclusion of J. H. Ropes in his edition of *The Text of Acts*, and of Lake and Cadbury in their *Commentary on Acts*.[5] Concerning the much disputed passage in Acts 1.4, involving συναλιζόμενος, Bowyer draws upon a suggestion of Hemsterhusius that the word should be read συναλιζομένοις, i.e., "He commanded them, being assembled together, not to depart." This solution of a troublesome crux does not appear to have been taken into account by the modern scholars who have dealt specially with this verse.[6]

[1] J. J. Griesbach, *Novum Testamentum Graece* (Halle and London, 1806), s.v.

[2] In the "Sylloge notabiliorum aut celebratiorum conjecturarum mutanda lectione in N.T." of his *Novum Testamentum Graece* (Halle, 1797).

[3] In some quite inexplicable way several scholars refer the conjecture to Bowyer's *first* edition (1763); so, e.g., Farmer (see n. 3, p. 158 above); Karl Gschwind. *Die Niederfahrt Christi in die Unterwelt* (Münster/W., 1911), p. 15; Urbanus Holzmeister, *Commentarius in Epistolas SS. Petri et Iudae apostolorum* (Paris, 1937), Part I, p. 310; E. J. Goodspeed, *Problems of New Testament Translation* (Chicago, 1945), p. 196; Werner Bieder, *Die Vorstellung von der Höllenfahrt Jesu Christi* (Zürich, 1949), p. 97. It is a fact, however, that neither the Greek text nor the section devoted to *Critical Conjectures* in the edition of 1763 contains the slightest mention of this emendation. One wonders whether these scholars, all of whom specifically mention the 1763 edition, had ever consulted a copy of this edition.

Who it was that suggested this conjecture to Bowyer (who marks it with the enigmatic siglum "S") appears to be quite an insoluble problem; for a discussion see Harris, *Expositor*, Ser. 6, VI (1902), 387-88.

[4] The validity of the conjecture, it goes without saying, is not increased by the multiplicity of scholars who repeat it. In this case, the introduction of a new subject in verse 19 ("Enoch") disturbs the otherwise smooth context. Harris himself acknowledged this when he confessed, "It must not be forgotten that when the emendation is made in the text, something has still to be done to restore continuity to the argument" (*Side-Lights on New Testament Research* [London, 1908], p. 209 n.). A conjecture which introduces an inappropriate and harsh transition into a passage which was perfectly consistent before can scarcely be correct. See also Carl Clemen's criticism of Harris's proposal, in *Expositor*, Ser. 6, VI (1902), 316-20, as well as Selwyn's objections, *The First Epistle of St. Peter* (London, 1949), pp. 197 f.

[5] Being respectively *The Beginnings of Christianity*, Part I, vol. III (London, 1926), 265-69, and *ibid.*, vol. IV (London, 1933), 177 and 181.

[6] E.g., W. H. P. Hatch, *JBL*, XXX (1911), 123-28; C. R. Bowen, *ZNW*, XIII (1912), 247-59; and H. J. Cadbury, *JBL*, XLV (1926), 310-17.

One of the most attractive of the numerous suggestions regarding changes in the received punctuation of the Greek text is at Mark 14.41. The stark inconcinnity of the traditional rendering of καθ-εύδετε κτλ. is obviated by Bowyer in taking the clause interrogatively, an interpretation which is adopted also by the Revised Standard Version (1946) and the New English Bible (1961).

In many respect William Bowyer was in advance of his time. A man of very small stature, he was, we are told, often referred to by his contemporaries as "the little man of great sufficiency."[1] When others saw the defects of the Textus Receptus of the New Testament but continued to print it unchanged, he boldly issued an edition which at many points anticipated the views of scholars more than a century later. Two circumstances account for the relatively slight impact which his critical opinions made upon contemporary scholars: the lack of a well-rounded theory of textual criticism based on a study of families of texts, and the over-powering hold which the time-honored Textus Receptus had gained upon both academic and clerical circles alike. Nevertheless, in the long view of the history of New Testament scholarship Bowyer's critical edition of 1763 stands out as a landmark of rare, though largely unappreciated, achievement.

[1] See the *Dictionary of National Biography*, VI, 85b.

INDEX OF NAMES

NEW TESTAMENT TOOLS AND STUDIES

EDITED BY

BRUCE M. METZGER, Ph.D., D.D., L.H.D.

20975

225.4
m59

Date Due